Palgrave Studies in the History of Social Movements

Series Editors
Stefan Berger, Institute for Social Movements, Ruhr University Bochum, Bochum, Germany

Holger Nehring, Contemporary European History, University of Stirling, Stirling, UK

Around the world, social movements have become legitimate, yet contested, actors in local, national and global politics and civil society, yet we still know relatively little about their longer histories and the trajectories of their development. This series seeks to promote innovative historical research on the history of social movements in the modern period since around 1750. We bring together conceptually-informed studies that analyse labour movements, new social movements and other forms of protest from early modernity to the present. We conceive of 'social movements' in the broadest possible sense, encompassing social formations that lie between formal organisations and mere protest events. We also offer a home for studies that systematically explore the political, social, economic and cultural conditions in which social movements can emerge. We are especially interested in transnational and global perspectives on the history of social movements, and in studies that engage critically and creatively with political, social and sociological theories in order to make historically grounded arguments about social movements. This new series seeks to offer innovative historical work on social movements, while also helping to historicise the concept of 'social movement'. It hopes to revitalise the conversation between historians and historical sociologists in analysing what Charles Tilly has called the 'dynamics of contention'.

Editorial Board

John Chalcraft (London School of Economics, UK)
Andreas Eckert (Humboldt-University, Germany)
Susan Eckstein (Boston University, USA)
Felicia Kornbluh (University of Vermont, USA)
Jie-Hyun Lim (Research Institute for Comparative History, Hanyang University Seoul, South Korea)
Marcel van der Linden (International Institute of Social History, The Netherlands)
Rochona Majumdar (University of Chicago, USA)
Sean Raymond Scalmer (University of Melbourne, Australia)
Alexander Sedlmaier (Bangor University, UK)

Magnus O. Bassey

Student Activism in 1960s America

Stories from Queens College

palgrave
macmillan

Magnus O. Bassey
Department of Secondary Education
and Youth Services
Queens College, CUNY
Queens, NY, USA

ISSN 2634-6559 ISSN 2634-6567 (electronic)
Palgrave Studies in the History of Social Movements
ISBN 978-3-031-54793-5 ISBN 978-3-031-54794-2 (eBook)
https://doi.org/10.1007/978-3-031-54794-2

© The Editor(s) (if applicable) and The Author(s), under exclusive license to Springer Nature Switzerland AG 2024

This work is subject to copyright. All rights are solely and exclusively licensed by the Publisher, whether the whole or part of the material is concerned, specifically the rights of translation, reprinting, reuse of illustrations, recitation, broadcasting, reproduction on microfilms or in any other physical way, and transmission or information storage and retrieval, electronic adaptation, computer software, or by similar or dissimilar methodology now known or hereafter developed.
The use of general descriptive names, registered names, trademarks, service marks, etc. in this publication does not imply, even in the absence of a specific statement, that such names are exempt from the relevant protective laws and regulations and therefore free for general use.
The publishers, the authors, and the editors are safe to assume that the advice and information in this book are believed to be true and accurate at the date of publication. Neither the publishers nor the authors or the editors give a warranty, expressed or implied, with respect to the material contained herein or for any errors or omissions that may have been made. The publishers remain neutral with regard to jurisdictional claims in published maps and institutional affiliations.

Cover illustration: Photo courtesy of Queens College

This Palgrave Macmillan imprint is published by the registered company Springer Nature Switzerland AG
The registered company address is: Gewerbestrasse 11, 6330 Cham, Switzerland

If disposing of this product, please recycle the paper.

Series Editors' Foreword

Around the world, social movements have become legitimate, yet contested, actors in local, national, and global politics and civil society, yet we still know relatively little about their longer histories and the trajectories of their development. Our series reacts to what can be described as a recent boom in the history of social movements. We can observe a development from the crisis of labor history in the 1980s to the boom in research on social movements in the 2000s. The rise of historical interests in the development of civil society and the role of strong civil societies as well as non-governmental organizations in stabilizing democratically constituted polities has strengthened the interest in social movements as a constituent element of civil societies.

In different parts of the world, social movements continue to have a strong influence on contemporary politics. In Latin America, trade unions, labor parties, and various left-of-center civil society organizations have succeeded in supporting left-of-center governments. In Europe, peace movements, ecological movements, and alliances intent on campaigning against poverty and racial discrimination and discrimination on the basis of gender and sexual orientation have been able to set important political agendas for decades. In other parts of the world, including Africa, India, and South East Asia, social movements have played a significant role in various forms of community building and community politics. The contemporary political relevance of social movements has undoubtedly contributed to a growing historical interest in the topic.

Contemporary historians are not only beginning to historicize these relatively recent political developments; they are also trying to relate them to a longer history of social movements, including traditional labor organizations, such as working-class parties and trade unions. In the longue durée, we recognize that social movements are by no means a recent phenomenon and are not even an exclusively modern phenomenon, although we realize that the onset of modernity emanating from Europe and North America across the wider world from the eighteenth century onwards marks an important departure point for the development of civil societies and social movements.

In the nineteenth and twentieth centuries, the dominance of national history over all other forms of history writing led to a thorough nationalization of the historical sciences. Hence social movements have been examined traditionally within the framework of the nation state. Only during the last two decades have historians begun to question the validity of such methodological nationalism and to explore the development of social movements in comparative, connective, and transnational perspectives taking into account processes of transfer, reception, and adaptation. While our book series does not preclude work that is still being carried out within national frameworks (for, clearly, there is a place for such studies, given the historical importance of the nation state in history), it hopes to encourage comparative and transnational histories on social movements.

At the same time, as historians have begun to research the history of those movements, a range of social theorists, from Jürgen Habermas to Pierre Bourdieu and from Slavoj Žižek to Alain Badiou as well as Ernesto Laclau and Chantal Mouffe to Miguel Abensour, to name but a few, have attempted to provide philosophical-cum-theoretical frameworks in which to place and contextualize the development of social movements. History has arguably been the most empirical of all the social and human sciences, but it will be necessary for historians to explore further to what extent these social theories can be helpful in guiding and framing the empirical work of the historian in making sense of the historical development of social movements. Hence the current series is also hoping to make a contribution to the ongoing dialogue between social theory and the history of social movements.

This series seeks to promote innovative historical research on the history of social movements in the modern period since around 1750. We bring together conceptually informed studies that analyze labor movements, new social movements, and other forms of protest from early modernity to the present. With this series, we seek to revive, within the context of historiographical developments since the 1970s, a conversation between historians on the one hand and sociologists, anthropologists, and political scientists on the other.

Unlike most of the concepts and theories developed by social scientists, we do not see social movements as directly linked, a priori, to processes of social and cultural change and therefore do not adhere to a view that distinguishes between old (labor) and new (middle-class) social movements. Instead, we want to establish the concept "social movement" as a heuristic device that allows historians of the nineteenth and twentieth centuries to investigate social and political protests in novel settings. Our aim is to historicize notions of social and political activism in order to highlight different notions of political and social protest on both left and right.

Hence, we conceive of "social movements" in the broadest possible sense, encompassing social formations that lie between formal organizations and mere protest events. But we also include processes of social and cultural change more generally in our understanding of social movements: this goes back to nineteenth-century understandings of "social movement" as processes of social and cultural change more generally. We also offer a home for studies that systematically explore the political, social, economic, and cultural conditions in which social movements can emerge. We are especially interested in transnational and global perspectives on the history of social movements, and in studies that engage critically and creatively with political, social, and sociological theories in order to make historically grounded arguments about social movements. In short, this series seeks to offer innovative historical work on social movements, while also helping to historicize the concept of "social movement." It also hopes to revitalize the conversation between historians and historical sociologists in analyzing what Charles Tilly has called the "dynamics of contention."

In his *Student Activism in 1960s America: Stories from Queens College*, Magnus Bassey traces the reasons why students became involved in social justice and antiwar campaigns over the course of the 1960s. Bassey's study "identifies the QC student activists of the 1960s; how and why they became activists, their activities, their achievement as activists, and what motivated them to think that they could make history themselves by confronting racism."

He thus unpacks grand social theories about social movement mobilization and, in particular, theories that highlight ideology as a key motivational factor, instead, he asks how these grand theories worked in practice and how ideology was put to work and created meaning among the activists. Instead of applying social movement theories, Bassey has unearthed activists' memories and tells their stories to explain why they decided to protest and what the protests meant to them.

Queens College is a good case study for such an endeavor. It was the only one of the City University of New York (CUNY) colleges that saw significant student activism. Queens College also saw campaigns for social justice that can be seen as pioneering in the context of other campaigns. The student strike at Queens College in November 1961 provided the foundational moment for later protests: the strike happened in protests against ban on speakers on campus that were deemed controversial and it was a way for the student activists "to fight power on campus, to fight racism and discrimination, and above all, to fight for students' rights which had been stifled by the propagation of *in loco parentis* by the QC administration." Queens College students also participated "in an ongoing fight to keep CUNY totally tuition-free." Such protests were also pioneers in the context of US student activism more generally: they happened before the mobilizations of the Free Speech Movement (FSM) that started at the University of California, Berkeley, as well as the large mobilizations at Columbia University around 1968: Mario Savio, a key FSM activist "worked as a picket captain during the student strike at QC in 1961."

A key theme in Bassey's richly documented work is connections between activists in the United States and beyond. For example, in 1963, the QC Student Help Project went to the southern United States and observed some of the civil rights organizing by the National Association for the Advancement of Colored People (NAACP) and the Student Nonviolent Coordinating Committee (SNCC) first hand. Also in 1963, Queens College students traveled to Mexico, specifically "to assist impoverished Mexicans to build a laundry facility in the town of Taxco."

As we witness debates about the freedom of speech, the relationship between research and activism, and student mobilizations in our own world as this book goes to press, this book might encourage us to reflect on the motivations of student activism that defy straightforward categorization. It also alerts us to the importance of personal, inter-generational, and collective memories in student mobilizations.

Bochum, Germany Stefan Berger
Stirling, UK Holger Nehring

Acknowledgments

The research for this book owes so much to so many people because it draws essentially from primary sources derived from archival materials housed at Benjamin S. Rosenthal Library at Queens College. With the gracious assistance of the archivists in the Department of Special Collections at Queens College Library, my research was made so very much easier. The archivists who contributed greatly to the success of this work include, Annie Tummino, now Head of Special Collections and Archives, Natalie Milbrodt, and Alexandra Dolan-Mescal. They were generous with their assistance, and I thank them all. I owe special thanks to Ben Alexander, former Head of Special Collections and Archives at Queens College Rosenthal Library who was kind enough to accommodate my many requests. A book written based on primary sources derived essentially from archival materials cannot but attest to the high quality of the resources at the Queens College Civil Rights archives. I am also grateful to Cindy Lawler, Archives Specialist at McCain Library and Archives, The University of Southern Mississippi, for sending copies of the *Mississippi Free Press* edited by Lucy Komisar to me after relevant payment for photocopying had been made. Above all, it is a pleasure for me to acknowledge the help I received from Mark Levy who introduced me to the Civil Rights Archives at Queens College that I did not even know existed. Mark's personal account of his participation in Freedom Summer (with his late wife, Betty), and our numerous e-mail correspondences have enriched the historical narrative in this book greatly. It is worth mentioning that Mark was the initiator/founder and the first contributor to the Queens College library's CRM Archive. A few words cannot begin to acknowledge my indebtedness to him. Mark was very generous with his assistance and magnanimous with his time. He was wonderfully supportive and encouraging in this effort.

I must also express my profound gratitude to Dr. Sidney B. Simon (now deceased), Rabbi Moshe Mitchell Shur, Joseph Liesner, Elliot Linzer, Joan Nestle, Michael R. Wenger, Stan F. Shaw, Dorothy M. Zellner, Arthur Gatti, Lucy Komisar, and Andrew Berman who either gracefully granted me interviews or responded to one or the other of my many questions and requests. I must also thank Eleanor Armour-Thomas, the former head of our department, for her incredible support through the years. My sincere thanks to Georgine Ingber, Andy Poon, and Ayesha Ali of Creative Services for their help with the cover photograph. I want to thank the blind reviewer whose comments and suggestions have made this a better book than I ever set out to write. To others, I thank them all. However, I assume full responsibility for the views expressed, and none of the above are responsible for any errors or misstatements in this book.

Contents

1	Introduction	1
2	Queens College: A History	27
3	The Pioneers	49
4	The Trailblazers	79
5	The Bridge Leaders	149
6	The Rebuilders	183
7	Those Who Volunteered and Why They Volunteered	221
8	Conclusion	235
Bibliography		255
Index		271

About the Author

Dr. Magnus O. Bassey is a Professor in the Department of Secondary Education and Youth Services at Queens College, The City University of New York. He is the author of *Western Education and Political Domination in Africa: A Study in Critical and Dialogical Pedagogy; Missionary Rivalry and Educational Expansion in Nigeria, 1885-1945; Malcolm X and African American Self-Consciousness.* Dr. Bassey has also authored numerous academic articles. His articles have appeared in rigorously peer reviewed journals.

List of Tables

Table 1.1	Research participants by theme/race/gender/number interviewed	15
Table 8.1	1960s QC activists in selected occupational groups	249

CHAPTER 1

Introduction

I was motivated by Queens College and its more than eight decades of alumni, and I wanted to become part of its story. The school boasts an inspiring legacy: generations of people embodying the motto, "Discimus ut Serviamus". ("We learn so that we may serve")
—Dr. Frank H. Wu, President, Queens College, 2020

David Farber described the 1960s as the age of great dreams and the era of revolt, rupture, and contradictions in America.[1] It was a decade of possibilities, grandeur, and tragedy. This period saw America's efforts to send astronauts into space, the establishment of the Peace Corps during the Administration of President John F. Kennedy, Dr. Martin Luther King, Jr.'s famous and prophetic, "I Have a Dream" speech, and Lyndon B. Johnson's commitment to the "Great Society."[2] However, as Richard Braungart and Margaret Braungart, have noted, "In the mid-1960s, the tide of hope and optimism began to give way to frustration and ugliness."[3] Frustration and ugliness in America in the mid-1960s emanated from the assassination of President John F. Kennedy and others,[4] the Vietnam War quagmire, the draft, and the Tet Offensive in Vietnam. Consequently, some Americans began to question their political leaders who had told them, for instance, that the Vietnam War would be over in a very short time. As a result, many began to lose faith in the efficacy of their government.

Based on injustices, hypocrisy, and ugliness that some students saw in their college campuses, in the country, and in the world at large, they began to question their political leaders. Students organized their discontents over three major issues namely, civil rights, free speech, and antiwar concerns. Their protests involved direct actions such as sit-ins, marches, picketing, and boycotts. They protested segregation and systemic racism. They pushed for an increase in college and university diversity, civil rights, voting rights, antidiscrimination laws, an inclusive environment for students of color, changes in college discriminatory policies, and a voice in administrative decision-making. They also protested racial and gender inequalities and against the Vietnam War. During the 1960s, student activists in American campuses could be heard chanting, "Peace in Vietnam Now!" "Power to the People." "Black Power." "Up Against the Wall." "Do not fold, spindle, or mutilate."[5] The first major revolt by college students against a school administration in the United States in the 1960s was the Free Speech Movement (FSM) led by Mario Savio[6] at the University of California, Berkeley, in 1964. The Berkeley demonstrations set the tone for other student demonstrations in the United States during this period.

The increasing US involvement in the Vietnam War brought the next phase of student protests that focused on the institutions that supported the Vietnam War efforts. Students and some faculty were incensed by the contributions their universities and colleges were making toward military research, the Vietnam War, and the military-industrial complex. In 1966 Students for a Democratic Society (SDS) sneered at Robert McNamara, the Secretary of Defense, and prevented his car from leaving Harvard campus. Campus unrests included protests and boycotts of Dow Chemical Company (the manufacturers of napalm and a major defense contractor), burning of draft cards, the closing of military draft induction centers, sit-ins, rallies, marches, and even a March on the Pentagon in 1967.[7] In the same year, 1967, students from the University of Wisconsin protested recruitment on their campus by Dow Chemical because it was a major defense contractor.[8] In April 1968, several hundred students led by Students for a Democratic Society (SDS), protested Columbia University's affiliation with the Institute for Defense Analyses (IDA) and Columbia's proposal to build a ten-story gymnasium in the recreational space of Morningside Park. Students at the University of Chicago organized a sit-in to protest Selective Service examinations being held on their campus. As if these were not enough, on August 28, 1968, antiwar protesters disrupted the Democratic Party National Convention in Chicago. Indeed, antiwar protests also took place at San Francisco State College and at the University of Wisconsin. There were student protests at Cornell University and at the University of California, Berkeley, in 1969. In the 1970s, student protests were reported at the University of California, Santa Barbara, and at Kent State University in Ohio. During the Kent State demonstrations, the National Guard fired into the crowd, killing four students, and wounding nine.[9] At Jackson State College in Mississippi, the state police fired at a dorm killing two students and wounding twelve. Students all over the United States mobilized for political reforms, and in all, there were protests in more than 700 college and university campuses nationwide.[10] As Alexander Cruden has stated, "Students on the front lines of the struggle…risked their scholarships, degrees, careers, and even their lives, yet generally kept their cool and made their case with thoughtful logic and nonviolent bravery."[11]

Student protests at Queens College (QC) predated the Free Speech Movement (FSM) of 1964.[12] As QC students moved away from the repressive McCarthy era of the 1950s, they began to confront and challenge those in power at the college. The defining characteristic of this break from the past was a student strike on November 16, 1961, in objection to the ban of controversial speakers who had been invited to campus by student clubs. This strike happened before the Free Speech Movement protest at the University of California, Berkeley, in 1964, and before the more famous student protest at Columbia University in 1968. The student strike at QC in 1961 gave the activists among them a direct and immediate way to fight power on campus, to fight racism and discrimination, and above all, to fight for students' rights which had been stifled by the propagation of *in loco parentis* by the QC administration. As one commentator noted, during the 1960s, QC "campus was vibrant with activism, which included organizing folk music festivals and antinuclear weapon rallies, fighting speaker ban laws, and supporting school programs in Prince Edward County, among other demonstrations and protests."[13]

Although studies on social movements and activism have been carried out by scholars from about the mid-1800s, in most of these studies, the processes of collective action are often lost in broad sweeping theories of social change.[14] Similarly, Richard G. Braungart and Margaret M. Braungart have argued that most of the studies on student movements are discipline-based and are often somewhat narrow in focus.[15] Since student movements of the 1960s cannot be attributed to a single explanation, it is therefore my position that to understand student movements of the 1960s, one must focus on individual historical contexts because in the critical study of social movements, motives cover a wide array of theoretical positions. The material in this study contributes to new research on student activism by shedding new light on the untold stories of individual QC student activists. The study presents first-person narratives from the actual participants, and tells their stories in their own voices, from their own records, and from the documents they left behind. It identifies the QC student activists of the 1960s; how and why they became activists, their activities, their achievement as activists, and what motivated them to think that they could make history themselves by confronting racism. It provides an intimate look at the students' lives and their social justice journey, beginning at Queens College and as they moved into their careers. The study also examines the organizing models of the student activists at QC in the 1960s.

* * *

It has been documented that participation in activism is often a product of ideological identification with the values of the movement together with a history of previous activism.[16] In this context, even before the 1964 activism heated up on campus, QC students were already at the forefront of social justice work. For instance, during the summer of 1963, about forty students from QC traveled to Mexico as part of the Queens College Mexico Volunteers, sponsored by the college's Newman House to assist impoverished Mexicans to build a laundry facility in the town of Taxco. On their second trip, the volunteers built a school that is still thriving in Mexico today.[17] Political consciousness of students on campus was further stirred up when the Student Association hired buses for a large delegation of QC students to attend the March on Washington, D.C., where Dr. Martin Luther King, Jr. delivered his "I Have a Dream" speech in August 1963. These students came back to campus having taken Dr. King's message to heart and were fired up. In addition, QC students were also involved in numerous protests in New York City during the early 1960s.

According to Michael J. Sandel, "Times of trouble prompt us to recall the ideals by which we live."[18] At QC, social justice became the students' guiding principle for activism and remains to this day the abiding counsel for moral and civic community work. For example, more than a matter of public debate or moral suasion, Lucy Komisar left QC between 1962 and 1963 to edit the *Mississippi Free Press* in Jackson, Mississippi despite the high levels of brutality meted out to civil rights workers in Mississippi. Lucy's example must have been instructive in the recruitment of QC volunteers for Prince Edward County during the summer of 1963 and for Freedom Summer in 1964. At about the same time, a former QC student, Dorothy M. Zellner was a full-time SNCC staff working in the South. As a student at QC, Dorothy was a writer and editor for a major student newspaper, *Crown*, influencing students on major social issues in her work against racism and discrimination. Under a different circumstance but related to activism, sixteen students from QC and one of their professors, Dr. Rachel Weddington, went to Farmville, Virginia, in the summer of 1963 to prepare Black students for classes for "free schools" that would be open to all students in the fall of 1963 because schools had been closed in Prince Edward County, Virginia, for four years by the state due to Virginia's "Massive Resistance" to integration.[19]

We see another example of QC activism after three civil rights workers were declared missing in Mississippi, the efforts by the leadership of the Student Help Project in highlighting and emphasizing profound shortcomings in Virginia and Mississippi generated intense catalytic resonance on campus.[20] This led to the establishment of "fast for freedom," during which seven QC students went on a five-day hunger strike to draw the attention of the press, television networks, and the public to what was happening in Mississippi. Another goal of the fast was to protest segregation and to put pressure on the federal government to protect civil rights workers. Some of the students involved in the fast included Gary Ackerman, a student newspaper editor (and, later, a member of the New York Senate from 1979 to 1983 and a member of the US House of Representatives from 1983 to 2013); Michael R. Wenger, chairman of the Student Help Project at QC 1964–1965 (who later served as the Deputy Director for Outreach and Program Development for President Clinton's Initiative on Race); and Ronald (Ron) F. Pollack, the Student Association President (who later was the Founding Executive Director of Families USA and the Founding Executive Director of the Food Research and Action Center (FRAC). Many of the QC student activists from the 1960s have brought their social values and political commitments into successful and meaningful careers in public service, activism, and social justice causes. Some of the QC activists have provided national leadership on antipoverty programs, parenting, school–family relationships, and helped in writing special education laws for other countries. Indeed, many of them have been teachers, lawyers, librarians, community organizers, union leaders, professors, writers, advocates, and the list goes on.[21]

The game-changers. Lucy Komisar, one of the 1960s QC activists noted in a 2009 lecture that her education at QC was a political and moral one, but these were not in the Queens College course catalog. From the interviews I have conducted with some of the QC activists of the 1960s, and the archival records I have reviewed, activism or social movement were not part of the Queens College curriculum or even listed in the catalog. However, many of the student activists told me and I have on record that Ms. Helen Hendricks, an African American College Office Assistant in the office of Student Activities at QC, was one of the driving forces in social justice activism at QC. Ms. Hendricks rose to the rank of Administrative Assistant in the Office of Student Activities, and in that capacity, she was able to support various student projects. She was closely connected to many students and was a driving force behind many student projects and activities on campus.[22] Mark levy, one of the Freedom Summer volunteers told me that Ms. Hendricks, in her quiet and effective ways, was particularly supportive of their activist endeavors at QC. Indeed, Mark stated that along with "Prof. Waddington, Ms. Hendricks was a key campus voice giving us kids the encouragement to invest time and take risks in doing the 'right' and 'just' things."[23] Michael Wenger, a QC student activist of the 1960s, affirmed that Ms. Hendricks was a driving force in most of their activist endeavors on campus. This view was reinforced in a written memo to me by Stan Shaw, one of the leaders and the chair of the Student Help Project (1963–1964) that Ms. Hendricks was aptly the mentor they needed and had at QC. This perception of Ms. Hendricks is widespread and entrenched among QC activists of the 1960s. Ms. Hendricks later became Assistant to the Dean of Student Affairs charged with the responsibility of supporting minority students interested in pursuing graduate programs. Through her efforts, there was a major increase in the admission and graduation rates of minority students in law and medical schools. She was promoted to Higher Education officer in 1986 before she retired in 1992. In a recent interview with Michael Wenger and Stan Shaw, two leaders of the Student Help Project at QC, Ms. Hendricks discussed her role in advising and mentoring students of different backgrounds while she was employed in the Office of Student Activities. She also talked about her experiences as one of the few African American female staff members on campus during the era of the social justice movements of the 1960s. In that interview, Stan Shaw, a Student Help Program leader in the 1960s, asked Ms. Hendricks about the tension that existed in her office between the college authorities who did not accept many of the things the student activists were doing on campus even though Ms. Hendricks was in support of most of them. She responded that in such instances she simply acted as a go-between to soften the blows from both sides. Another personality who provided critical support for student activism on QC campus in the 1960s was a well-respected African American professor, Dr. Rachel Weddington (deceased). As one student activist, Stan Shaw said, "As young leaders, we had the vision and energy to change the world but not the wisdom and maturity to make things happen. Dr. Weddington had an abundance of those latter traits."[24] Dr. Weddington was a mentor to most of the Civil Rights groups at QC. She even traveled with QC students to Prince Edward County, Virginia. It is noted that her calming presence and relationship with the Black community were keys to the effectiveness of the Prince Edward County project. It is no wonder that Dr. Weddington was a member of the committee that designed the Freedom School curriculum which was devised to improve African American educational needs in Mississippi. In a recent interview, Ms. Hendricks expressed the view that some of the Civil Rights activities on campus went smoothly because the Dean of Students and members of the Academic Senate respected the views of Dr. Weddington who was the faculty advisor to many of the civil rights student groups.[25] Another important influence on student activism at QC in the 1960s was Dr. Sidney Simon (deceased). Like Rachel Weddington, Dr. Simon was the faculty advisor for some of the civil rights groups at QC. He mentored and trained students who were preparing to tutor students in Prince Edward County, Virginia in the summer of 1963. He led several training sessions for the students out of his house in Long Beach, Long Island, New York. His well-known motto was, "deed should always match creeds."[26] Michael Wenger, one of the leaders of the Student Help Project recollected the important part Dr. Simon played in encouraging them to do more for social justice. He said, "Sid was telling us that [the Student Help Project in South Jamaica and Prince Edward County] weren't enough. If our commitment to freedom and justice was truly a deeply held value, we had to act repeatedly over time, incorporating our commitment into our everyday activities."[27] In short, Dr. Simon was telling these students that it was not enough for them to shout their beliefs from the rooftops or to act on their beliefs whimsically but to get out of their comfort zones regularly to back up their words with action.[28] Stan Shaw and Michael Wenger maintained in a book chapter that the CORE faculty advisers, three members of the education department accelerated their understanding that social justice was part of a healthy society and instigated the activist process by challenging them to do more than just protest.[29] Michael Wenger credits Helen Hendricks, Sidney (Sid) Simon, and Rachel Weddington with turning them from young impetuous, immature, and somewhat disrespectful young people into more mature, more respectful, more responsible, and thoughtful adults.[30] Lucy Komisar in her personal narrative in 2009 told her audience at QC how Michael Harrington held weekly public meetings with them at Deb's Hall during which time they debated and shared their concerns about ideology, social movements, social justice issues, and inequality in American society.[31]

A reviewer had asked, just as many others have asked me, what made QC such a rich site for student activism in the 1960s although other CUNY college campuses had influential student programs like the Student Help Project, CORE, student newspapers, and others, but activism was not as intense as in QC? My answer is that unlike other CUNY campuses, members of the QC Student Help Project went to the South in 1963 as a group and saw the National Association for the Advancement of Colored People (NAACP) and the Student Nonviolent Coordinating Committee (SNCC) officials organize protests, boycotts, pickets, sit-ins, and resistance in Prince Edward County. As we will see elsewhere in this book, while in Virginia, members of the QC Student Help Project were equipped with the courage, information, and organizational tools to confront power, and they shared these skills with others when they returned to campus in 1963. They showed their colleagues at QC how they could confront systemic racism and become agents of change. These volunteers were able to connect protests to QC students' profound thoughts of activism as democratic action on campus. The students who went South realized that they could channel their energies and power to bring about change. This is how Michael R. Wenger and Stan F. Shaw, two leaders of the Student Help Project who went to Prince Edward County, Virginia in 1963 made this point:

1 INTRODUCTION 9

> Through our Prince Edward County experience, we not only learned that we could be change agents, but we learned how to be change agents. We developed skills in communication, goal setting, team building, planning, fund-raising, political organization, community organization, teaching, and advocacy.[32]

Back on campus after the Virginia project, Wenger states, "We intensified our activities as we sought to generate wider and stronger support for the civil rights movement among students, and to raise their awareness of the persistent double standard with which our society viewed the value of a human life."[33] Stefan M. Bradley in his book, *Harlem vs. Columbia University: Black Student Power in the Late 1960s* documented similar findings at Columbia University some years later in 1968. This is what he said:

> Many of these young people had been exposed to the Civil Rights movement in the South. Students, white and black, had traveled throughout the South, participating in freedom rides, registering voters, and even teaching in inadequate schools. After witnessing firsthand, the ugliness of racial discrimination and oppression, many of the student protesters believed that it was their obligation to change society...These black and white students, taking their cue from the Civil Rights movement, formed coalitions to fight racism in the early 1960s.[34]

It is important to point out here that the student activists at QC in the 1960s were by no means representatives of the campus community or even somewhere in-between, rather they were outliers who were often labeled "troublemakers"[35] by the college administration and many of the other students on campus because QC campus in the 1960s was conservative to the core.[36] Despite overwhelming odds, these activists did not succumb to the machination of their adversaries. Joan Nestle, one of the student activists at QC in the 1960s confirmed in a correspondence with me that they were called the scum of the earth at QC, but even then, they kept on going.[37] A lot of the students at QC at this time cared very little or not at all about social justice issues because they were inherently conservative. They were more preoccupied with their schoolwork and a few extracurricular activities. However, as Mark Levy recollected, it was only a very small group of artsy, poetry-reading, guitar-playing bohemians and beatniks that brought activism and activist backgrounds with them to

QC as "red-diaper babies."[38] Joan Nestle, one of the QC activists of the 1960s told me,

> We stand in the embers of near history—the McCarthy 50s with its hate mongering, its fear of complicated thought, its believe that difference was treason, was my grounding for seeking out others who wanted to see a different America. It was at Queens College that I met my first community of activists, those who were called red diaper babies —because their parents had been involved in the labor struggles of the 1930s and 40s. They had experience in organizing protests, they taught me that our struggles had a history, had its poets like Brecht, its singers like Odetta, that there was a culture of resistance.[39]

In my research and findings, many of the student activists at QC in the 1960s had parents who were civil rights activists themselves or had parents who were supportive of civil rights causes.[40] Indeed, from available archival records and the oral interviews conducted, I found out, just as Doug McAdam and Jon N. Hale uncovered in their own studies, that the values of the student activists at QC were consistent with the core values that the volunteers learned at home.[41] As Michael Wenger (a student activist himself) remembered, QC in his day had a predominantly White student body, some of whose parents were Jewish immigrants and working-class families. Some of these parents were Holocaust survivors who felt a deep commitment to social justice which they passed on to their children. Additionally, for some of the parents, bigotry in the South was a clear reminder of the persecution that they had fled from Europe and other parts of the world. And as they saw it, if what was happening to Blacks in the South was allowed to continue, then the same could happen to Jews who were out of line. On the other hand, some people were just perplexed by the sheer brutality in the South. This group which included Michael Wenger himself, "simply could not understand how a desire for basic human rights could generate such brutality. How could other human beings use police dogs, billy clubs, fire hoses, and cattle prods against peacefully protesting human beings who were practicing nonviolence?"[42] they wondered. Wenger believes that these are some of the explanations, among many, why:

> On a small tree-lined campus in the heart of a bustling, growing, residential part of New York City, the children of these immigrants marched to protest the brutality in the South, conducted fund-raising drives to support the

freedom riders and the lunch-counter protestors, and arranged lectures and 'teach-in' activities on campus to raise student awareness and implore the federal government to do more to support racial justice.[43]

Let me at this juncture briefly comment on my research data and methodology. This research is based on primary sources derived essentially from archival materials collected at QC Rosenthal Library. To begin my research, I visited the QC Civil Rights and activist archives at Rosenthal Library and consulted the QC Roll Call of Queens College Students and Faculty who participated in the southern Civil Rights Movement of the 1960s created by Mark Levy for the QC Library Archives.[44] Next, I reviewed a comprehensive list of QC activists of the 1960s in *Veterans of the Civil Rights Movement* also created by Mark Levy. Finally, I reviewed Queens College CORE newsletter parts 1 and 2.[45] From the collated list, I was able to identify 45 subjects including four professors who served as mentors to the various student groups. After an extensive and a thorough review of archival records, I earmarked 31 activists for this study based on available archival materials and records of their activism. Of this number, three of the student activists on my list and one professor had died, but there were sufficient archival materials about their activism in the library to warrant their inclusion in the study. With the help of Mark Levy and other available resources, I was able to get the e-mail addresses of 26 QC student activists and one professor (totaling 27) and sent them e-mails. In the e-mail, I explained my mission as a researcher interested in studying student activism at QC in the 1960s. Each e-mail was accompanied by a set of questionnaires consisting of eighteen questions that asked the volunteers about their experiences at QC as activists. I wanted to know the number of years each volunteer spent at QC. I also wanted to know why they became activists, what or who influenced them, their major in college, where they served, information explaining their duties and assignments, their areas of deployment, their service experiences, information about the nature of the students they taught (for those who were teachers), their hosts, cooperation from their hosts, newspaper publications, memorabilia, copies of memos, letters and any information that would advance the cause of the research. I received responses from five student participants, and one Professor, Dr. Sidney Simon (now deceased). During the research, I interviewed six additional student activists who did not return their questionnaires but were interested in talking to me about their activism at QC.[46] To my greatest surprise, one of the respondents was a person whose information I needed the most because I had almost nothing relating to his Freedom Summer service in the QC archives. On the other hand, there were abundant archival materials including biographies, printed materials, clippings, correspondence, photographs, curriculum, lesson plans, preparatory and training materials, Freedom Summer documents, Mississippi Freedom Democratic Party (MFDP) documents, memorandums, newspaper clippings, personal letters, memorabilia, souvenirs, Freedom Summer anniversaries, and reunions among other documents in the QC archives for about 30 participants. We have this trove of information in the QC Civil Rights archives not by accident but because Mark Levy (himself a Freedom Summer volunteer) who was one of the coordinators of the Civil Rights archives at Queens College, had created a QC Roll Call of activist alumni and faculty who served in the southern Civil Rights Movement and persuaded the QC activists of the 1960s to donate their personal CRM-related documents and materials to the QC archives, which most of them did so very graciously.[47] Some of these documents were arranged and indexed, others were not. To conduct this research, then, I waded through piles of boxes intermittently and sorted out what I needed over a period of four years. Yes, you heard it right, four years, for it is often said that archival research is not only a difficult art but it is perhaps the most demanding task of the historian.

An in-depth examination of the lives of the student activists, a thorough review of extensive material from the archives, and interviews conducted uncover a previously untold story of the 1960s student activism at QC. Reviewing archival records, documents, interviews (oral and print), and relevant secondary sources over the course of four years has allowed me to write this book. This study is based on sources derived from records of 31 QC subjects who through their written records, archival materials, and personal interviews have told their own stories. In conformity with modern academic historiography, the research for this book is based on primary sources from archival materials collected from the Benjamin S. Rosenthal Library at QC, whose Department of Special Collections and Archives contains an impressive collection. Also important, were the archival records I examined from the University of Southern Mississippi—McCain Library and Archives. Among those records reviewed are copies of the *Mississippi Free Press* edited by Lucy Komisar, a QC student who took a year off from her studies to write and edit for the paper from 1962 to 1963. This research has also benefitted from the *Student Movements of the 1960s Project: The Reminiscences of Mario Savio*. The Savio interview was undertaken under the auspices of the Oral History Research Office at Columbia University. *KZSU Project South Interviews* (SCOPE Chapter 33, Mickey Shur) from the Department of Special Collections and University Archives, Stanford University Libraries, Stanford, California, proved helpful as well. The *KZSU* interviews were conducted by eight students from Stanford University during the summer of 1965 and were sponsored by *KZSU*, Stanford's student radio station. Other records reviewed include the *Tully-Crenshaw Feminist Oral History Project* Schlesinger Library, Radcliffe College, and Interview with Lucy Komisar conducted by Julie Altman. Some documents from the Martin Luther King, Jr. Center for Nonviolent Social Change, and the Mississippi Department of Archives and History in Jackson, Mississippi were also reviewed. Other documents that have enriched the narrative in this book include the history of the Freedom Summer Project, private papers, diaries, correspondence, letters, memos, editorials, articles, letters to editors, mementos, letters to and from friends and family members of participants, memorabilia, flyers, curricular materials, and teaching aids that shed light on the contributions of QC students to the 1960s activism. Most of these materials were donated by the student activists themselves to the QC library. Some of the participants were interviewed to record their stories in their own voices. Where permitted, the attempt was made to tape the interviews for oral history and for posterity. The stories of the participants are told in their own voices and in the voices of the local people they encountered. I have identified and elaborated on the strategic moments that connect the archival materials at QC to events in the 1960s. The important questions this research is trying to answer are: Who are the QC student activists of 1960s? What catalyzed them to become activists? What did they achieve during their mission? What prompted them to think that they could make history themselves by confronting racism?

Obviously, a study of this nature required that I speak with some of the people involved. Fortunately, I was able to interview eleven subjects and one professor, Dr. Sidney B. Simon, for this book. Those interviewed were primarily people who had returned their questionnaires to me and agreed to do personal interviews with me or those who responded to some of the many questions I asked the activists on my list in the process of the research. I interviewed the eleven activists and one professor through e-mail correspondence, phone conversations, and/or face-to-face discussions. The phone and face-to-face interviews generally lasted between one and two hours at a time and were repeated in many instances as needed. In one case, the interviews included numerous e-mail correspondence, numerous phone calls, and a lot of face-to-face conversations that have continued almost ad infinitum.[48] I must mention the fact that Dr. Simon gave me permission to tape his interviews, but the taping did not go well because of my inability to handle the taping equipment properly.

Since this is historical research based on archival sources and materials, I have adopted the chronological or sequential structure methodology. However, because of the nature of the data available to me, I have added thematic frameworks to the study to make for clarity and ease of understanding. The narratives are organized around specific themes that best define the events. These themes provide a fit within the historical sequence of events during the period under study and demarcate the historical construction of individual events. Conceptually and theoretically, I considered four thematic groundings for this book. Accordingly, I have created themes such as the *Pioneers*, who represent some of the first QC student volunteers who were engaged in activism at QC and went to the South for social justice advocacy from 1962 to 1963. They constituted the vanguard of social justice activism at QC in the 1960s. The *Trailblazers* were among the first group of QC volunteers who answered the call from SNCC and COFO for social justice activism in Mississippi in 1964. These were Freedom Summer activists who were part of the initiative designed to bring attention of the nation to the plight of African Americans in Mississippi. "These were deeply idealistic individuals, dedicated to achieving equal rights and human dignity for all."[49] They, in my view, were risk-takers who suffered intimidation and reprisals, spoke truth to power, and risked their lives to make a difference. They are those Howard Zinn said were not ashamed to be called "troublemakers," and "like the abolitionists of old; … they were proud of their ability to confront racism directly but nonviolently."[50] Bridge *Leaders* were social justice recruiters on and off QC campus. *Bridge Leaders* persuaded those who were already predisposed, to take the initial steps to participate in activism among QC students. Indeed, *Bridge Leaders* acted as middle managers who translated the organization's goals and objectives to the rank and file. Doug McAdam describes *Bridge Leaders* "as midwives to the recruitment process."[51] The *Rebuilders* were student activists and QC professors who went to Mississippi in 1965 to help rebuild Black churches that had been burned or bombed during Freedom Summer.[52]

Table 1.1 Research participants by theme/race/gender/number interviewed

Theme	Number of Participants	White	Black	Male	Female	No. Interviewed
Pioneers	9	8	1	3	6	3
Trailblazers	8	8	0	5	3	2
Bridge Leaders	4	3	1	2	2	3
Rebuilders	8	5	3	5	3	3
Professors	2	1	1	1	1	1
Total	31	25	6	16	15	12

For lack of a better designation, I have included in this theme those activists connected to QC who participated in one form of activism or the other from 1965 onwards. Table 1.1 shows the spread of each identity theme. Of this number, twelve subjects or 39% of the cohort were interviewed.

This book has eight chapters that are topically and chronologically arranged beginning with Chapter 1, which presents the structural narrative of the book's material. In Chapter 2, I argue that the late 1950s saw the end of the era of McCarthyism and conformity and the 1960s transitioned into the era of youth empowerment and social justice at QC. The speaker ban strike, anti-HUAC demonstrations, Women Strike for Peace, and the antinuclear movement activities preceded the civil rights efforts at the college. In Chapter 3, I maintain that the pioneer work done by Lucy Komisar and the Student Help Project (SHP) at Queens College were antecedents of the greater social justice activism that were undertaken by students at QC in the 1960s. Chapter 4 proclaims the 1964 summer volunteers from QC as trailblazers because they were among some of the first to answer the clarion calls from the Student Nonviolent Coordinating Committee (SNCC) and Council of Federated Organizations (COFO) for civil rights activism against racial segregation and the struggle for social justice in Mississippi.[53] The chapter argues that the underlying motivation for these volunteers was their inexhaustible dedication to righting the wrongs of the past. In Chapter 5, I identify individuals who led activist recruitment efforts and created activist consciousness on and off campus. These are the kinds of people Belinda Robnett calls bridge leaders, or links between community and organization.[54] The chapter also details the contributions of many others who crystalized and enhanced activism on and off QC campus during the period. Chapter 6 focuses on the critical role that QC students and professors played in rebuilding burned-down African American churches in Mississippi in 1965. It also brings into light, the body of evidence of other QC individuals who were involved in different activist causes between 1965 and 1970. In Chapter 7, I sketch in very rapid strokes some of the answers the research has uncovered on why some White students (a good number of them Jewish) from QC and throughout the country were attracted to the movement of the 1960s. In Chapter 8 which is the conclusion of the book, I note that since the "March for Our Lives" in 2018 and the "Black Lives Matter" protests after the murder of George Floyd in 2020, social activism has again entered many students' consciousness. Indeed, the chapter compares the social activism of the 1960s with the social movements of today in the United States. It also explores how the activist movement of the 1960s fits within today's social activism framework, and whether the lessons learned by activists in the 1960s can be replicated by today's activist student leaders. The section ends by exploring how technology has affected and impacted student activism in the United States in the twenty-first century and concludes by asking some of the QC student activists of the 1960s about the enduring effects of student activism and guide for a new generation of student activists. In relevant chapters in the book, I provide intimate case studies as to why these participants were drawn into activism and use the stories told, letters reproduced, and activism uncovered to piece together their motivation.

This documentation will be an invaluable resource for scholars and researchers interested in the ever-evolving scholarship on social movements throughout the world. It will also supplement works on the milestones of student activism particularly regarding a portion of the story never told before as articulately, for example, that of students from Queens College and other Liberal Arts institutions. Additionally, the book brings to light memos and correspondence from the volunteers, their students, parents, government officials, friends, and family members of the major players that have never been published before. The work also reveals public reactions to the efforts of the volunteers through letters of support, condemnations, and hate mails as well as correspondence to and from the volunteers to their students and their hosts. It details and makes public personal narratives never published before.

* * *

In discussing the contributions of these activists, the book explains and interweaves into their personal stories why each of them was so motivated to participate in activism even at great personal risks. Readers will notice that I have followed the careers of the activists under study through to the present day because for most, if not all of them, their activist work in the 1960s had led them to a lifetime work of social justice advocacy. It has indeed been said that activists not only help to transform the world, but they are themselves transformed by the work they do.[55] For example, many of the 1960s activists, "have gone on to lives devoted to the common good: ministers of diverse faiths, college professors, writers, midwives, public radio workers, publishers, prison educators, founders of interreligious committees working for peace in the Middle East, and corporate lawyers who do courageous pro bono legal and advocacy work."[56] Another reason for following the QC activists is based on Doug McAdam's position that participation in activism in the 1960s radicalized the volunteers and increased their integration into political organizations or that 1960s activism laid a strong foundation in the pursuit of activist careers in later life by the volunteers.[57] In which case, the 1960s activists "emerged from the experience more committed to activism than ever before."[58] Mark Levy, a QC student activist of the 1960s once stated, "The lessons of that summer have shaped the rest of my life and confirmed for me—and for so many of us who were there—our ongoing commitments to social change. Betty and I and many others came back North and continued—in various ways—to participate in the struggle for social justice." He went on to say, "I am grateful to have been at QC throughout a period of hope, vision, and struggle of the student rights and subsequent social movements of the '60s and '70s and also to have served as a 1964 Freedom Summer volunteer in Mississippi."[59] In a number of his writings, Mark maintains that he learned from his participation in the movements even more than he learned from his classes. However, to unearth the interconnectedness between student activism in the 1960s and the activists' later lives is to review and unpack their individual stories. There is also the need to see if there is continuity in the lives of the QC student activists after 60 years, and whether they have continued to voice the same political views and values as they advocated in the 1960s. It is also important to see, through their individual stories, if these volunteers have lived up to their 1960s values,[60] and whether they were concentrated "in the teaching or other 'helping professions,'"[61] as McAdam suggested (see the conclusion in this book).

By the end of this book, readers will have an intimate understanding of the motivations behind student activism and advocacy at QC in the 1960s. However, it is important to point out that although many of the subjects of this study were often invited to participate in Civil Rights efforts, this book is about social protests and student activism at Queens College and not about Civil Rights.

How I Came to Write This Book

I wish to acknowledge how I came to write this book because many have asked me, including one academic reviewer, how I came to write the book. This book is a child of necessity; the necessity to write the Queens College's own story; the story that had been neglected for decades. In writing this book, therefore, I spent considerable amount of time at the Queens College archives putting the pieces together. The published and unpublished materials found in the archival collection on Civil Rights form the backbone for this work. And indeed, evidence from these archival sources has been primarily helpful in illuminating the contributions of those courageous and fearless students from Queens College, and a tribute to all the other colleges whose students staged their own fights for social justice in America. Secondary and oral sources from Mark Levy have been of considerable assistance to me in writing this book. Mark and I came to know each other through mutual curiosity. In a meeting of the Black History Month organizing committee on December 15, 2011, Rikki Asher, a colleague of mine in the Department of Secondary Education and Youth Services, pitched a joint presentation to be made by both of us (Rikki and I) on the topic, *The Education of Malcolm X with Reflections from John Dewey* to the committee. Mark Levy who was a member of the organizing committee requested through Rikki to see my earlier published article entitled, *What Would John Dewey Say about the Educational Metamorphoses of Malcolm X?* Upon Mark's request, I sent him the article, and in his acknowledgment, he remarked:

> Thanks so much for sending the article! I thought you might be interested in the fact that last month was the 50th anniversary at Queens College of a student strike in 1961 protesting QC administration's ban on selected speakers invited by student groups—chief among them was the banning of Malcolm X as being "too controversial." There's info in the QC archives about all that. *That QC connection might be useful for your presentation.*[62]

Mark went on to add, "I'm a QC alumnus who taught in the QC SEEK program for a while—back when Bill Sales was one of QC SEEK's key faculty—and we used Malcolm's speeches as class texts. So, I enjoyed your article and its appreciation of Malcolm X's development and contributions."[63] But then he queried:

> PS: I left classroom and college teaching to enter a second career as a union organizer before retiring recently and working now with QC's civil rights archive, so the memory of some of my academic reading from long ago is a bit fuzzy. You touch on issues I'm still interested in and bring up things I haven't thought about for a long while. I don't remember exactly, but wasn't a lot of John Dewey's emphasis on participation and democracy originally based on his view of schools as a place to assimilate and integrate recent immigrants into the industrial workforce? Did Dewey ever talk about race? How useful do you find the more critical Paulo Freire framework for appreciating Malcolm's education, ideas, and roles? I haven't read it yet, so I was wondering if there was anything useful for your discussion in the new Manning Marable biography?[64]

In my response, I thanked Mark and noted that when I return from my trip to Nigeria in about four weeks, I would be happy to know more about his kind of work at the college Civil Rights archives. Here is my response which is worth reproducing at length.

> Thank you for your interesting historical note. I will be interested to know about that angle of the college. As you may be aware, what happened some 50 years ago is still rearing its ugly head and is perfectly in force today though covert. I do not know what the reaction of the college administration to our presentation will be, but I can assure you that there will be at best passive resistance and indeed even research on Malcolm X has its price. I will be traveling out of the country, but when I return, I would like to know more about your kind of work in the college. Yes, John Dewey wrote about "school as a place to assimilate and integrate recent immigrants into the industrial workforce," but he also wrote about other things including the place of experience in education which is going to be the focus of our discussion on February 1, 2012. With respect to Paulo Freire's framework on Malcolm's education, I have published two books which address that connection. The books are: 1. *Malcolm X and African American Self-Consciousness* (Lewiston, New York: The Edwin Mellen Press, 2005). 2. *Malcolm X: The Seeker of Justice*. (Philadelphia: PA: Xlibris Corporation, 2003). Finally, concerning Marable's book, I have a copy and have read

it extensively but since my last publication on Malcolm was in 2009, I strongly hope there will be other scholars with the courage to continue with this important line of research.[65]

On February 1st after our presentation organized by the Black History Month committee, I met Mark for the first time. After the usual pleasantries, we agreed to meet someday to discuss issues relating to Civil Rights and social justice at Queens College in his days. But before we agreed on the date to meet, Mark had sent me a pack of documents entitled, *Personal Background Documents about Mississippi Freedom Summer'64: Selected Letters and Articles from the Collection of Mark Levy in the Queens College/CUNY Civil Rights Archives.* The collection contained Mark's transcriptions of some of his and his late wife's 1964 Mississippi letters and a few articles which he and his late wife (Betty) were quoted in and a short introduction to create a short Word file packet. He also posted photos which he and his friend took in 1964. There were also 1964 images from Meridian and Mississippi Summer. Mark and I agreed on a formal meeting on April 3, 2012, the date Mark was making a presentation to Professor Evelyn Julmisse's class. Since the presentation was scheduled for 4:30 pm, Mark and I met at 2:00 pm in my office. The following day, after the meeting and his presentation, I received this correspondence from Mark: "I enjoyed our conversations yesterday and appreciate your interest in exploring writing a 'QC-Narrative' using materials in the QC archives. Please contact me whenever you think I can be of assistance. Here are some ideas and materials that might be of interest."[66] Mark's e-mail was accompanied by his piece entitled, *QC 50s-70s Activist Student Narrative.* This was the beginning of what was to be many years of active collaboration as I searched the Queens College archives and sent Mark numerous e-mails, phone calls, and face-to-face meetings in search of information on activism at QC while writing this book. Now, you know.

* * *

Activism at Queens college in the 1960s. Queens college students' historic March on Washington D.C. for jobs & freedom, August 28, 1963. (Photograph, Courtesy of Mark Levy)

NOTES

1. David Farber, *The Age of Great Dreams: America in the 1960s*. New York, NY: Hill and Wang, 1994.
2. The 1960s was an era of massive social reforms intended to improve the social and economic status of the masses. President Lyndon B. Johnson was able to put into place enormous social programs including civil rights, welfare programs, education (Elementary and Secondary Education Act, 1965), manpower training, and health care services. See Richard G. Braungart and Margaret M. Braungart, "Political Generational Themes in the American Student Movements of the 1930s and 1960s." *Journal of Political and Military Sociology* (177–230), Vol. 18 (Winter), 1990, p. 197.
3. Richard G. Braungart and Margaret M. Braungart, "Political Generational Themes in the American Student Movements of the 1930s and 1960s." *Journal of Political and Military Sociology* (177–230), Vol. 18 (Winter), 1990, p. 197.

4. Apart from the assassination of President John F. Kennedy, other leaders were also assassinated during the 1960s: Medgar Evers, June 12, 1963; Martin Luther King, Jr., April 4, 1968; Robert F. Kennedy, June 6, 1968. On August 28, 1968, youthful demonstrators disrupted the Democratic National Convention in Chicago.
5. See Richard G. Braungart and Margaret M. Braungart, "Political Generational Themes," p. 177.
6. See "An Overview of US Student Activism in the 1960s: American Decades." In Alexander Cruden, ed. *Perspectives on Modern World History: Student Movements of the 1960s.* Farmington Hills, MI: Greenhaven Press, 2012, p. 13. Note also that Mario Savio was a former student at Queens College, 1961–1963.
7. Richard G. Braungart and Margaret M. Braungart, "Political Generational Themes," p. 204. See also, Alexander Cruden (ed.). *Perspectives on Modern World History: Student Movements of the 1960s.* Farmington Hills, MI: Greenhaven Press, 2012, pp. 17–18.
8. See Cruden, *Perspectives on Modern World History*, p. 18.
9. During this incident in Kent State, the National Guard fired its weapons into the crowd of demonstrators, killing four students and wounding nine of them.
10. Richard G. Braungart and Margaret M. Braungart, "Political Generational Themes," p. 205.
11. Alexander Cruden (ed.). *Perspectives on Modern World History: Student Movements of the 1960s.* Farmington Hills, MI: Greenhaven Press, 2012, p. 5.
12. QC students went on strike in 1961 in objection to the ban of controversial speakers on campus by the college administration. The students also went to Albany to protest the attempt to introduce tuition into CUNY colleges. QC students were involved in an ongoing fight to keep CUNY totally tuition-free. It is important also to point out that Mario Savio of the FSM at the University of California, Berkeley fame worked as a picket captain during the student strike at QC in 1961. He also went to Albany with other QC students to protest the effort to introduce tuition into CUNY colleges.
13. Mark Levy cited in Jon N. Hale, *The Freedom Schools: Student Activists in The Mississippi Civil Rights Movement.* New York, NY: Columbia University Press, 2018, pp. 83–84.

14. See Steven M. Buechler, *Social Movements in Advanced Capitalism: The Political Economy and Cultural Construction of Social Activism.* New York, NY: Oxford University Press, 2000.
15. Richard G. Braungart and Margaret M. Braungart, "Political Generational Themes," p. 179.
16. Doug McAdam, "Recruitment to High-Risk Activism: The Case of Freedom Summer." *American Journal of Sociology*, Vol. 92, No. 1, 1986.
17. See Kevin Donnellan, "GOODMAN." An unpublished paper, 1993.
18. Michael J. Sandel, *Democracy's Discontent: America in Search of a Public Philosophy.* Cambridge, MA: Harvard University Press, 1996, p. 3.
19. Virginia segregationists met the *Brown* decision and integration with fierce resistance by closing the Prince Edward County Public Schools from 1959 to 1963–64 academic year.
20. See Michael R. Wenger and Stan F. Shaw, "Northerners in a Jim Crow World: Queens College Summer Experience." In Terence Hicks and Abul Pitre, eds. *The Educational Lockout of African Americans in Prince Edward County, Virginia (1959–1964): Personal Accounts and Reflections.* Lanham, MD, University Press of America, 2010. See also, Michael R. Wenger. *My Black Family, My White Privilege: A White Man's Journey through the Nation's Racial Minefield.* Bloomington, IN: iUniverse, Inc., 2012.
21. See Michael R. Wenger and Stan F. Shaw, "Northerners in a Jim Crow World," p. 65.
22. Oral History and Queens Memory Project with Ms. Helen Hendricks. 2019 Queens Library.
23. Mark Levy, Campus Antecedents to the Summer of 1964, n.d.
24. Stan Shaw cited in Queens College Libraries: "Civil Rights: The Queens College Student Help Project.".
25. Oral History and Queens College Project.
26. Queens College Libraries: "Civil Rights: The Queens College Student Help Project.".
27. Michael R. Wenger, *My Black Family, My White Privilege*, p. 40.
28. Ibid.
29. Michael R. Wegner and Stan F. Shaw, "Northerners in a Jim Crow World: Queens College Summer Experience." In Terence Hicks

and Abul Pitre, eds. *The Educational Lockout of African Americans in Prince Edward County, Virginia (1959–1964): Personal Accounts and Reflections* (Lanham, MD: University Press of America, 2010), p. 58.
30. Michael Wenger, *Interview with Helen Hendricks* "Student Help: Lived Experience Project.".
31. Lucy Komisar, "A Personal History of Civil Rights and Feminism," talk at panel on "Women, Queens College, and the Civil Rights Movement," March 16, 2009, Queens College. See Doug McAdam's discussion of Michael Harrington in the resurgence of the Left during the Sixties. *Freedom Summer*, p. 236.
32. Michael R. Wegner and Stan F. Shaw, "Northerners in a Jim Crow World: Queens College Summer Experience." In Terence Hicks and Abul Pitre, eds. *The Educational Lockout of African Americans in Prince Edward County, Virginia (1959–1964): Personal Accounts and Reflections* (Lanham, MD: University Press of America, 2010), p. 65.
33. Michael R. Wenger, *My Black Family, My White Privilege: A White Man's Journey through the Nation's Racial Minefield*, Bloomington, IN: iUniverse, 2012, p. 41.
34. Stefan M. Bradley, *Harlem vs. Columbia University: Black Student Power in the Late 1960s*, Urbana, IL: University of Illinois Press, 2009, p. 64.
35. See Hale, *The Freedom Schools*, p. 84. See also Bradley, *Harlem vs. Columbia*, p. 65.
36. See "Dear Faculty Member," Box 10, folder 1, Michael Wreszin Collection. Department of Special Collections and Archives, Queens College, City University of New York.
37. Joan Nestle's correspondence with the author August 22, 2023.
38. Mark Levy, "QC 50s-70s Activist Student Narrative, n.d. Joan Nestle confirmed Mark Levy's recollection.
39. Joan Nestle's communication with the author August 22, 2023.
40. See also Stan Shaw's conversation with me August 21, 2023.
41. Doug McAdam, *Freedom Summer*., New York, NY: Oxford University Press, 1988, p. 49; Jon N. Hale, *The Freedom Schools*, p. 89.
42. Michael R. Wenger, *My Black Family, My White Privilege*, p. 24. It should be noted that these images were captured on national

television and broadcast throughout the United States and all over the world.
43. Ibid.
44. Mark Levy served as one of the coordinators of the Civil Rights archives at Queens College after his retirement as Executive Director of the Committee of Interns and Residents in 2008.
45. Queens College CORE was originally Queens College chapter of NAACP. This group switched over to CORE during the 1962–1963 academic year.
46. During the research, I had correspondences with four other respondents.
47. Mark Levy (himself a Freedom Summer volunteer) was one of the coordinators of the Civil Rights archives at Queens College. This feat by Mark Levy supports Doug McAdam's contention that activism does not only radicalize participants but puts them in contact with like-minded people embedded in a set of relationships and an emerging activist subculture. Indeed, as soon as Mark Levy relocated to Rhode Island with his wife, he wrote to tell me, "I've also initiated a project to find RI residents and college students who went South in the 1960's for civil rights projects like (MS) Freedom Summer 1964 and (AL) SCOPE Project 1965.".
48. Between 3/14/2012 and 7/8/23, I counted 67 e-mail correspondences, numerous face-to face meetings, and very many phone calls between Mark Levy and I.
49. McAdam, *Freedom Summer*, p. 46.
50. Cited in Bradley, *Harlem vs. Columbia*, p. 65.
51. Doug McAdam, "Recruitment to High-Risk Activism: The Case of Freedom Summer." *American Journal of Sociology*, Vol. 92, No. 1, 1986, pp. 64–90, p. 76.
52. According to Manning Marable, thirty-seven African American churches had been firebombed during Freedom Summer. See Manning Marable. "Searching for Restorative Justice: The Trial of Edgar Ray Killen" *Souls*, Vol. 10. No. 2, 2008, p. 156.
53. See Manning Marable. "Searching for Restorative Justice: The Trial of Edgar Ray Killen" *Souls*, Vol. 10. No. 2, 2008, p. 155.
54. Belinda Robnett, *How Long? How Long?: African-American Women in the Struggle for Civil Rights*. New York: NY: Oxford University Press, 1999.

55. Rob Rosenthal and Lois Brown, "Then and Now: Comparing Today's Student Activism With the 1960s," *HuffPost*, August 27, 2014, Updated October 27, 2014.
56. Ibid., p. 2.
57. Doug McAdam, "The Biographical Consequences of Activism." *American Sociological Review*, Vol. 54, No. 5, 1989, pp. 752–753; See also, Doug McAdam, *Freedom Summer*, p. 234.
58. This is the conclusion Doug McAdam came to in his many studies: "The Biographical Consequences of Activism." *American Sociological Review*, Vol. 54, No. 5, 1989, pp. 744–760; Doug McAdam, *Freedom Summer*. New York, NY: Oxford University Press, 1988; Doug McAdam, "Recruitment to High-Risk Activism: The Case of Freedom Summer." *American Journal of Sociology*, Vol. 92, No. 1, 1986, pp. 64–90.
59. Mark Levy, "QC 50s-70s activist student narrative." (n. d).
60. Doug McAdam, "The Biographical Consequences of Activism." *American Sociological Review*, Vol. 54, No. 5, 1989, pp. 744–760. Doug McAdam, *Freedom Summer*. New York, NY: Oxford University Press, 1988.
61. Doug McAdam, "The Biographical Consequences of Activism," p. 755. See also, Jerusha O. Conner, *The New Student Activists: The Rise of Neoactivism on College Campuses*. Baltimore, MD: Johns Hopkins University Press.
62. E-mail correspondence from Mark Levy to the author, January 1, 2012.
63. Ibid.
64. Ibid.
65. Correspondence to Mark. Levy, January 2, 2012. Up to this point, I did not know that Mark levy was a White man. I thought he was a Black professor who did not want to take his own risk.
66. Correspondence from Mark Levy, April 4, 2012.

CHAPTER 2

Queens College: A History

> *My education at Queens (College) was a political and moral education, moving from the civil rights movement to the women's movement to what I do now. It wasn't in the course catalog, but that education has been the basis for everything I've done in my life. The issue for students and others here is whether you make political and moral values part of yours.*
> —Lucy Komisar
>
> *Because the students went out into the larger community each day, as residents, family members, and jobholders, they were always part of the real world, and responded to it immediately and fully.*
> —Lee Cogan

The pursuit of knowledge and the desire to serve and support others are ingrained in the history of Queens College (QC). Located on a beautiful piece of land on a hill in Flushing, Queens, QC was established with "the goal of offering a first-rate education to all people regardless of background or financial means,"[1] specifically within the growing population in the borough of Queens. Parents in Queens who could not afford to send their children away for college felt a pressing need to still see their children receive a college education. Although the population of the borough of Queens had grown to 1,250,000 by 1935, Queens had no public college or university of its own.[2] After a series of meetings held over the span

© The Author(s), under exclusive license to Springer Nature Switzerland AG 2024
M. O. Bassey, *Student Activism in 1960s America*, Palgrave Studies in the History of Social Movements,
https://doi.org/10.1007/978-3-031-54794-2_2

of two years, the people of Queens decided to form a "Committee for a Free City College" with Queens County Judge Charles S. Colden as its chairperson. A fact-finding committee chaired by Dr. Samuel A. Rutledge was set up by Judge Colden to establish the need for and the means of funding such an institution. This committee affirmed the need for a college in Queens, emphasizing that "statistics about high school graduates and Queens students either in attendance at, or turned away for lack of space from, the existing city colleges—City, Hunter, and Brooklyn,"[3] was tremendous. The report of the committee went on to say that,

> the City of New York has available an ideal college plant, the Parental School, which belongs to its educational facilities... Located on one of the highest and most central points in Queens, this plot of 107 acres presents the possibility of development into one of the most beautiful college campuses in America giving adequate room for growth and sports fields for the next 50 years.[4]

The interesting story in the history of QC is that with the closure of the Parental School in 1935, the fact-finding committee proposed establishing a city college in its place. Having amassed reasons for the creation of the college, Judge Colden moved on to mobilize citizens to canvass for the establishment of an institution of higher learning in Queens.[5]

Based on the fact-finding report and after extensive study and reviews, members of the Committee for a Queens Free College forwarded a petition to Mayor Fiorello LaGuardia of the City of New York and members of the Board of Higher Education,[6] requesting a college in Queens. The petition read:

> We, the undersigned, residents of Queens County respectfully PETITION the honorable persons and bodies hereinbefore named to take all steps necessary for the establishment of a free city college for the borough of Queens at the site of the old Parental School in Flushing.[7]

An informal poll taken by the *Brooklyn Eagle* newspaper, together with other surveys and committee reports, showed overwhelming support by the public regarding the establishment of the college. Supporters included religious leaders; civic, social, cultural, and educational organizations; public officials; citizens with no affiliations; and social and welfare officers and workers. Due to the overwhelming nature of the support for the college, a local newspaper concluded, "The proposed free college in

Queens may rise as the University of the Future."[8] The people's expectations were met on December 25, 1936, when Mayor LaGuardia accepted the establishment of QC using the facilities of the Parental School, which had been abandoned for about a year. On April 6, 1937, the Board of Higher Education of the City of New York created Queens College with the following pronouncements: "that the Board...does hereby create and establish an educational unit or center in the County and Borough of Queens to be known as Queens College." The pronouncement went on to add that the college would be "a college of liberal arts and sciences."[9] A budget of $424,000 for the "proposed Queens College reconstruction..."[10] was approved by the Board of Estimate. The college opened its doors for the first registration of students on October 4, 1937, and had four hundred students across sixteen departments in three divisions: Arts, Social Sciences, Mathematics and the Natural Sciences. At its outset, there were thirty-four faculty members and fifty-six staff.[11] During a board meeting on May 25, 1937, Dr. Paul Klapper, who was then Dean of the School of Education at City College, was elected the first president of QC, and Dr. Margaret V. Kiely, the former principal of Bridgeport Normal School in Connecticut, was named the first Dean of the College. Dr. Klapper envisioned the new college as "a community of scholars serving others," by his personal choice of the motto, *Discimus ut Serviamus*: We learn so that we may serve.[12] In a speech at the testimonial dinner given by Queens College Association at Pomonok Country Club in his honor on June 17, 1937, Dr. Klapper stated,

> It is our hope to make of Queens College a great intellectual center. We hope that it will give the residents of Queens an opportunity to hear the leaders in American thought; that its auditorium will welcome the best that America has to offer in music and drama; that its exhibition halls will exhibit the best in representational and plastic arts...We have our dream, but reality is only a dream realized.[13]

Sharing a sentiment that would later drive QC students in support of activism with louder resonance, Klapper conscientized them to translate their quality education into service; to make service to their communities highly visible. And to the college's beginning class, he stated, "We are the pioneers of a new institution. We have no history to look back to, but we can look forward to progress."[14] During the First Dedication Day ceremonies on October 26, 1937, Mayor LaGuardia vocalized his support of QC, advising the institution to be a quintessential fortress of learning, its aspirations, hopes, and ideals high. The year 1941 witnessed major events at the college: QC received full accreditation from the New York State Department of Education and the Alumni Association was founded. It held its first commencement in the same year, wherein Dr. Klapper declared: "A great city has reaffirmed its faith in youth." Of importance also was the publication of the college yearbook, *Silhouette*, as well as QC's accreditation by the Middle States Association of Colleges and Secondary Schools.

QC is one of the senior colleges in the City University of New York system.[15] Queens College is nationally rated for its liberal arts and sciences as well as for its preprofessional programs, giving it the title of "the jewel of the CUNY system."[16] It occupies eighty acres of land between Kissena Boulevard and Main Street in Flushing. The college has grown substantially in the number of students and educational standards from its humble beginning of four hundred students in 1937 to a student enrollment of about seventeen thousand today, made up of undergraduate and graduate students organized into four divisions: Arts and Humanities; Mathematics and the Natural Sciences; the Social Sciences; and Education. A recent college publication shows that the student body is comprised of people from over 150 countries.[17] QC students speak many languages, and the college prides itself as the most diverse campus in the state of New York and indeed in the entire country. Regarding ethnic diversity in both the borough of Queens and at Queens College, Dr. James L. Muyskens, president of the college (2002–2013) in a publication once stated:

> The new diversity in the borough led to an explosion of new businesses and a blooming of ethnic and language studies at Flushing's own institute of higher education, Queens College. We now have programs, centers, and institutes that study the rich histories of Asians, Jews, the Irish, Italians, Greeks, Latinos, African Americans, and others, and offer a thriving English as a Second Language program. Our New Immigrants and Old Americans project has published six books on the effects of this new wave of immigration.[18]

* * *

So how, then, did such a relatively small liberal arts college in New York become a hotbed of student activism in the 1960s? As we now know, QC started as a small, conservative liberal arts college.[19] According to Rosalyn Terborg-Penn, a former QC student activist,[20] the image of Queens College students in the 1960s as an enlightened radical student body was deceiving because,

> Only a few students came to the college radicalized by their parents' politics. For most of us, our formal secondary education had been just as conservative as any other consensus system of the 1950s and early 1960s, both intellectually and politically. Our college education was similarly conservative, as we battled against the status quo in our search for "truth."[21]

Not surprisingly, given its conservative credentials, in 1959 two campus student papers, *Crown* and *Rampart*, were suspended by the college administration for being too radical and confrontational. The conservative nature of the college can be gleaned further from the fact that in 1960, the college administration imposed a dress code on women students (no shorts, no slacks, or "similar attire" based on the theory of *in loco parentis*—in place of parents). Through their interpretation of *in loco parentis*, Queens College administration arrogated to itself the duty and authority to act in the place of parents. This authority, the administration argued, extended from setting dress codes, demanding students always carry ID cards, and denying students any say in the school curriculum.[22] Mark Levy, president of the QC Student Association (1962–1963) was suspended briefly for challenging a Queens College Dean's right to demand his ID card. Levy explained that the confrontation with the Dean happened as he was having a deep conversation with a student who was about to reveal to him how he (the student) functioned as an FBI agent who reported events and individuals on campus to the FBI.[23] During the presidency of Dr. John J. Theobald (1949–1958), he had made it absolutely clear that "he would not tolerate left-wing or collectivist activism at Queens College,"[24] by wielding extraordinary power that he had created for himself. Accordingly, in 1950, he suspended four student organizations, their members, and the elected Student Council representatives for inviting Celia Zitron, a representative of the Teachers Union who had been suspended by the Board of Education, to speak on campus. Twenty-two other students who distributed fliers condemning the president's high-handedness were disciplined with probation as well.[25] President Theobald justified his actions in a mimeographed letter written on May

27, 1950, to students and faculty that "It appears that all the individuals concerned suffered under the misconception that they were acting in defense of democracy and did not realize that in defying law and order they were, in fact, evoking 'lynch law' and dealing the most serious blow possible to democracy."[26] Indeed, in those days, even the Teachers Union was considered subversive. A left-wing student organization, the American Youth for Democracy, was denied a charter of association by the college. Similarly, Howard Fast, a renowned left-leaning novelist, was forced to speak outside the gate of the college, even though a student organization had officially invited him to deliver the talk.[27]

Faculty and staff were not exempt from these draconian policies. Harold Lenz, Dean of Students, a man who believed in freedom of speech, freedom of opinion, and freedom of association was immediately removed from his position when President Theobald took office.[28] In October 1952, Dr. Vera Shlakman, assistant professor of economics, was terminated from the college because she refused to testify before the Senate Internal Security Subcommittee of the Judiciary Committee about Communist Party membership. The following year, Dr. Oscar Shaftel,[29] assistant professor of English and one of the original faculty members at Queens College, was also terminated from his position for refusing to say whether he had been a member of the Communist Party after testifying before the Senate Internal Security Subcommittee. Finally, Dudley P. Straus, an instructor in English, was similarly relieved of his post in 1955, purportedly because of his Communist Party affiliation as well.[30] These professors were dismissed from the college under Section 903 of the New York City charter: a resolution of the New York City Council that prohibited employees from asserting their Fifth Amendment rights or from refusing to answer questions from a court or properly constituted committee of inquiry. These three professors were relieved of their posts because they were active trade unionists, which had nothing to do with their reputations as teachers and scholars of international repute. They were never charged with influencing students in their classrooms in any negative way.

"The firing of the three professors was only one manifestation of the repression of faculty, albeit the most visible," noted Lawrence Kaplan. "All faculty members now had to sign a loyalty oath as a condition of employment. Conservative administrators denied tenure to instructors whose politics were deemed unacceptable."[31] The communist hysteria on campus during this period caused a student reporter to write in the 1957 college yearbook (*Silhouette*) that the college was "surrounded for three years by unparalleled political turmoil. We witnessed the dismissal of some of our favorite instructors, and were swept up in an aura of fear. While some were dancing to the rhythms of the juke box, others were fighting for 'academic freedom,' political tolerance, arguing about the rights of teachers and administrators."[32]

These draconian policies continued into the early 1960s, with the college administration under President Harold W. Stoke barring the QC Marxist Discussion club from inviting the Communist Party national secretary, Benjamin J. Davis, to speak on campus on October 9, 1961. Similarly, the Queens College administration banned the young Nation of Islam's spokesperson, Malcolm X,[33] from speaking on campus at the invitation of the Queens College chapter of the NAACP in 1961. To maintain a sense of fairness because of student agitation, rather than by conviction another student club was barred from inviting the conservative leader William F. Buckley, Jr., to campus by the college administration.[34] Just as with the strict dress code for women, this, the administration argued, was justified based on the principle of *in loco parentis*.

* * *

The brief introduction above leaves one to wonder how students from this traditionally conservative institution were at the forefront of social activism and social justice struggles in the 1960s. Mark Levy, a former QC student activist, explained that it was the subgroup of artsy, poetry-reading, guitar-playing bohemians,[35] and beatniks[36] who brought activism and activist backgrounds onto QC campus as "red-diaper babies."[37] Most of the bohemians and red-diaper babies, Levy affirmed, had known one another from attending progressive summer camps as children. He maintained, and I agree, that "the story of Queens College student activism should be told in the historical context of the campus of the period that preceded it."[38] It is therefore safe to say that a series of events in the early 1960s were precursors to Queens College students' galvanization into action in search of social justice. First in this series of events was the anti-communist witch-hunt by QC administration that forced student clubs to disinvite their guest speakers. The Administrative Council of the City University of New York, CUNY governing body "upheld the cancelation (of invited speakers) on the grounds that inviting a Communist to speak on campus would violate the University's obligation to 'obey the laws of the state and the nation.'"[39] QC student union protested the ban based on academic freedom and free speech.[40] While the American Civil Liberties Union contested the ban in court, Dr. Stoke, then president of Queens College, explained that "the ban on Communists would probably not apply to visiting dignitaries from Communist countries," because "[a] speech by a foreign Communist would have educational value…while a speech by a native member of the party could only be aimed at propagandizing among students."[41] QC students organized a rally on October 25 that was followed by a one-day strike on November 16, 1961, in which "Ban the ban" signs, posters, and leaflets were posted throughout the campus. The student association led by Kenneth (Kenny) Warner organized the strike, though it was supported by other social clubs, fraternities, sororities, and house-plans. According to published reports in *Phoenix*, the student newspaper, over 72% of the students refused to attend classes on that day.[42] The paper justified the strike by noting, "It's plain and simple—we want to choose our speakers. We aren't concerned with either Communists or Muslims." The paper went on to state, "We're striking against unintellectual prejudgments made against 'dangerous' ideologies—we're striking for a broader spectrum of selection than our administration allows."[43] Seth Cagin and Philip Dray noted, "For many students the Queens College strike was a heady introduction to the efficacy of confrontational politics, a declaration of independence from the older generation."[44] The student protest was a visible social critique of the overbearing policies of the college administration, and provided the students a direct and immediate way of thinking they could change the direction of the institution themselves. In a letter addressed to President Stoke, Mark Levy, then a third-year student, accused the president of creating an atmosphere of fear and intimidation, effectively trampling on academic freedom and the civil liberties of students and faculty on campus. "Whether I espouse the causes of Lincoln Rockwell, Ben Davis, or Robert Welch," Levy wrote, "is of no relevance to believing that they have the right to speak and be heard."[45] To support his contention of intimidation and the culture of fear created by the president, Levy went on to say:

> What disturbs me most is that while circulating the petition [...] urging the City University presidents to maintain an open speaker policy, I met many students who were afraid to sign even though they said that they

believed that what we were asking for was right. They were afraid that if they expressed their opinions publicly, they might be hurt when trying to enter a profession or graduate school.[46]

As Levy saw it, "When a person cannot feel free to express his opinion in our democratic society, there is something deathly wrong... because when you forbid one person to speak, many people become afraid to speak."[47] He told the president that it disturbed him greatly when he confronted students who were gripped by fear because "no true scholarship can exist in such an atmosphere."[48] Levy made it quite clear to the president that he was even more frustrated when he encountered faculty members who were scared to speak their minds for fear of reprisal. And in a defiant but somber tone, he stated:

> Several teachers whom I have approached have shown this same fear and hesitation. I feel that I have been let down and that my teachers have failed me. In history, philosophy, contemporary civilization, music, art, language, English, science, and education courses, my teachers have told me about the conflict of ideas and about the struggles of great men against apathy and suppression of thought. My teachers tell me about the greatness of our country, our ideals, our rights, and our liberties and freedoms. But when it comes right down to a direct application or personal exertion, their teachings become just so many meaningless words.[49]

Levy reminded the president that academic freedom must exist on campus because the "whole history of education has been a fight for the free expression of ideas."[50] He concluded by stating categorically that any change in the open speaker policy in the City University system would not only hinder free inquiry but would increase an intolerable and frightening atmosphere of fear.[51]

Another major event that crystallized and energized student protests at Queens College was the introduction of tuition in CUNY colleges by the state government. Before now, there was no tuition paid at any of the CUNY colleges. Arguably, this issue brought the concept of social class, economic self-interest, and social justice to students' consciousness and reverberated throughout CUNY colleges and beyond. The Queens College Student Association made its position on the imposition of tuition at the city colleges and universities clear by the production and distribution of **"Our Position—No Tuition"** buttons that students wore throughout campus.[52] This legacy has continued, with buttons worn city-wide for union issues. QC students embarked on letter writing campaigns, lobbying, and demonstrations, all to halt the state's imposition of fees on CUNY students. QC students reached out to other students from Hunter, City College, and Brooklyn College for support, thus facilitating cooperation with the other CUNY colleges.

Student upheavals against totalitarian rules of the Queens College administration, the anti-McCarthyism fight of the Cold War era, and the tuition fight at CUNY colleges provided the framework and breeding ground for student activism. On this, Mark Levy stated:

> The self-interest-driven, student rights activism around *in loco parentis* and tuition issues of the early '60s, provided a necessary break from the quietude of the McCarthy period. That experience created the space for the transitions into the civil rights, anti-war, anti-imperialism, and feminist activity that followed—and introduced many QC students (beyond the "small caf" groups) to their first taste of organizing and speaking out. For me personally, it led me to become active in student government and become Student Association President in 1962–63.[53]

Queens College students played a leading role in the anti-CUNY tuition hike imbroglio, and interestingly, the fight against tuition helped to connect campuses together into a national student movement around several issues.[54]

* * *

As we now know, student activism does not arise in a vacuum. A variety of social and racial issues appear to have galvanized students at QC at the time, including the House Un-American Activities Committee (HUAC) hearing and the anti-HUAC demonstrations in San Francisco, California, as well as the local Queens College student chapter of Women Strike for Peace (WSP), which raised questions and concerns about the hazards posed by nuclear testing to children's health. This group of women activists had as their slogan, "End the Arms Race not the Human Race." These activists invited guest speakers to campus to speak on the impending nuclear catastrophe in the world. Activists were also invited to speak on the Cuban missile crisis. Also, of importance to the growing social consciousness on campus, were events in the South such as the Montgomery Bus boycott. The determination of those who were prepared to fight for racial justice convinced a group of Queens College students of the intrinsic essence of racial justice and the abolition of Jim Crow oppression.[55] Michael Wenger and Stan Shaw, two QC student activists have argued that even though discrimination and injustices existed in the North, these paled in comparison to the barefaced deprivation of Black people's fundamental human rights that ran rampant in the South, contradicting the country's declaration that all people are created equal. QC students watched White people's vicious attacks on Black students in Little Rock, Arkansas; bus burnings in Anniston, Alabama; the sight of Birmingham, Alabama firefighters and police officers using police dogs and water hoses on Black children. This agglomeration of inequality added steam to the moral outrage of some QC students who understood American civic tradition to mean freedom from coercion. Considering these events, the Queens College chapter of the Congress of Racial Equality (CORE) was born with the objective of actively supporting "the courageous young black-and-white protesters in the South."[56] Following the bans on political advocacy and free speech on college campuses at a time of intense surge in student activism, student groups began a series of protests in the summer of 1964. However, I want to argue here that students at Queens College, as was the case with college students all over the country during the 1960s, were involved in rebellious behaviors as a sort of passive resistance to authority and agency, by expanding the boundaries of dissent and challenging the status quo. At QC, Stephen Stepanchev noted, "There was a stretching of limits, even in matters of dress," perhaps as a way of distinguishing between the generations. On campus, Stepanchev said, "Men and women wore blue jeans in and out of the classroom, shorts, long hair, and beads. The men also wore beards and sometimes a single earring. Black students wore Afro haircuts."[57]

The March on Washington during the summer of 1963, which a good number of QC students attended, also served as a great impetus for activism for those who attended because, as one of the QC participants in the March later revealed, "It was an inspiring day, one I feel lucky to have participated in."[58] Those who participated in the March took Reverend King's message to heart and were prepared to confront institutional racism through peaceful means. King's message awakened these groups of students to the racial injustice and oppression in the country.

* * *

What has not been emphasized enough regarding students' motivation to action and activism at QC is the student press. Unlike other liberal arts colleges, QC had and still has a vibrant and combative student press. These independent and grassroots publications included *The Crown, Rampart, The Phoenix, The Activist, Graffitti, Queens College Underground Press, The Castle, The Free Press, Knightbeat* later known as *Newsbeat*, and more. A number of these papers were recognized by the college administration, but many others were underground. Indeed, the history of these publications with the college administration was sometimes stormy at best if not outright rocky at times, culminating in the college administration ending the publication of *Crown* and *Rampart* in 1959 by vote from the college's faculty council, even though *Crown* had been published since Queens College was founded in 1937 and *Rampart* came about a decade later. The two student papers were replaced by *Phoenix*, and *Phoenix* itself was engulfed in several disputes with the administration, which placed the *Phoenix* editorial board on suspension at some point. The *Free Press* in one of its editorials maintained that "Freedom of the press is one of the most basic rights that can be granted to students—- and one that they must fight for when it is denied."[59] The quotation below serves as a notable reminder of the combative nature of QC students' desire for a free and enlightened press:

> The Queens College campus was hit by a double-barreled blow against a one-newspaper policy this week. The first attack came last Friday, when the College's Student Senate voted unanimously to recommend to an administrative committee that the seven-year-old one-newspaper policy be ended. The second attack was begun this morning, with the first issue of the *Free Press*. The paper is an independent weekly, which will cover news of the Queens College campus and events of interest to students. The paper was produced by a group of student leaders, headed by Student Association President Harvey Weiner, in an attempt to show the Queens administrators that there was a need for a second newspaper...[60]

Arguing against both the dress code and the concept of *in loco parentis*, the *Free Press* wrote:

> [S]tudent activities are expected to enhance the intellectual and cultural life of the college community, provide opportunities for students to assume positions of responsible leadership, provide opportunities for students to participate as members of a democratic organization, and foster a high level

of community morale through faculty-student cooperation in planning and conducting community affairs. Beginning with their own basic assumptions one must conclude that men and women of good intentions are able to determine appropriate dress for themselves.[61]

The paper concluded, "More important, how can dress regulations be justified as a means of enhancing anyone's intellectual or cultural life?"[62] Reporting on the student protests against the dress code, the *Free Press* stated, "Today, in direct violation of Queens College dress regulations, coeds are attending classes, frequenting the library, the College Memorial Center, and the cafeteria in slacks. The demonstration was called for by campus leaders and the Queens College Student Senate in order to demonstrate active student support for the revocation of dress regulations."[63]

* * *

It is therefore no wonder when Rosalyn Terborg-Penn, herself a QC alumnus and a member of the Student Help Project, wrote about student activism at QC in the following words:

In the 1960s, the image some had of Queens College of the City University of New York was of enlightened radical students, many of whom struck against academic freedom violations and attacked discrimination against Black people by participating in the civil rights movement. At home some of us joined the northern student movement, while others went south to work with SNCC.[64]

As one commentator noted, "Students at Queens College were far from passive in the period 1960–1975. Activism was in the air.... Students took part in strikes, demonstrations, sit-ins, teach-ins, marches, and debates; they passed resolutions, made demands, and distributed leaflets on and off campus."[65] He went on to conclude that the students, "seemed to be moved by a desire for individual freedom and social justice.... They supported academic freedom, civil rights for minorities, women's liberation, gay liberation, [and] student representation on the College governing bodies."[66]

A major campus event that drew the public's attention, (including that of the *New York Times* and local television stations in New York), to the oppression, exploitation, and disenfranchisement of Blacks being perpetuated in Mississippi and other parts of the South occurred in 1964 when it was heard that three civil rights volunteers (one of them, Andrew Goodman, a QC student) went missing in Mississippi.[67] Seven students from Queens College went on a five-day hunger strike (*Fast for Freedom*) to draw attention to the plight of these missing civil rights activists. The memo announcing *Fast for Freedom* had Michael Wenger, chair of the Student Help Project, and Ronald (Ron) Pollack, president of the Student Association, as contacts. This protest evoked anger and resentment toward those who were responsible for the atrocities in Mississippi. Utilizing the weapon of moral suasion, the protest efforts under the leadership of Michael Wenger's Student Help Project, Carolyn Hubbard's CORE, and the Queens College Student Association led by Ronald Pollack sparked great resentment on the Queens College campus among the students against the perpetrators.[68] The fast was to dramatize the students' demands for federal intervention in Mississippi and to help create a moral climate in which federal intervention was possible. Starting July 2, 1964, at 3:00 p.m., the fasting students consumed nothing but water thereby putting their bodies and health on the line.[69] According to a statement written by the organizers, several students were to undergo *Fast for Freedom* in the hope that it would start a chain of similar events on other campuses.[70] The organizers passed out leaflets to motivate others to action. The seven students involved in the five-day hunger strike included: Gary Ackerman, Steve Brooks, Ronald Pollack, Eric Rosenthal, Howard Schwartz, Michael Wenger, and Charles Simmons.[71] The fasting students lived together in the basement at the First Methodist Church in Flushing at night. During weekdays they had their headquarters in the Alumni Room at the College Memorial Center on campus from 8:00 a.m. to 10:00 p.m., Monday through Thursday, and from 8:00 a.m. to 4:00 p.m., on Friday. They did continue to attend classes during the weekdays though.[72] The fasting students reminded the nation that the fight for freedom in Mississippi was a fight for democracy, which could only be won through a combination of internal state initiatives, heightened national consensus, and massive federal intervention to guarantee the fundamental rights of Black people in Mississippi. Appealing to the better side of the nation, the students reiterated the necessity that something could and must be done by the federal government. Many of the QC students who were not fasting were involved in press releases, publicity, outreach, and lobbying to support the request for federal protection for the Civil Rights workers in Mississippi. To say the least, these efforts were rewarded because shortly after, Senator Kenneth B. Keating, US senator from New York and a member of the Committee on the Judiciary, sent the following correspondence to the students:

Dear Friend:
Many thanks for your recent message concerning the students who are spending the summer in Mississippi in a voter registration drive. Please be assured that I stand ready and willing to assist any New York student whose own civil rights are violated in the course of this work. In this connection, the enclosed telegram may be of interest to you. Please do not hesitate to get in touch with me again if I can be of further assistance. I regret that the great pressures of mail I am receiving dictate this form of reply. I know you will understand.
Very sincerely yours,
Kenneth B. Keating[73]

In a telegram to Robert F. Kennedy, the attorney general, dated June 23, 1964, Senator Keating wrote:

HONORABLE ROBERT F. KENNEDY
THE ATTORNEY GENERAL
DEPARTMENT OF JUSTICE
WASHINGTON, D. C.
TWO NEW YORKERS, MICHAEL SCHWERNER AND ANDREW GOODMAN WHO ARE IN MISSISSIPPI TO ASSIST IN A VOTER REGISTRATION DRIVE HAVE DISAPPEARED AND ARE THE SUBJECT OF A WIDE SEARCH.
THE PRESIDENT HAS INDICATED THAT EVERYTHING POSSIBLE WILL BE DONE TO INVESTIGATE THIS DISAPPEARANCE. I AM CONFIDENT THAT YOU WILL MAKE THE FACILITIES OF YOUR OFFICE FULLY AVAILABLE FOR THAT PURPOSE.
MAY I SUGGEST THAT U.S. MARSHALS BE ASSIGNED TO PROTECT THE CONSTITUTIONAL RIGHTS OF THE YOUNG PEOPLE WHO ARE IN MISSISSIPPI IN CONNECTION WITH VOTER REGISTRATION DRIVES. I WOULD APPRECIATE YOUR REACTION TO THIS SUGGESTION.
KENNETH B. KEATING
U.S. SENATOR[74]

Following the efforts of the Student Help Project leadership in raising political and social awareness about the missing civil rights volunteers in Mississippi and for keeping the memories of the slain civil rights workers alive, the parents of Andrew Goodman poignantly declared in a letter dated October 2, 1964, addressed to both Michael Wenger and Stan Shaw (two leaders of the Student Help Project and CORE) noting: "Time cannot change our loss, but you have softened its sharpness with your own expressions of love and hope, purpose and action."[75] The couple went on to write:

> Your tributes to Andy, to James and Michael are proper tributes to yourself, and to the continued, fearless commitment of our youth in this cause. They are the living promise of America and James, Michael and Andrew will always be alive in this promise. An old spirit has been renewed and is aboard once more in our land. It is certain now we shall overcome! They and you are the strong but tender voices of humanity that have reached us from all parts of our country and many countries of the world.....[76]

The couple concluded, "And so together our lives have been touched by this immortality and because of it we shall never forget!".[77]

The contributions of Ms. Helen Hendricks in encouraging students to participate in the activist movement, and in the recruitment efforts on campus must also be acknowledged. According to Mark Levy, one of the Freedom Summer volunteers from QC, Ms. Hendricks, an Administrative Assistant in the office of Student Affairs, "was a key campus voice giving us kids the encouragement to invest time and take risks in doing the 'right' and 'just' things."[78] Finally, Jerusha O. Conner argues that to understand why some students turn to activism, one must understand the dialectical relation between the student activists and their higher educational institution. This is because students are challenged and changed through their coursework, and in their interaction with faculty, staff, and their peers.[79] Conner explains that professors impact students in infinite ways through the kinds of knowledge, analysis, language, and pedagogy that they use in their classes. Lucy Komisar, a QC student activist, stated in a lecture in 2009, that her education at QC was a political and a moral one even though these were not written in the college catalog. She remembered particularly well Michael Harrington who held weekly public meetings with them at Deb's Hall where they talked and debated ideology, history, politics, and social movements.[80]

Indeed, campus climate shapes the context in which perceptions, attitudes, expectations, and behavior are produced. Michael Wenger in his book, *My Black Family, My White Privilege: A White Man's Journey through the Nation's Racial Minefield*, maintained that in a call to action, Dr. Sidney B. Simon (1927–2023), a professor, and CORE adviser at QC, often said to them, "That's the sound of a police billy club on a child's head. Now, what are you going to do about it?"[81] On reflection, Wenger, one of Dr. Simon's students and a volunteer for the Jamaica and Virginia Student Help Projects, thinks that Dr. Simon, in effect, was telling them to back up their words with action. These are Wenger's direct words, "But Sid was telling us that this wasn't enough. If our commitment to freedom and justice was truly a deeply held value, we had to act repeatedly over time…"[82] In another example, a 1964 QC student activist remembered Dr. Weddington (a QC professor and student advisor) who often persuaded them (students), "to do the right thing," and join the fight for human dignity.[83] It is important to note also that the Freedom Week at QC campus was a period of consciousness-raising and ideological commitment to the cause of student activism in the college. It was a period where beliefs about activism were created and reinforced and a period where activism was incubated at the college. Throughout the remaining chapters of this book, we will see the dialectical relationship between QC and student activism as well as the sociopolitical conditions that shaped and propelled some QC students into activism in the 1960s.

NOTES

1. *Queens College, City University of New York*. Wikipedia (Accessed 6/27/2019).
2. Queens College. *Queens College of the City University of New York, 1937–1962* written by Lee Cogan; Harold W. Stoke, President, New York, Queens College, 1963, p. 12.
3. Ibid., p. 16.
4. Ibid., pp. 16 & 19.
5. Queens College: *The People's College on the Hill: Fifty Years at Queens College, 1937–1987*; edited by Stephen Stepanchev, Shirley Strum Kenny, President, New York, Queens College, 1988.
6. Other organizations to which the petition was addressed include: The Board of Estimate and Apportionment of the City of New

York; The Board of Aldermen of the City of New York; The Municipal Assembly of the City of New York; The Board of Higher Education of the City of New York; The Board of Education of the City of New York. See Petition Book, Department of Special Collections and Archives, Queens College, City University of New York.
7. Petition Book, Department of Special Collections and Archives, Queens College, City University of New York.
8. Queens College: *Queens College of the City University of New York, 1937–1962,* New York, Queens College, 1963, p. 16.
9. Ibid., p. 21.
10. Ibid., p. 16.
11. See Ibid., p. 25.
12. See Lee Cogan, In *The People's College on the Hill: Fifty Years at Queens College, 1937–1987*, edited by Stephen Stepanchev. New York, Queens College, 1988, p. 9.
13. Stephen Stepanchev ed. *The People's College on the Hill: Fifty Years at Queens College, 1937–1987*, p. 12.
14. Ibid.
15. The City University of New York is the largest urban public university in the United States. It has seven community colleges, 11 senior colleges, and seven graduate or professional institutions spread throughout New York City. It serves more than 260,000 undergraduate and graduate students and awards 55,000 degrees each year.
16. Wikipedia, Queens College, City University of New York. From Wikipedia, the free encyclopedia. http://en.wikipedia.org/wiki/Queens_College_City_University_of_New_York (Accessed 5/2/2012).
17. About QC. http://www.qc.cuny.edu/about/Pages/default.aspx
18. Cited in President Muyskens' page, Queens College Web Page. Originally published with the title, "Religious Diversity in Queens." In Ellen Freudenheim, ed. *Queens: What to Do, Where to Go (and How Not to Get Lost) in New York's Undiscovered Borough,* New York: St. Martin's Press, 2006. http://www.qc.cuny.edu/about/administration/president/Pages/NewsArchive.aspx?ItemID=1... (Accessed 5/9/2012).
19. Mark Levy wrote in his notes in, "QC 50s–70s activist student narrative," "The campus, when I came in 1960, was pretty quiet

and conservative except for a few artsy, poetry-reading, guitar-playing bohemians and beatniks whom I came to hang out with, in the 'small caf.'".
20. Rosalyn Terborg-Penn was a 1963 graduate from Queens College, see chapter two.
21. Rosalyn Terborg-Penn, "A Black History Journey: Encountering Aptheker along the Way." *Nature, Society, and Thought*, Volume 10 Issue 1&2, 1997, p. 189. Another QC student, Mark Levy also reported that when he first came to QC, the campus was pretty quiet and conservative.
22. Mark Levy, "QC 50s-70s Activist Student Narrative." (n.d.).
23. Ibid.
24. Stephen Stepanchev (ed.), *The People's College on the Hill*, p. 58.
25. Ibid.
26. Ibid.
27. Lawrence Kaplan, "McCarthyism at Queens College." *Unpublished Paper Deposited in Queens College Archives,* (n.d.), p. 2.
28. Ibid., p. 1.
29. Professor Shaftel was reinstated to his position in 1982.
30. Stepanchev (ed.), *The People's College on the Hill*, p. 60.
31. Lawrence Kaplan, "McCarthyism at Queens College" *Unpublished paper deposited in Queens College Archives*, (n.d.), p. 4.
32. Stepanchev (ed.), *The People's College on the Hill*, p. 60.
33. Malcolm X was invited to speak at Queens College by QC chapter of NAACP. See Seth Cagin and Philip Dray, *We Are Not Afraid: The Story of Goodman, Schwerner, and Chaney, and the Civil Rights Campaign for Mississippi*. New York: Nation Books, 2006, p. 101.
34. See Mark Levy, "QC 50s-70s Activist Student Narrative." (n.d.).
35. This referred to students with unconventional lifestyle.
36. Those students who developed youth counterculture.
37. These were sons and daughters of Jewish intellectuals or labor unionists whose parents or relatives had joined revolutionary and socialist movements and communicated to their children and wards radical political values that made the Civil Rights movement an attractive option.
38. Mark Levy, "QC 50s-70s Activist Student Narrative."
39. J. Lee Auspitz, "Crimson's Ad Protests Ban on Speeches: Queens College Paper Runs Editors' Appeal." Published: Tuesday,

November 21, 1961. http://www.thecrimson.com/article/1961/11/21/crimsons-ad-protests-ban-on-speeches/ (Accessed 5/4/2012).
40. See "Speaker Policy." Box 2 folder 21, Michael Wenger Collection, Department of Special Collections and Archives, Queens College, City University of New York.
41. J. Lee Auspitz, "Crimson's Ad Protests Ban on Speeches."
42. Mark Levy, "QC 50s-70s Activist Student Narrative." See also Seth Cagin and Philip Dray, *We Are Not Afraid: The Story of Goodman, Schwerner, and Chaney and the Civil Rights Campaign for Mississippi*. New York: Nation Books, 2006, p. 103.
43. Stephanchev (ed.), *The People's College on the Hill*, p. 66.
44. Seth Cagin and Philip Dray, *We Are Not Afraid: The Story of Goodman, Schwerner, and Chaney and the Civil Rights Campaign for Mississippi*. New York: Nation Books, 2006, p. 103.
45. Dear President Stoke." Box 1, folder 2002, Mark Levy Collection, Department of Special Collections and Archives, Queens College, City University of New York.
46. Ibid.
47. Ibid.
48. Ibid.
49. Ibid.
50. Ibid.
51. Ibid.
52. Mark Levy, "QC 50s–70s Activist Student Narrative," p. 2.
53. Ibid., p. 3.
54. Ibid.
55. Michael R. Wenger and Stan F. Shaw, "Northerners in a Jim Crow World: Queens College Summer Experience." In Terence Hicks and Abul Pitre, eds. *The Educational Lockout of African Americans in Prince Edward County, Virginia (1959–1964): Personal Accounts and Reflections*. Lanham, MD: University Press of America, 2010, p. 56.
56. Ibid.
57. Stepanchev (ed.), *The People's College on the Hill*, p. 66.
58. Mark Levy, "QC 50s–70s Activist Student Narrative," p. 7.
59. "Renegade Newspaper Hits Queens Campus." Box 1, folder 12, Andrew Berman Collection, Department of Special Collections and Archives, Queens College, City University of New York.

60. "Queens Gets New (s) Paper." Box 1, folder 12, Andrew Berman Collection, Department of Special Collections and Archives, Queens College, City University of New York.
61. "The Free Press: End of a Vestige." Box 1, folder 12, Andrew Berman Collection, Department of Special Collections and Archives, Queens College, City University of New York.
62. Ibid.
63. "Students Protest Dress Rules." Box 1, folder 12, Andrew Berman Collection, Department of Special Collections and Archives, Queens College, City University of New York.
64. Rosalyn Terborg-Penn, "A Black History Journey: Encountering Aptheker along the Way." *Nature, Society, and Thought*, Vol. 10, No. 1 & 2, 1997, p. 189.
65. Leo Hershkowitz,, "Demonstrations and Debates." In Stephen Stepanchev, ed. *The People's College on the Hill: Fifty Years at Queens College, 1937–1987*. New York: Queens College of the City University of New York, 1988, p. 66.
66. Ibid.
67. Michael R. Wenger, *My Black Family, My White Privilege: A White Man's Journey through the Nation's Racial Minefield*. Bloomington, IN: iUniverse, 2012, p. 43.
68. Ibid.
69. Ibid. See also "Fast for Freedom." Box 2, folder 16, Michael Wenger Collection, Department of Special Collections and Archives, Queens College, City University of New York.
70. Ibid.
71. "Fast for Freedom." Box 2, folder 16, Michael Wenger Collection, Department of Special Collections and Archives, Queens College, City University of New York.
72. "Student Association of Queens College." Box 2, folder 16, Michael Wenger Collection, Department of Special Collections and Archives, Queens College, City University of New York.
73. "Letter from Senator Kenneth B. Keating of New York." Box 1, folder 4, Arthur Gatti Collection, Department of Special Collections and Archives, Queens College, City University of New York.
74. "Telegram from Senator Kenneth B. Keating of New York to Attorney General Robert F. Kennedy." Box 1, folder 4, Arthur Gatti Collection, Department of Special Collections and Archives,

Queens College, City University of New York. Another member of Congress from New York, James R. Grover, Jr. wrote to the US President asking him to offer protection to the students who were in Mississippi, see Box 1, folder 1, Robert Masters Collection, Department of Special Collections and Archives, Queens College, City University of New York.
75. "Carolyn and Robert Goodman." Box 1 folder 3, Stan Shaw Collection, Department of Special Collections and Archives, Queens College, City University of New York.
76. Ibid.
77. Ibid.
78. Levy, "About Freedom Summer'64 and Q.C.," p. 3.
79. Jerusha O. Conner, *The New Student Activists: The Rise of Neoactivism on College Campuses.* Baltimore, MD: Johns Hopkins University Press, 2020.
80. It is important to point out that Michael Harrington was appointed a professor of political science at QC in 1972 where he taught until his death in 1989.
81. Wenger, *My Black Family,* p. 39.
82. Ibid., p. 40.
83. Levy "About Freedom Summer'64 and QC," p. 3.

CHAPTER 3

The Pioneers

I wanted to make more of a contribution than participating in occasional demonstrations.

—Lucy Komisar

In this chapter, I will examine how Lucy Komisar's activism, and the advocacy of members of the Students Help Project set the tone for vigorous student activism and protests at QC in the 1960s. I consider these activists pioneers because they were the first group of students to leave QC campus to the South for activist and social justice work aimed at confronting power. The chapter will examine how Lucy Komisar's activism, and the advocacy of members of the Student Help Project set the tone for vigorous student activism and protests at QC in the 1960s. In the narrative, I will first highlight Lucy's involvement on campus, as well as how her work in Mississippi propelled her into a life of social justice activism and change before turning to the Students Help Project, both of which, I argue, paved the way for profound student activism at QC campus during the Freedom Summer of 1964. Indeed, there is a clear nexus between Lucy's activism, the advocacy of members of the Student Help Project, and the intensification of student protests at QC campus in the 1960s, although this nexus has never been clearly attributed until this research. Historical validation of the nexus between Lucy Komisar and activism on QC campus, for instance, can be found in her work as the editor of the *Mississippi Free Press* and how she dedicated herself with zeal to the cause of social justice after she had returned to campus in 1963. Lucy founded the Dissent Forum as a venue to invite speakers to Queens College. She participated in the campus free speech protest against attempt by the QC administration to censor the *Phoenix* newspaper for running a poem about abortion. She remembered carrying a petition against the House Un-American Activities Committee (HUAC) and asking her fellow students to sign. Some refused to sign because they were afraid that it would prevent them from ever getting a government job. This, Lucy said, was part of her political consciousness that made her decide, "now for the rest of my life …I will do what I believe in and not be silenced by fear of not getting a job."[1]

Lucy Komisar was born in New York in 1942. Her father, David, was a salesman, and her mother, Frances, was at first a secretary and later a housewife.[2] Her grandparents emigrated from Russia and Eastern Europe to New York City in the early 1900s. She attended public schools both in the Bronx and on Long Island. She was a bright student who obtained exceptionally good grades in school. After graduating from high school, she entered Queens College in 1959, eventually obtaining her B.A. degree in 1964. However, in the spring of 1960 she attended a Yale University "Challenge Colloquium" wherein college students gathered to discuss current events. Though she initially wanted to become a Spanish or French teacher, she found herself also involved in activist causes while in college. During the Yale conference, she met members of the Young People's Socialist League, also known as YPSL.[3] The Young People's Socialist League (YPSL) was the youth group of the Socialist Party, a democratic socialist organization led by Norman Thomas.[4] A few months later, Lucy drove in her old Plymouth car with Michael Harrington, a member of the Socialist Party, Paul DuBrul, a YPSL, and Jack Newfeld (who was not a YPSL but had worked with fellow student Paul DuBrul on the Hunter College newspaper[5]), to Raleigh, North Carolina where Southern student leaders would found the Student Nonviolent Coordinating Committee (SNCC). Later, Lucy, with other YPSLs, served as a volunteer staff for Bayard Rustin's Committee to Defend Martin Luther King.[6] Back at Queens College, Lucy got involved in student politics and was chosen to represent the student government at the National Student Association Congress which was held every summer.[7]

Lucy was one among many protesters who picketed the ABC Paramount Corporation's offices in Manhattan at 7 West 66 Street in 1961 because the Paramount Theaters in Austin were segregated. During this protest, Lucy was one of four young protesters who held a sit-in in the company's executive offices. Although fifteen protesters were arrested during this event, Lucy was not one of them. Along with a group of peace activists, Lucy took part in a sit-in at the Russian Embassy in New York to protest the Soviet detonation of a fifty-megaton bomb.[8] In another protest, Lucy was arrested on a charge of criminal trespass in Elkton, Maryland, for eating with Walter Lively (an African American) in a segregated restaurant during the US Route 40 freedom rides organized by CORE. Lucy and Walter Lively spent three days in jail.[9] In 1962, Lucy participated in a sit-in with other members of the YPSL at Beth-el Hospital in Brooklyn in support of workers at the hospital who were not allowed to form unions, a right given to others by New York State law. Lucy and thirty-three others were arrested during this event including Stokely Carmichael (later known as Kwame Ture), who later became a leader in the SNCC. Lucy also took part in a protest in New York against segregated Woolworth's stores in the South. Although Lucy credits Allard Lowenstein with changing her worldview toward activism,[10] it was at the Young People's Socialist League (YPSL) meetings that she took her first steps toward political activism. During the annual Midwest meeting of the National Student Association Congress in 1962, Lucy met William L. Higgs, a lawyer from Mississippi, who had helped found a small alternative newspaper, the *Mississippi Free Press*. Higgs needed reporters for the paper, and Lucy, who had worked on newspapers in high school and college, offered to go to Mississippi to help. She took a year's leave of absence from QC to go to Jackson, Mississippi to work on the *Mississippi Free Press* as its editor with Charlie Butts as the publisher. From 1962 to 1963, she wrote and edited a good deal of the newspaper almost completely by herself until she returned to college in 1963. Central to Lucy's editorial duties was her avid advocacy for the minority's right to vote in Mississippi. In one of her editorials in the *Mississippi Free Press* of Saturday, June 29, 1963, captioned, "*IF YOU DON'T VOTE...YOU DON'T COUNT*," she stated:

> Last week, the Federal Bureau of Investigation arrested a man in connection with the murder of Medgar Evers. It is the first time that we recall seeing an arrest resulting from the many investigations the FBI has made in

regard to the abuses of the rights of people in Mississippi. There have been many other shootings in the state that can be clearly and directly connected with the attempts of [Blacks] to seek their right to vote. In most instances, the FBI has made some investigations, but we do not recall any previous arrests. ... The only sure way to have any government agency work for you is to be registered. Then when you squawk about something, that agency is going to do something (for fear you will use your voting power to see that someone takes their jobs).[11]

In another editorial of June 15, 1963, she wrote,

The selfish and corrupt government of the state is clearly to blame for the death of Medgar Evers. He died because he stood in defiance of the interests that wish to see Mississippi remain in its past...No one could know Medgar Evers and not hear him prod, urge, cajole, and encourage all people to register and vote so that they could end injustice and suffering in Mississippi.[12]

And in the editorial of June 1, 1963, captioned *"After the Storm,"* Lucy stated, "Of course, we hope that something permanent and fine will come out and be left after the storm. And we have no doubt, there will be several changes—several improvements. But the only way to really assure that any improvements remain and the only way to really be able to get at the root of the trouble, is with the ballot."[13]

In a eulogy to Medgar Evers, Lucy extolled the virtues of the deceased as one of the finest "polling rights" advocates, and said,

Medgar Evers gave his life to building the kind of unity that would show up at the polls with greater and greater strength at each election. He knew that the only way to bring about the kind of state he envisioned was to get the deprived people of Jackson and Mississippi unified at the ballot box so that they could put into office reasonable and humane men on both the state and local level.[14]

The *Asbury Park Press* reported that for about a year, Lucy and Charlie Butts "drew weekly salaries of $20 each," to which Lucy responded, "It wasn't much money, but there aren't many ways to spend money in Jackson anyway."[15] Writing and covering the news for the *Mississippi Free Press* was not without its risks. Indeed, when Lucy spoke with John Doar, the deputy attorney general for civil rights, after she had been out covering the Civil Rights march in Jackson, Mississippi, Doar told Lucy, "Look, you'd better watch out, because our people who were in the street are telling us that they heard white men there talking about you. They know who you are. So, watch out."[16] She also experienced some harassment from the police in Mississippi.[17] Lucy left Mississippi in August 1963. On her way home, she stopped over in Washington, DC for the March on Washington and heard Rev. Martin Luther King Jr., give his famous "I Have a Dream" speech. Back on campus during her senior year, Lucy participated in several activist causes. Apart from founding the Dissent Forum, she participated in many activist events such as carrying petitions and stopping students on the QC quad to sign. To Lucy's bewilderment, many students refused to sign because they were too afraid of the government.[18] Lucy was particularly disturbed by this kind of behavior on campus because she knew that the bridge to political power and change can only be built through the cooperation of students, faculty, and the people.[19]

After graduating from Queens College in 1964, she worked for the *New York Post* as a copy girl and later for *Village Voice* as a freelance writer. She also worked for the hat workers' union. She was a writer for the United Hat, Cap, and Millinery Workers. During her search for work, she came face-to-face with unacceptable levels of employment discrimination against women,[20] which led her to become involved with the National Organization for Women (NOW) to push for tougher antidiscrimination laws in the workplace. She soon became the public relations person for NOW, and in 1970 she was elected NOW public relations vice president. During her tenure, she devoted most of her energies to writing and speaking about feminism, advising those who wanted to start new chapters of NOW and other activist organizations, speaking at colleges and clubs because she believed that using her talents in this way was more rewarding and fruitful. Lucy's accomplishments included getting the US government to change its contract compliance rules in the early 1970s to include women.[21] Working with others, she was also able to get the Federal Communications Commission to require affirmative action for women's employment in radio and TV stations.

Lucy worked as NOW public relations vice president for about eighteen months and decided to direct her efforts to other pressing issues. Going forward, she devoted a great deal of her attention to journalism, mostly freelance writing. She also took interest in journalism concerned with foreign politics because through working in developing countries she "became aware of the use of the tax haven system to help dictators loot those countries of assets, and corporations cheat on taxes."[22] According to one biographer:

> In the 1980s and 1990s, she (Lucy) wrote about international affairs, with a focus on movements for democracy in the developing world. In that context she reported from Central America, the Philippines, Zaire and elsewhere in Asia, the Middle East, and Latin America. She also wrote about European politics and foreign policy and covered dissident movements in the Soviet Union and Eastern Europe. She was banned from East Germany and harassed by security police in Zaire.[23]

Lucy is an investigative journalist and activist whose work covers a wide array of topics from financial corruption to corporate fraud to offshore banking, international corruption, international crimes, looting of countries, etc.[24]

As a journalist, Lucy has written for numerous papers.[25] She was a member of PEN (Organization of Poets, Playwrights, Essayists, Editors, and Novelists), and was a member of the organization's board of directors until 1996. Her PEN membership included her serving on the Freedom to Write Committee and visiting Uruguay under dictatorship to report on repression of the press. The Freedom to Write Committee offers support to writers, journalists, and editors who have been jailed, persecuted, or censored for their writing.[26] Lucy was also a member of the American Civil Liberties Union, among others.[27] During her prolific career, Lucy has won several distinguished journalism awards.[28] Lucy's other distinctions include working as the campaign manager for James McNamara for New York City Council in 1965. She also worked as special assistant to the deputy administrator, Human Resources Administration, New York City, 1967–1968. She was the press secretary for Allard Lowenstein's Congressional primary campaign for the 5th District of Long Island, New York, in 1968. She served as the press secretary in the City Council President campaign of Elinor Guggenheimer in 1969. Lucy has worked as a writer, reporter, and producer of several documentaries. Currently, she is a freelance writer and has written several books and belongs to several professional organizations. She was one of three women who broke down the "no women allowed" barrier at McSorley's, a men's only bar in Manhattan in the 1970s to test the new public accommodations law in New York City.[29] She is the author of the report, *Citigroup: A*

History and Culture of Tax Evasion (2006). Her investigative reporting has indicted major American banks and corporations in assisting third world dictators to loot their countries of assets and cheat on their taxes.[30] On this aspect of her work, she once said:

> Through my work in developing countries, I became aware of the use of the tax haven system to help dictators loot those countries of assets and corporations cheat on taxes. And I turned my attention a dozen years ago to investigating the offshore bank and corporate secrecy system. I found that it was run by the big international banks to help tax evasion by corporations and the mega rich, to hide and launder the money of drug and arms traffickers and other criminals, to help dictators of mineral-rich countries steal revenues, to enable international corporations bribe corrupt officials to get contract, to help divorcing men hide their incomes.[31]

Lucy is presently a member of the Council on Foreign Relations and has published many revelations about governmental fraud in America and abroad.[32]

* * *

Though events such as those mentioned above galvanized students at Queens College into activism, it appears to me that other national events added impetus to the sweeping student activist movement at QC in the 1960s. Of great significance here was the contribution of the Student Help Project volunteers in connecting protests to students' profound thoughts of activism as democratic action on campus. Because members of the Student Help Project had been exposed to Civil Rights activism when they went to the South, they were able to provide students on QC campus when they returned with informational and organizational tools to understand how they might confront systemic racism and become agents of change.[33]

The Student Help Project was a program in which QC students volunteered to tutor minority and low-income students in Jamaica, Queens, with Professors Rachel T. Weddington, Sidney B. Simon, and Mickey Brody of the education department acting as their advisers.[34] These faculty members also mentored QC students who went to Virginia, where schools were shut down by orders from the state for the purpose of stopping school integration. Following the unanimous decision of the US Supreme Court in *Brown v. Board of Education* (1954), that "separate but equal," has no place in public education, Virginia embarked on "Massive Resistance" to integration, which resulted in the closure of Prince Edward County public schools from 1959 to 1964. During this period, Black children in Prince Edward County suffered immensely as approximately 1700 of them were deprived of public-school education in the county. At the invitation of Rev. L. Francis Griffin, sixteen students from QC[35] and one professor participated in the Prince Edward County Tutorial Project. The role of the QC volunteers in Prince Edward County was to get Black children ready for the opening of "Free Schools" in the fall of 1963 after four years of being deprived of public education.[36]

On arrival in Prince Edward County, the student leaders arranged through Black ministers and the NAACP for the volunteers to live with Black families and to use church and community facilities for classes.[37] The volunteers lived with Black families,[38] and as soon as the last group of volunteers arrived, they set out to register students for the program with the help of Dr. Robert Lee Green of Michigan State University. Dr. Green was the head of a psychological testing group working in Mississippi under a federal grant for Michigan State University to study the effects of the closed schools.[39] More than six hundred students were registered for the program.[40] Eight centers were established with the help of Rev. L. Francis Griffin of First Baptist Church. Classes were held in churches and church basements.[41] While some makeshift classrooms could accommodate up to 110 students, others held "four classes of fifteen pupils each in the same room."[42] According to a survey conducted by Michigan State University, in 1959 only about 3% of Black children aged five to twenty-two in Prince Edward County could not read and write; that rate had risen to 23% by 1963.[43] Indeed, the Michigan researchers found some seven-year-old children who could not hold a pencil or even mark an X in a book. In Farmville, the volunteers held classes in the Beulah A.M.E. Church and the First Baptist Church. In Levi, classes were held in an abandoned schoolhouse. In Hampden-Sydney, they set up shop in a Sunday school. Despite the great distance traveled by some students, the children "flocked to school in such numbers that teachers had to cut off enrollment at 500."[44] The ratio of students to teachers was about one teacher to about fifteen students, though this ratio varied according to the number of students on a particular grade level. Members of the project exposed students to creative learning. Because the students in these "schools" were encouraged to take part in and enjoy what they were doing, these gave them self-esteem, a feeling of accomplishment as well as love of knowledge and learning.[45]

* * *

The volunteers encountered issues in Prince Edward County schools like those in public schools anywhere in the United States. However, the social problems were compounded by the fact that four years of educational deprivation had left some of the students without basic skills. Even a physical education teacher discovered to his utter dismay that "four years without organized athletics could rob many students of muscle coordination."[46] A report titled, *Student Help Project: A Summer in Prince Edward County*, listed what was, what should have been, and what was lacking in the social and academic skills of the children in Prince Edward County as the volunteers saw them when they arrived. On the whole, the volunteers found some reasons for hope, as the students were enthusiastic and eager to learn, "Upon their arrival, the Queens College students-turned-teachers encountered bright smiles and a tremendous desire to learn, a desire that had grown out of a four-year educational vacuum."[47] The report went on to say that the volunteers were amazed at the children's joyousness and their enthusiasm in performing even the most rudimentary tasks. However, eagerness could not override four years of educational deprivation. So, the volunteers had to start the students with exceedingly small baby steps in reading, arithmetic, spelling, and geography because most of the students worked far below their grade levels. Initially, the students were divided according to the grade and the level they last attained when they were in school some four years earlier before establishing their cogent skills level. The entire process was flexible enough for students to be grouped according to their needs and academic ability. As one observer remarked, "By now the kids are scrawling their names in script, and one teacher has his charges deep in simple 'science experiments.' The chief effect is a bright-eyed attentiveness worthy of West Point."[48] A teacher, Lou Mercado described his experiences in Prince Edward County this way: "All they need is the teaching. Motivation here is very high. We don't get the ordinary discipline problems."[49]

* * *

With respect to their security in Prince Edward County, Michael Wenger must have spoken for all members of his team when he reported that although the volunteers did not experience any physical violence, "they were constantly subjected to hostile stares and verbal abuse from some white members of the community, but this didn't deter them from persevering with their program, which was eagerly attended by 600 [Black] youths, ranging in age from six to 20."[50] A New York City paper reported on June 16, 1964:

> A unique Queens College project goes into its second summer this year with honors from three organizations for its short history of helping children of the borough and in Prince Edward County, Va. The Self-Help project, serving more than 1,000 youngsters in 22 Queens centers and others in Virginia, already has received the Human Relations Award from B'nai B'rith and recognition from the National Student Assn. and the Anti-Defamation League.[51]

* * *

While in Virginia, members of the Student Help Project were equipped with the courage, information, and organizational tools to confront power, and they shared these skills with other students when they returned to QC campus in 1963. Indeed, although the Queens College volunteers were advised not to get involved in any demonstrations while in Virginia, they nonetheless witnessed field workers for the SNCC train teenagers for marches and sit-ins in Farmville and they shared this with QC students when they returned to campus. Indeed, the early activities of the members of the Student Help Project at QC prompted the vast mobilization of students for Freedom Summer 1964 at QC. Members of the Student Help Project gave the Freedom Summer volunteers increased courage to go to Mississippi,[52] because as Eric L. Hirsch has made known, consciousness-raising, collective empowerment, participation, and group decision-making are the necessary ingredients for protest movements to germinate and grow.[53] Michael Wenger and Stan Shaw maintain in one of their book chapters that their experience in Prince Edward County taught them that they could confront danger and survive and that they could be comfortable with people who lived vastly different lives than theirs. Above all, they came to the realization that they could make a difference,[54] and as such, they began to change inside. In a recent book, Wenger wrote,

As we headed for home, our neat vision of the world and our plans for the rest of our lives had been forever altered. We would no longer be so smug about our own virtue. Our arrogance had been permanently muted. On the other hand, our passion had intensified. The sting of racism now had a more personal feel to it, and it became difficult to identify with white people anywhere who were not actively engaged in the struggle.[55]

Wenger must have spoken for the group when he said that while in Virginia, they became aware of the economic and physical intimidation used by Whites in the South to subdue Blacks. Likewise, they also understood the humiliating deference required of Black men and women to keep their jobs. They realized that some White men and women in the South were quite unhappy with the scheme of things but felt helpless to do anything about it. This is to say, members of the Student Help Project understood white privilege upon returning to campus.

It's not surprising that it was during Stan Shaw's (one of the leaders of the Student Help Project) tenure as the chairman[56] of NAACP at Queens College that he decided to switch the group's affiliation to CORE because, according to him, "NAACP, then like now, did not have much involvement with student activism whereas CORE was the up-and-coming activist organization supporting freedom rides and sit-ins during the '60s."[57] Therefore, when this group of students moved into leadership positions in CORE and the Student Help Project at Queens College, they, together with others in SNCC, organized sit-ins and demonstrations at the New York World's Fair in 1964—mimicking similar demonstrations in the South. They were also at the forefront in the recruitment of volunteers for Freedom Summer 1964 on campus. Michael Wenger maintained that their Prince Edward County experience strengthened their resolve and gave the Black struggle in the South a personal meaning. He went on to say, "We knew and now counted as friends some of the people who were being so grievously devalued and mistreated. Abandoning the struggle was not an option."[58] Accordingly, as a forceful reminder, members of the Student Help Project met in the spring of 1964 to mentor Queens College students who were about to go to Mississippi in the summer to register Black voters. Members of the SHP who met in the Student Help Project Office to mentor the Freedom Summer volunteers in the Spring of 1964 included: Carolyn Hubbard, John Irvine, Michael Wenger, Stan Shaw, Rosalind Weinstock, Gerald Gliber, Barbara Jones, and Michael Schenkler.[59] Michael Wenger explained the part they played in preparing the Freedom Summer volunteers in readiness to go to Mississippi in the following words: "In the spring of 1964, we met with a group of Queens College students who were planning to spend the summer registering [Black] voters in Mississippi." Wenger went on to say, "They had volunteered for the SNCC-inspired Mississippi Freedom Summer, and they were anxious to hear from others who'd been in the South. We shared our Prince Edward County experiences and what we'd learned from them."[60] Members of the Student Help Project who had been exposed to Civil Rights activism in the South believed that it was their obligation to work for change, and that they could act without waiting for others. Wenger aptly described their involvement in the struggle, and explained that on arrival from Virginia they intensified their activities on campus to generate wider and stronger support for the civil rights movement among QC students, because they wanted to raise student awareness of the double standards in American society and the failure of the federal government to use its vast resources to help Blacks in the South.[61] And indeed, from Spring 1964, many members of the Student Help Project were more concerned with student activism and the Freedom Summer Project than with the Student Help Project of earlier years. The protest efforts and advocacy of the leadership of the Student Help Project sparked *Fast for Freedom* on QC campus after three Freedom Summer volunteers were declared missing and later found dead in Mississippi, including one of their own, Andrew Goodman.[62] During *Fast for Freedom*, seven students from Queens College went on a five-day hunger strike to draw attention of the nation to the plight of civil rights workers in Mississippi.

* * *

It is often said that activists not only transform the world, they, themselves are often transformed by the work they do. With this in mind, I aim to bring to light the faces and stories of some of those who were involved in the Student Help Project; those who, I argue, formed the foundation of student activism at Queens College in the 1960s. The students who went to Prince Edward County at the invitation of Rev. L. Francis Griffin were: Michael Wenger, Stan Shaw, Phyllis Padow-Sederbaum (then Phyllis Padow), Deborah (Debby) Yaffe, Rosalind Andrews (then Rosalind Silverman), Jean L. Konzal (then Jean L. Stein), Michael Barbera, Sheila Hartman, Ina Gold, Leonard Hausman, Donna Brass, Carolyn Hubbard, Marjorie Sulkes, Mark Blumberg, June

Tauber, and Rhoda Maidanick.[63] Dr. Rachel Weddington went with the students as the faculty adviser. Of the sixteen students who went to Virginia, fifteen were White, and one student, Carolyn Hubbard, was the only Black volunteer. Carolyn later became chairman of CORE and chairman of the Student Help Project at QC. The group that went to Virginia consisted of 11 women and 5 men. They ranged in age from 17 to 22.[64] By highlighting their stories, I hope to show the legacy of QC's history at the forefront of change, social justice, and activism.[65]

* * *

We begin with Michael R. Wenger, one of the leaders of the Student Help Project at Queens College. Wenger was born in Brooklyn, New York, in 1942. He joined Queens College formally as a full-time student in the fall of 1962 and graduated in 1965 with a degree in political science with a minor in education. He served as the Chairman of CORE at Queens College from 1963 to 1964 and Chairman of the Student Help Project from 1964 to 1965. He took part in tutoring students in South Jamaica during the academic year, and in Prince Edward County, Virginia, during the summer of 1963. On Wenger's return from Virginia, he and Stan Shaw received the B'nai B'rith Human Relations Award in 1964 for their services in tutoring about one thousand minority students in South Jamaica and about six hundred Black students in Prince Edward County, Virginia. In 1964, Wenger helped to organize the Freedom Week, whose purpose was to inform students and faculty at Queens College about the Mississippi Freedom Summer Project as well as recruit volunteers and raise money for the project. Wenger was also involved in organizing *Fast for Freedom* and participated in the fast for the purpose of drawing the federal government's attention to the deplorable conditions in Mississippi, and for the government to provide Freedom Summer 1964 volunteers with federal protection. Progressive politics animated Michael Wenger whose parents were progressives who hosted a fundraising event for Aaron Henry, head of the Mississippi Freedom Democratic Party (MFDP) in Michael Wenger's former high school. Henry even spent the night in Michael Wenger's parents' home.[66]

After his graduation in 1965, Wenger took appointment as a special education teacher in South Huntington, Long Island, New York from 1965 to 1967. He moved to Beckley, West Virginia in 1967 to serve as the director of an antipoverty program known as the Community

Education Program. Between 1967 and 1981 Wenger served the people of West Virginia in various capacities including as the Commissioner of the West Virginia Department of Employment Security, and Deputy Commissioner of the West Virginia Department of Welfare. In 1981, he was appointed States' Washington Representative at the Appalachian Regional Commission (ARC). While serving on the commission, he wrote a biweekly column on race relations for the *Prince George's Journal*. In September 1997, Wenger was appointed Deputy Director for Outreach and Program Development for President Clinton's Initiative on Race. Wenger is a Senior Fellow and Acting Vice President and Director of the Civic Engagement and Governance Institute at the Joint Center for Political and Economic Studies. He is also an adjunct faculty member in the Department of Sociology at The George Washington University.

* * *

Another QC student activist of the 1960s was Stan F. Shaw. He was the first Chairman of the Student Help Project at QC. Stan Shaw was born in Utica, New York, on August 18, 1943, but grew up in Cambria Heights, Queens. He graduated from QC with a B.A. degree in sociology and education in 1965. When Stan Shaw became Chairman of the Queens College chapter of NAACP, he decided to switch the group's affiliation to CORE because CORE was supporting freedom rides and sit-ins during the 1960s. Shaw was Chairman of CORE from 1962 to 1963 and the first Chairman of the Student Help Project at QC from 1963 to 1964. As Chairman of the Student Help Project, Stan Shaw was one of the volunteers who tutored students in South Jamaica, Queens, and participated in the Tutorial Project in Prince Edward County, Virginia during the summer of 1963. Shaw received the B'nai B'rith Human Relations Award in 1964 with Michael Wenger for their services in tutoring poor minority students in South Jamaica, and for getting Black students in Prince Edward County, Virginia ready for the reopening of "Free Schools" in the fall of 1963.

After graduating from QC in 1965, Stan Shaw obtained a master's degree in special education from the University of Northern Colorado in 1968 and a Ph.D. degree in Special Education and Disadvantaged Youth from the University of Oregon in 1971. He has pursued a career in special education as a researcher, professor, and policy advocate. Stan

Shaw is currently a Senior Research Scholar at the Center on Postsecondary Education and Disability and Professor Emeritus, Department of Educational Psychology, Neag School of Education. He is the author, co-author, or lead author of several academic books and articles on Students with Disabilities. He is a former editor of the *Journal of Postsecondary Education and Disability* (JPED). He serves on the editorial boards of several academic journals.

* * *

Another QC student activist of note in the 1960s was Ronald (Ron) Pollack. Ronald Pollack was born in 1944 and grew up in Kew Gardens, New York. He majored in political science and was the Queens College Student Association President, 1964–1965. He participated in *Fast for Freedom* at Queens College. After graduating from QC, Ronald Pollack received a law degree from New York University. He was the Founding Executive Director of the Food Research and Action Center (FRAC), which is a leading national nonprofit organization that is working to eradicate poverty-related hunger and malnutrition in the United States. He also founded and ran another organization with national standing called, Families USA. The nonprofit, nonpartisan organization serves health care consumers, and believes in "a nation where everyone has access to the best health care." Until early 2017, Pollack was the founding executive director of Families USA. He now serves as Chair Emeritus of the organization. Before then, he was the Dean of the Antioch University School of Law. In 1997, President Bill Clinton appointed Mr. Pollack as the sole consumer representative on the Presidential Advisory Commission on Consumer Protection and Quality in the Health Care Industry. As a result, Pollack helped to prepare the Patients' Bill of Rights, which has been enacted by many state legislatures in the United States. In 2007, he received the Common Ground co-award for bringing together disparate groups of insurers, hospitals, physicians, nurse groups, the pharmaceutical industry, business, and labor groups together and reaching a consensus proposal for expanded health coverage for the uninsured.

Pollack is a national voice for health care protection in the United States. His opinion on healthcare is often sought after by national television shows, radio programs, and newspapers. President Barack Obama credited Ronald Pollack and Families USA for playing a pivotal role in the passage of the Affordable Care Act (ACA) also known as Obamacare.

"On a printed copy of the ACA displayed in Families USA's office, Obama wrote, 'To Ron and Families USA – You made this happen!'"[67]

* * *

Another personality worthy of mention concerning activism on QC campus was Professor Rachel T. Weddington (1917–2010). Professor Weddington served as faculty adviser for the Student Help Project and was a Queens College CORE adviser as well. She was one of the professors at QC encouraging students to do the right thing by taking part in movement campaigns. Professor Weddington was born on March 9, 1917. She was the daughter of Ralph and Laura Weddington of Atlantic City. She graduated from Atlantic City High School with honors and attended Howard University where she obtained both her bachelor's and master's degrees. She obtained her doctorate from the University of Chicago in Illinois in 1958 and taught at Howard University and at the Merrill Palmer Skillman Institute. She later joined Queens College where two students pitched the proposal for the Student Help Project to her. The purpose of the Project was not only to provide tutorial services to minority children in South Jamaica, Queens, but also to expose White students to minorities and to African American culture.[68] The Student Help Project in South Jamaica served as a precursor to the Prince Edward County Tutorial Project, and Dr. Weddington was one of the student advisers who mentored the student volunteers in both projects. Dr. Weddington was uncompromising in her demand for virtue and diligence from the volunteers during their trip to Prince Edward County, Virginia, and warned the students against going off task. According to Michael Wenger and Stan Shaw, Dr. Weddington made their role clear: They were to work with the children to help them get ready for the new "free schools" that were due to open in the fall of 1963. "Deviation from that plan, no matter what else was occurring in Prince Edward County, was not part of the mission."[69] It is therefore not surprising that Dr. Weddington was one of the fifty-three conferees invited to help develop the curriculum and the prospectus for Freedom Summer 1964.[70] Dr. Weddington worked at QC for many years before taking up appointment as the Dean of Teacher Education at the City University of New York (CUNY). She held this position until her retirement in 1985. She was the second African American tenure-track line professor at Queens College.

Dr. Weddington moved to Portland, Oregon, during her retirement years. She died in 2010.

* * *

Another member of the Student Help Project was Jean L. Konzal (then Jean L. Stein). Jean was born in 1944.[71] As a student at Queens College, she volunteered for the Student Help Project in Jamaica, Queens, and went with the group of sixteen QC students to Prince Edward County. Jean attributes her activism to being born and raised "in a working-class Jewish family with deep roots in the progressive movements of the early twentieth century."[72] She particularly attributed her own activism to her aunt, Jean, after whom she was named. According to Jean Konzal, her aunt was a self-educated woman who became active in the radical movements. While traveling to New Llano, Louisiana in the early 1920s, she wrote scathing reports in her diary "of the oppression of African Americans that she witnessed along the way."[73] Jean Konzal credits her aunt for making her the type of woman she wanted to be. Jean was also influenced by biographies of historic and legendary figures such as Joan of Arc, Queen Esther, and George Washington Carver because each of them "acted in ways unexpected of them." In addition, as she recollected some years later, students in the 1960s were swept by the optimism of the John F. Kennedy administration, which enjoined Americans to "Ask not what your country can do for you--ask what you can do for your country."[74] Such optimism, Jean imagined, inspired some college students to think that they could change the course of history and make a difference in the world. Jean went to Prince Edward County because she thought that the situation in the South was worth rectifying by making a difference in the lives of the children she was about to teach. According to her, they were able to douse their parents' fears about the dangers of the trip to Prince Edward County, by promising to be an educational group only and not participate in any demonstrations, because "if we did, we would jeopardize our position as teachers in the (Black) and (White) communities."[75]

On their way back from Prince Edward County, Jean and the other volunteers attended the March on Washington on August 28, 1963. In 1964 when James Chaney, Michael Schwerner, and Andrew Goodman were reported missing, she participated in a campus-wide protest with other students.[76] She also participated in the summer workshop led by Dr.

Sidney Simon and Dr. Rachel Weddington on human relations at Rutgers University in 1964.[77]

Jean holds a Doctorate degree. She served as a classroom teacher, a reading teacher, a staff developer, and a consultant for more than forty years and was the chair of the Department of Elementary and Early Childhood Education at The College of New Jersey (TCNJ) from where she retired some years ago. During her career, she coauthored two books dealing with family and school relationships and published a number of academic articles and papers. Now, she serves as an adjunct professor for TCNJ's Global Master's program. She lives in Maine with her husband. In her retirement, she devotes most of her time to gardening, reading, theater work, and volunteering for political campaigns.[78] In her unique way, Jean Konzal donated some of her original Prince Edward County papers and photos to the Robert Russa Moton Museum,[79] which is "a center for the study of Civil Rights in education" in Farmville, Virginia.

* * *

Deborah (Debby) Yaffe was born in 1945. She started attending Queens College at the age of sixteen in 1962 and joined the Student Help Project where she was assigned to tutor students in South Jamaica, Queens. At seventeen, she volunteered for the Student Help Project in Prince Edward County, Virginia. In Prince Edward County, she served as the project's librarian. As the librarian, she ensured that all the assigned locations were supplied with books and materials in all the subject areas. These were books that publishers from New York had donated before the students left for Farmville, Virginia. On returning to Queens, she actively participated in civil rights and social justice causes including her membership in Students for a Democratic Society (SDS). She attended civil rights meetings, marches, and rallies and continued to work with students in Jamaica, Queens, New York. She juggled study and work in book publishing, and finally graduated from Queens College in 1969 with a B.A. degree in English and a minor in education. After graduation, she continued to pursue a career in children's book publishing until 1985 when she obtained her master's degree in library science (M.L.S.) from St. John's University. Having obtained her M.L.S., Debby accepted appointment as a research librarian. She retired in 2010 and went back to her first passion—tutoring, working in an adult literacy program.

* * *

Rosalyn Terborg[80] (later Rosalyn Terborg-Penn) (1941–2018) was born on October 22, 1941, in Brooklyn, New York. Her family moved to Queens, New York in 1951. She graduated from John Adams High School in 1959 and entered Queens College where she obtained her B.A. degree in history in 1963. Rosalyn worked with the committee that developed the South Jamaica Student Help Project in 1962. She helped to set up the project in her church, St. Albans Congregational Church on Linden Boulevard in Jamaica. As she recollected later, the Student Help Project was not only to tutor Black students but also to expose White students who had no real exposure to Black people and African American culture to relate to Black people.[81] Because of her conviction, she was one of the supporting members of NAACP at Queens College and belonged to the Northern Student Movement. She was also a member of the Committee for a Sane Nuclear Policy (SANE), and a member of the Young People's Socialist League.[82] She unwaveringly stood among a group of students who picketed the large Woolworth's store in downtown Manhattan in New York City every Saturday for months in support of the 1960 sit-ins by students of North Carolina Agricultural and Technical State University in Greensboro.[83] She was part of a coalition of radical students who invited both Malcolm X and Herbert Aptheker to give lectures at Queens College. However, when the college authorities refused to allow Malcolm X to speak on campus in 1961, she was part of the protest on campus to challenge the decision until the ban was lifted. It is therefore no surprise that when Malcolm X was eventually allowed to speak on campus, Rosalyn was exhilarated because according to her, "The exhortation by the charismatic Malcolm X was an emotional experience that incited anger and reproach, feelings I had long held repressed when outside of my own community."[84] About Aptheker, she said,

> He opened a whole new world to me, however, not just by talking positively about Negro accomplishments, something I had heard at home, but by discussing what was then called "Negro history" as a legitimate field of inquiry, a topic worthy of serious analysis that challenged the consensus school we all hated, but could not seem to revise adequately.[85]

While at QC, Rosalyn took numerous road trips aimed at dislodging discrimination in the South and was an active member of the Student Help Project. She even served on the tutorial group's governing committee, and her church, St. Albans Congregational Church on Linden

Boulevard in Jamaica, Queens, was one of the churches that participated in the South Jamaica Tutorial Project through her personal initiative.[86] She helped set up the project in her church before she left New York in the summer of 1963 to go to graduate school at George Washington University in Washington, DC. She obtained a master's degree in history from George Washington University in 1967 and a Ph.D. in African American history from Howard University in 1977. While Rosalyn was in Washington, DC, she joined the "DC Students for Civil Rights" group that lobbied Congress for the passage of the Civil Rights Act of 1964. She started working at Morgan State University in 1969. She was a professor of history and former director of the history Ph.D. program and director of the Oral History Project at Morgan State University. She co-founded and was the first national director of the Association of Black Women Historians (ABWH). During her career, she published seven books and more than 40 articles. Dr. Rosalyn Terborg-Penn retired from Morgan State in 2006. She died in 2018.

* * *

Born in 1943, Rosalind Andrews (then Rosalind Silverman) was raised in Jackson Heights, Queens, where she attended Bryant High School. She entered Queens College in 1960, attending night classes and working during the day. She matriculated the following year into the history program, graduating in 1965 with a History major and an Education minor. As a student, she participated in the Student Help Project and went to Prince Edward County, Virginia. She also attended the March on Washington for Jobs and Freedom in 1963. Rosalind was involved in numerous civic causes while she was a student at QC including the anti-Vietnam war movement.[87]

After graduating from college, she lived in India for nine months with her husband who was on a Fulbright scholarship. On her return to the United States, she taught history for three years at Long Island City High School in Queens. She moved to Washington, DC, and in 1972 obtained her master's degree in psychology from Catholic University. She was employed as a US probation officer whose portfolio included "supervising people convicted of federal crimes, writing pre-sentencing reports, and making recommendations for sentencing."[88] After serving for two years as a Programs Specialist at the Administrative Office of the Federal Courts, she was promoted to the rank of Chief US Probation Officer for the Eastern District of Tennessee (being only the second woman to attain that rank at that time). During her employment she received the Director's Award for Outstanding Leadership. She retired in 2000. She now works as a mitigation specialist with emphases on death penalty cases.

* * *

Phyllis Padow-Sederbaum (then Phyllis Padow) was raised in Merrick, Long Island, and graduated from Sanford H. Calhoun High School in 1961. She attended Queens College and graduated in 1965 with a B.A. degree with honors in sociology. As a student at QC, she signed up to work with the Student Help Project and was among the group of sixteen student volunteers who went to Prince Edward County. While in Virginia, she lived with a Black family in Farmville and tutored African American children in Prince Edward County.

Phyllis obtained her master's degree in Sociology from the University of Pennsylvania in 1970. For many years, she worked as a researcher and has been a community volunteer for at least thirty years. As a former volunteer in Prince Edward County, she supports the Robert Russa Moton Museum, which is a center for the study of Civil Rights in education in Farmville, Virginia. According to Lacy Ward, Jr., former director of the museum, "The Robert Russa Moton Museum is dedicated to the preservation and positive interpretation of the history of Civil Rights in Education, specifically as it relates to Prince Edward County and the role its citizens played in America's struggle to move from a segregated to an integrated society."[89] Phyllis Padow-Sederbaum is a member of the SH Calhoun High School Alumni Association. She now resides in her hometown of Merrick, New York.

In this chapter, I present a portrait of engagement by the early QC student activists who were bold enough to venture outside the Queens College campus. The chapter highlights the political engagements of two groups of student activists who ventured out of QC to do social justice work from 1962 to 1963. It illuminates and sheds light on the influence that these group of student activists had in co-constructing activist synergy on their return to QC campus, which led to more activist endeavors and participation in a campus that was largely untouched by student activism before then.

Michael Wenger, left, and Stanley Shaw, right, receiving the B'nai B'rith Human Relations Award from Mrs. Belema Reiner on behalf of the Student Help Project for providing tutoring services for more than 1000 students from South Jamaica and about 600 Black students from Prince Edward County, Virginia (Photograph, Courtesy of Michael Wenger, and Stanley Shaw Collections)

Notes

1. Lucy Komisar: A Personal History of Civil Rights and Feminism, talk at panel on "Women, Queens College, and the Civil Rights Movement," March 16, 2009, Queens College, p. 1.
2. Biography—Komisar, Lucy (1942–): Contemporary Authors— January 1, 2004, p. 1.
3. See Seth Cagin and Philip Dray, *We Are Not Afraid: The Story of Goodman, Schwerner, and Chaney and the Civil Rights Campaign for Mississippi*. New York, NY: Nation Books, 2006, p. 104. See

also, Lucy Komisar: A Personal History of Civil Rights and Feminism, Talk at Panel on "Women, Queens College, and the Civil Rights Movement," March 16, 2009, Queens College.
4. Lucy Komisar: A Personal History of Civil Rights and Feminism, Talk at Panel on "Women, Queens College, and the Civil Rights Movement," March 16, 2009, Queens College.
5. Note also that Harrington had a connection to the Village Voice, and was friends with the editor for which Newfeld wrote.
6. Cagin and Dray, *We Are Not Afraid*, p. 105.
7. Correspondence with Lucy Komisar, June 12, 2024.
8. Komisar, "A Personal History of Civil Rights and Feminism," p. 2.
9. See Cagin and Dray, *We Are Not Afraid*, p. 105. Lucy was jailed with Walter Lively, an African American student from Philadelphia who was also a member of YPSL. Lucy Komisar, "A Personal History," p. 3.
10. See Julie Altman, "Tully-Crenshaw Feminist Oral History Project (interview with Lucy Komisar, October 1991)," p. 5. Lucy also credits the political and moral education she received at Queens College for her activism.
11. Lucille Komisar, *Editorial Page: Mississippi Free Press*, Komisar (Lucy) Civil Rights Collection Number M395, folder 4, McCain Library and Archives, The University of Southern Mississippi, June 29, 1963. While in most of her records, she is addressed as Lucy, in the editorial page of *Mississippi Free Press*, she is addressed as Lucille.
12. Ibid., June 15, 1963.
13. Lucille Komisar, *Editorial Page: Mississippi Free Press:* Komisar (Lucy) Civil Rights Collection, Number M 395, folder 4, McCain Library and Archives, The University of Southern Mississippi. June 1, 1963.
14. Lucille Komisar, *Editorial Page: Mississippi Free Press*, Komisar (Lucy) Civil Rights Collection, Number M395 folder 4, McCain Library and Archives, University of Southern Mississippi. Mississippi Free Press, June 22, 1963.
15. "Young Editor of Negro Newspaper Walks Tightrope in Mississippi." Komisar (Lucy) Civil Rights Collection, Number M 395, folder 6, McCain Library and Archives, University of Southern Mississippi.

16. Tully-Crenshaw Feminist Oral History Project (interview with Lucy Komisar, October 1991), Collection Number M395, folder 1. McCain Library and Archives. The University of Southern Mississippi.
17. Lucy Komisar: A Personal History of Civil Rights and Feminism, talk at panel on "Women, Queens College, and the Civil Rights Movement," March 16, 2009, Queens College, p. 3.
18. Ibid., p. 1.
19. Ibid.
20. See Lucy Komisar: A Personal History of Civil Rights and Feminism, talk at panel on "Women, Queens College, and the Civil Rights Movement," March 16, 2009, Queens College, p. 4. Tully-Crenshaw Feminist Oral History Project (interview with Lucy Komisar, October 1991) Number M395 folder 1. McCain Library and Archives. The University of Southern Mississippi.
21. Ibid., p. 5.
22. Ibid.
23. *Lucy Komisar*. Wikipedia, the free encyclopedia. http://en.wikipedia.org/wiki/Lucy_komisar (Accessed 8/3/2012).
24. *Lucy Komisar*. OffshoreAlert Conference Miami 2019. https://events.bizzabo.com210247/agenda/speakers/384015 (Accessed 10/8/2019). See also, *Lucy Komisar*, From Wikipedia, the free encyclopedia. http://en.wikipedia.org/wiki/Lucy_Komisar (Accessed 8/3/2012).
25. See "Komisar (Lucy) Civil Rights Collection." Collection Number, Biographical/Historical Sketch: McCain Library and Archives, University of Southern Mississippi.
26. Ibid.
27. Biography—Komisar, Lucy (1942–) Contemporary Authors— January 1, 2004.
28. See *Lucy Komisar*. Wikipedia, the free encyclopedia. http://en.wikipedia.org/wiki/Lucy_komisar (Accessed, 8/3/ 2012).
29. Tully-Crenshaw Feminist Oral History Project (interview with Lucy Komisar, October 1991) Number M395 folder 1. McCain Library and Archives. The University of Southern Mississippi.
30. *Lucy Komisar*. From Wikipedia, the free encyclopedia. http://en.wikipedia.org/wiki/Lucy_komisar (Accessed 8/3/2012).

31. Lucy Komisar: A Personal History of Civil Rights and Feminism, Talk at Panel on "Women, Queens College, and the Civil Rights Movement," March 16, 2009, Queens College, pp. 5–6.
32. *Lucy Komisar*. From Wikipedia, the free encyclopedia. http://en.wikipedia.org/wiki/Lucy_komisar (Accessed 8/3/2012); Biography—Komisar, Lucy (1942–). Contemporary Authors—January 1, 2004. http://media-server.amazom.com/exec/drm/amzproxy.cgi/MjQwIMCaQ6B5X2EWRuqzIpy7.
33. See also Stefan M. Bradley, *Harlem v. Columbia University: Black Student Power in the Late 1960s.* Urbana, IL: University of Illinois Press, 2009, p. 64.
34. The tutoring program was also to expose White would-be teachers to Black culture.
35. Of the sixteen volunteers, 15 were White, and one was an African American female. They consisted of 5 men and 11 women. Their ages ranged from 17 to 22. See Michael R. Wenger and Stan F. Shaw, "Northerners in a Jim Crow World: Queens College Summer Experience." In Terence Hicks and Abul Pitre, eds. *The Educational Lockout of African Americans in Prince Edward County, Virginia (1959–1964): Personal Accounts and Reflections.* Lanham, MD: University Press of America, 2010, p. 57.
36. Michael R. Wenger, *My Black Family, My White Privilege: A White Man's Journey Through the Nation's Racial Minefield.* Bloomington, IN: iUniverse, Inc., 2012, p. 28. While schools were closed, Rev. Griffin pleaded with Attorney General Robert Kennedy to persuade the Ford Foundation to support financially the reopening of "free schools" in the fall of 1963 in Prince Edward County that all students could attend.
37. "'Student Help' Aids Many at Home, Virginia." Box 2 Folder 1, Michael Wenger Collection, Department of Special Collections and Archives, Queens College, City University of New York.
38. The advantage for this arrangement was that it restricted the volunteers' activities to those in which their hosts could participate, and enhanced the reception given to the volunteers in the Black community. See "Undated Speech Given by Jean Stein (now L. Konzal) entitled, "Upon Return from Prince Edward County"." Box 1, folder 16, Jean L Konzal Papers, Department of Special Collections and Archives, Queens College, City University of New York. Also see Wenger Box 1, folder 10.

39. Bob Smith, *They Closed Their Schools: Prince Edward County, Virginia, 1951–1964*. Farmville, VA: Martha E. Forrester, Council of Women, 1996, p. 237.
40. "Student Help Project: A Summer in Prince Edward County." Box 1 folder 10, Michael Wenger Collection, Department of Special Collections and Archives, Queens College, City University of New York.
41. "Student Help Project: A Summer in Prince Edward County." Box 1 folder 10, Michael Wenger Collection, Department of Special Collections and Archives, Queens College, City University of New York.
42. Ibid.
43. *Time Magazine*, August 9, 1963. Box 1 folder 10, Stan Shaw Collection, Department of Special Collections and Archives, Queens College, City University of New York.
44. "Schools Catching Up in Prince Edward." Box 1 folder 10, Stan Shaw Collection, Department of Special Collections and Archives, Queens College, City University of New York.
45. See "Student Help Project: A Summer in Prince Edward County." Box 1, folder 10, Michael Wenger Collection, Department of Special Collections and Archives, Queens College, City University of New York.
46. "Teachers on Loan in Va. Find They Learn as Well." Box 2, folder 1, Michael Wenger Collection, Department of Special Collections and Archives, Queens College, City University of New York.
47. "Student Help Project: A Summer in Prince Edward County." Box 1 folder 10, Michael Wenger Collection, Department of Special Collections and Archives, Queens College, City University of New York.
48. *Time*, August 9, 1963. Box 1, folder 10, Stan Shaw Collection, Department of Special Collections and Archives, Queens College, City University of New York.
49. Ibid.
50. "Classes in Churches." Box 2, folder 1, Michael Wenger Collection, Department of Special Collections and Archives, Queens College, City University of New York. Indeed, other volunteers reported similar incidents.

51. "Students Help Others Help Selves." Box 2, folder 1, Michael Wenger Collection, Department of Special Collections and Archives, Queens College, City University of New York.
52. Wenger, *My Black Family*, p. 41.
53. Eric L. Hirsch, "Sacrifice for the Cause: Group Processes, Recruitment, and Commitment in a Student Social Movement." *American Sociological Review*, Vol. 55, No. 2, 1990, pp. 243–254.
54. Wegner and Shaw, "Northerners in a Jim Crow World," p. 65.
55. Wenger, *My Black Family*, pp. 37–38.
56. Note that Mr. Shaw was one of the leaders of the Jamaica and Virginia Tutorial Projects.
57. E-mail correspondence between Annie Tummino of the Queens College Library Archives and Stan Shaw. See also Annie Tummino's e-mail correspondence with the author on 5/22/12.
58. Michael Wenger, *My Black Family*, p. 41.
59. Correspondence with Mark Levy.
60. Michael Wenger, *My Black Family*, pp. 41–42. These meetings were generally held in the Student Help Project Office on campus.
61. Wenger, *My Black Family*, p. 41.
62. Wenger, *My Black Family*, p. 43.
63. The list of participants could not be found in the QC archives. This list was compiled by Michael Wenger, Stan Shaw, and Phyllis Padow-Sederbaum [leaders of the Student Help Project] from memory. The list was given to me, courtesy of Annie Tummino, Head of Special Collections and Archives, Queens College, CUNY. It is important to note that this list is not arranged in any particular order.
64. Wenger and Shaw, "Northerners in a Jim Crow World," p. 57.
65. Unfortunately, I have biographical updates only on seven of the members of the Student Help Project. These are those who through their written records, archival materials, or personal interviews have told their own stories. Some of the members for whom I have information are: Jean L. Konzal, Debby Yaffe, Rosalyn Terborg-Penn, Rosalind (Silverman) Andrews, Phyllis Padow-Sederbaum, Michael Wenger, and Stan Shaw. However, it is important to point out that I tried unsuccessfully to obtain information on the others.
66. Michael R. Wenger, *My Black Family*, p. 43.

67. Wikipedia, "Families USA." https://en.wikipedia.org/wiki/Families_USA (Accessed 2/21/2020).
68. See correspondence between Rosalyn Terborg-Penn and Mark Levy, 9/2/08.
69. Wenger and Shaw, "Northerners in a Jim Crow World," p. 58.
70. Sandra E. Adickes, *The Legacy of a Freedom School*. New York: Palgrave Macmillan, 2005, p. 35.
71. See "The 3 Rs After 4 Years." Box I, folder 10, Jean L. Konzal Papers, Department of Special Collections and Archives, Queens College, City University of New York, p. 2.
72. "Questions for Queens College Students Regarding Prince Edward County Project." Box 1, folder 3, Jean L. Konzal Papers, Department of Special Collections and Archives, Queens College, City University of New York.
73. Ibid.
74. See ibid.
75. "Undated speech given by Jean Stein upon return from Prince Edward County." Box 1, folder 16, Jean L. Konzal Papers, Department of Special Collections and Archives, Queens College, City University of New York.
76. "Collection of Documents, Photos, and Other Memorabilia from Prince Edward County Summer 1963." Box 1, folder 1, Jean L. Konzal Papers, Department of Special Collections and Archives, Queens College, City University of New York.
77. Ibid.
78. "Jean Stein Konzal: Autobiographical Note." Jean L. Konzal Papers, Box 1, folder 2, Department of Special Collections and Archives, Queens College, City University of New York.
79. "Collection of Documents, Photos, and Other Memorabilia from Prince Edward County Summer 1963, Jean Leanore (Stein) Konzal." Box 1, folder 1, Jean L. Konzal Papers, Department of Special Collections and Archives, Queens College, City University of New York.
80. Rosalyn Terborg did not go to Farmville, Virginia but she was in the planning committee that designed the South Jamaica Student Help Project.
81. See correspondence between Mark Levy and Rosalyn Terborg-Penn 7/23/08.

82. Rosalyn Terborg-Penn, "A Black History Journey: Encountering Aptheker Along the Way." *Nature, society, and Thought*, Vol. 10, No. 1 and 2, 1997, p. 189. See also Dr. Terborg-Penn's correspondence with Mark Levy, 7/23/08.
83. See her e-mail correspondence with Mark Levy 7/23/08.
84. Terborg-Penn, "A Black History Journey," p. 190.
85. Ibid.
86. According to Rosalyn, when the idea of the South Jamaica Project was made, she contacted her pastor, Robert Ross Johnson in her church, St. Albans Congregational Church on Linden Blvd, who checked with officers of the church and they agreed for the tutorial program to begin in 1963, see her e-mail correspondence with Mark Levy, 9/2/08.
87. Another one of Rosalind Andrews' causes was the "Cleanup at Long Beach." Box 1, folder 5, Rosalind Andrews Collection, Department of Special Collections and Archives, Queens College, City University of New York.
88. Cited from information processed by Lige Rushing, edited and approved by Annie Tummino, Spring 2012, Department of Special Collections and Archives, Queens College, City University of New York.
89. Lacy Ward, Jr., "Robert Russa Moton Museum Farmville, Virginia." In Terence Hicks and Abul Pitre, eds. *The Educational Lockout of African Americans in Prince Edward County, Virginia (1959–1964): Personal Accounts and Reflections.* Lanham, MD: University Press of America, 2010, p. xiii.

CHAPTER 4

The Trailblazers

Our goal was to organize and confront power -- and not just 'do good.' We made changes, and were changed. Mississippi is not the same; but it took a while. Those changes are not complete. We went to oppose segregation and to support voting rights -- and learned that the Movement encompassed a much broader vision of social justice. 'Freedom Summer' was but one moment in a long and ongoing struggle!

—Mark Levy

Many of the volunteers who attended the two one-week training sessions in Oxford, Ohio were young, but they had the fortitude to set aside their own needs for a prophetic vision of change, a change that will forever benefit generations to come.

—Keith Beauchamp

SOCIAL ACTIVISM AT QUEENS COLLEGE: THE FREEDOM SUMMER

Scholars have studied social movements and activism from about the early nineteenth century, but to understand these phenomena, most of the "processes of collective action [have been] lost somewhere between

© The Author(s), under exclusive license to Springer Nature Switzerland AG 2024
M. O. Bassey, *Student Activism in 1960s America*, Palgrave Studies in the History of Social Movements,
https://doi.org/10.1007/978-3-031-54794-2_4

broad, sweeping theories of social change that have obscured the role of human agency ...."[1] Similarly, Jerusha O. Conner argues that student activists' identities and the causes that they embrace cannot be understood by focusing only on a single dimension of their identity or politics.[2] And in the words of Belinda Robnett, the commendable power of existing social movement theories is compromised when the interpretation of any component concept inadequately reflects or misconstrues the substance of real cases.[3] In light of the above, my position is that to begin to understand social movements, it is necessary to focus on historical contexts and social spaces by studying the individual actors and events assiduously because, in the critical study of social movements, motives cover a wide array of theoretical positions.[4] This being the case, I contend that it will be possible for us to begin to understand social movements and social activism of the 1960s by historical and interpretive mappings of the actual events through the voices, lenses, and records of participants.

We will now move from the foundational Students Help Project to the Freedom Summer 1964 activist movement at QC. Like the previous chapter, based on my review of archival records, correspondence, and a series of interviews, I have identified, highlighted, and discussed the remarkable contributions and challenges of eight trailblazers from Queens College who were involved in social justice activism in 1964. Validation for calling these volunteers trailblazers derives from a central component that they were among the first group of volunteers from Queens College to answer the clarion call from the *Student Nonviolent Coordinating Committee* (SNCC) and the Council of Federated Organizations (COFO) for social justice activism, particularly in making moves against racial segregation, and the struggle for social justice to secure for African Americans the right to vote in Mississippi. I want to state here that Freedom Summer 1964 was only one in a prolonged and ongoing struggle by African Americans for social justice in the United States.[5] Although many of these activists joined the movement for completely different reasons, most of them saw tremendous evil and risked their lives to combat it. They envisioned that it was up to them to challenge and change the country's direction in a mass activist movement that involved millions of Black people fighting for social changes. Undergirding their abiding faith was their immeasurable dedication to righting the wrongs of the past, and with a conviction of confraternity and ethical and moral commitments, these young men and women spoke truth to power because they saw a nation clogged by prejudice and wracked by contradictions. These QC activists went to support grassroots movement efforts in Mississippi because they perhaps understood as Emma Lazarus once said and repeated by one of the Freedom Summer volunteers that, "none of us can be free until all of us are free."[6] Through the efforts of the Queens College chapter of the Congress of Racial Equality (CORE), the Civil Rights Coordinating Council (CRCC), and the Student Help Project (SHP) leadership, intense recruitment campaigns for Freedom Summer volunteers took place on the Queens College campus.[7] In this chapter we are going to identify the Freedom Summer 1964 activists from QC, their motivation for participation, their previous experiences with activism, and their challenges and achievements. The chapter will examine how these activists were made and remade by visible and invisible interactions within their institution and their environment because activism does not arise in a vacuum.

* * *

One of these volunteers from QC, Andrew Goodman accepted the challenge of going to Mississippi to participate in the anti-racist activism and paid the ultimate price.[8] Of all the volunteer activists from QC for Freedom Summer 1964, the best known is Andrew Goodman, who was among the first group of Freedom Summer volunteers to leave for training in Oxford, Ohio. Goodman was born in New York City on November 23, 1943, into a liberal Jewish family. His father, Robert Goodman, was a civil engineer and a writer, and his mother, Carolyn Goodman, was a clinical psychologist and social activist. Goodman's grandfather, a highly successful attorney, hired the first Black lawyer to work in his firm. Goodman's family and community "were steeped in intellectual and socially progressive activism and were devoted to social justice."[9] Besides, Andrew attended the innovative and progressive Walden School located on Central Park West at 88th Street which encouraged creative expression and self-motivated learning. While in high school, Andrew's interests ranged from drama to poetry to the study of the Holocaust.[10] He was an anthropology major at Queens College and wanted to go to Mexico in the summer of 1964 to help build a school but changed his mind when he heard Allard Lowenstein give an exhilarating speech at Queens College in which he laid out an offensive for tackling the civil rights problem in Mississippi through voter registration.[11] Imbued with a high sense of mission to serve, Andrew told his father that he wanted to go to Mississippi "because this is the most important thing going on in this country! If someone says he cares about people, how can he not be concerned about this?"[12] he asked soberly.

Andrew's father, captured by his son's passion, pledged to support the effort by promising to pay the $150 needed for his expenses. "We couldn't turn our backs on the values we had instilled in him at home,"[13] Robert Goodman later said. But Andrew took a job loading trucks at the United Parcel Service to earn the money he needed to support himself during the summer in Mississippi. In his application as a volunteer to the project, he expressed his interest in voter registration and pointed out that he had very good "experience with racial and religious prejudice in the North and South."[14] Andrew was "a born activist,"[15] his mother remarked some years later. Yes, indeed, he was. He had earlier taken part in demonstrations at the New York World's Fair and marched in demonstrations for equal rights at New York City's Woolworth's on Thirty-fourth Street. Although he was scared, as some of his friends later recalled, he was determined to go to Mississippi. Indeed, he wanted to participate in the noble struggle for social justice because he believed that to defend the rights of others meant to defend his own rights and his own life.[16] Andrew was interviewed as a summer volunteer by Jim Monsonis on April 15, 1964, with the following recommendation to the Jackson, Mississippi, office: "I've talked with him here and feel he ought to be accepted. He is a white student with some political sophistication and knowledge about the state, is particularly interested in voter registration work and the political campaigns."[17]

In June 1964, Goodman left for training in Oxford, Ohio. Before he departed, he hugged his mother, Carolyn, and said, "Mom, look, this is something I believe in and you believe in. All your life, you and Dad have said that this is not right—the Constitution is being violated."[18] After his orientation, Goodman was billed to work in Vicksburg, but he was enlisted by Michael Schwerner and James Chaney, CORE staffers to work with them in Meridian instead. With this offer, Andrew said to his parents,

"Don't worry, I'm going to a CORE area. It's safer."[19] Again on June 21, he elaborated in a letter to his parents from Meridian, Mississippi:

> Dear Mom and Dad,
> I have arrived safely in Meridian, Miss. This is a wonderful town, and the weather is fine. I wish you were here. The people in this city are wonderful, and our reception was very good.
> All my love,
> Andy[20]

After his orientation at Western College for Women in Oxford, Ohio, Andrew Goodman was chosen to accompany Michael Schwerner and James Chaney (CORE staff members) to Meridian on Saturday, June 20 to prepare for others who were to follow them. On Sunday, June 21, 1964, Andrew accompanied Michael and James to investigate a church bombing near Philadelphia, Mississippi. On their way, they were arrested by Neshoba deputy sheriff, Cecil Price on the outskirts of Philadelphia, Mississippi after 3:00 p.m. and locked up in Sheriff Lawrence Rainey's jail. They were released at about 10:30 p.m. but were rearrested by the same Deputy Sheriff Price. This time, the deputy sheriff released the three young men to an angry mob.[21] The bodies of Andrew Goodman, Michael Schwerner, and James Chaney were found many weeks later, on August 4, 1964, near Philadelphia, Mississippi, buried under an earthen dam under construction in a remote area of Neshoba County.[22] The FBI discovered their bodies only after they (FBI) had offered a $30,000 reward.[23]

Goodman was a young man with an unwavering belief in fairness and social justice who saw evil and decided to do something about it. Leo Hershkowitz had this to say about him:

> He surely understood, perhaps more clearly than his friends, that the hatred in Mississippi and bigotry North and South did not just affect blacks. If there were a lesson to be learned from the Holocaust or lynching and atom bombs it was that all people suffer from blind, consuming hatred.[24]

Hershkowitz continued by stating, "Fear and ignorance breed terror and murder. To defend the rights of others means to defend your own rights and your own life."[25] To Andrew's murderers, he warned, "Commitment to social justice, to social values as applied to all members of society equally, is part of being an individual."[26] He explained to all that, "Commitment is rooted in actions of human accomplishment. It includes a respect for the sacredness of life. It is the impetus for a meaningful contribution to society."[27] A classmate who knew him described Andrew as a young man who read a lot and was interested in the theater. He acted in a campus production of *Doctor Faustus* and had a speaking part in an off-Broadway play.[28] Another colleague remembered him as a high school athletic star who played both basketball and soccer in high school. In a term paper he wrote for his sociology class on the subject, *The Black Muslims: A Phenomenon of Negro Reaction*, Andrew disagreed vehemently with Black Muslims in their characterization of White people as devils but cautioned that such a characterization by Black Muslims may derive from how Blacks were treated in the United States. "The source and cause of this need for reaction can be attributed to white contempt and neglect,"[29] he wrote in a term paper. He expressed similar views in a poem he wrote in a paper for a writing course taught by Professor Mary Doyle Curran, one of his professors at Queens College.

After Andrew's death, facing an array of news cameras and reporters in their 161 West Eighty-Sixth Street apartment, Robert and Carolyn Goodman discussed the loss and regretted the death of their son, Andrew. They asked that others continue the cause that Andrew died for and wished that those so involved would be protected in their noble mission. Reading from a prepared statement to the press, Mr. Goodman stated, "Our grief, though personal, belongs to our nation. The values our son expressed in his simple action of going to Mississippi are still the bonds that bind this nation together—its Constitution, its law, its Bill of Rights."[30] "Throughout our history," Mr. Goodman continued, "countless Americans have died in the continuing struggle for equality. We shall continue to work for this goal, and we fervently hope that Americans so engaged will be aided and protected in this noble mission."[31] Mr. Goodman told reporters that he and his family were in Washington, DC, a fourth night earlier where they made a "pilgrimage" to the Lincoln Memorial in which they found written, emblazoned in black letters on white marble: "It is for us the living to dedicate ourselves that these dead shall not have died in vain."[32]

Andrew, Michael, and James were jailed and murdered to halt the type of work they were doing, and to scare and intimidate the other volunteer activists who came to Mississippi for the summer. Mark Levy, one of the Freedom Summer activists from QC remarked, "Each of us knew it could have been any of us just as easily. But as part of a larger, dynamic, and committed movement, most of us carried on - a very few turned back."[33] The above statement bears testimony to the fact that Andrew Goodman and the others did not die in vain, they died for a noble cause: that is, for the restoration of the human spirit, human dignity, and service to humanity. Indeed, the signing of the Voting Rights Act in 1965 by President Lyndon B. Johnson bears testimony to some of the legislative accomplishments fueled by the flames the trio died for.

A classmate of Andrew Goodman, Michael Wenger, one of the organizers of the Freedom Week, stated that Andrew knew there was some danger, but he felt he wanted to go.[34] In an interview conducted by Shomial Ahmad many years later, Barbara (Jones) Omolade, the QC senior who recruited Andrew Goodman for Freedom Summer said that Andrew "was a regular student [but] what he did was extra brave."[35] The untimely death of the three young men emboldened the struggle for social justice at QC. According to one student commentator at QC, "Many things can be said about the Goodman tragedy and the whole Mississippi story. One thing, though, is sure, the events of the Mississippi summer acted to spur social justice activities on campus; the memory of Goodman kept the movement going; and the shock of the murder fed the work here with an element of seriousness and devotion that is seldom seen in college affairs."[36] Though the murder stretched the students' patience thin, it did not deter their determination, and as one student said, "'Shock' was the word used by most to describe the mood here; but if that was the prevailing emotion, it was not of the numbing variety."[37] Indeed, "letters immediately began going out from QC students to the President, then to Attorney General Robert Kennedy and members of Congress asking for more federal protection for rights workers."[38] More petitions were signed by hundreds of QC students and presented to Senator Kenneth Keating of New York asking for federal protection for civil rights workers after Andrew's death.

In 2014, President Barack Obama presented a posthumous Presidential Medal of Freedom to Andrew Goodman, James Chaney, and Michael Schwerner. Of this honor, Obama stated, "James, Andrew and Michael could not have known the impact they would have on the civil rights movement or on future generations. And here, today, inspired by their sacrifice, we continue to fight for the ideals of equality and justice for which they gave their lives." In a letter to Andrew's family to honor the occasion, President Obama concluded: "I am one of the many who stand on the shoulders of giants like Andy. His death forever changed our

Nation, and in his example, we are reminded of the difference we each can make when we summon the courage to lift up the lives of others."

However, just as a caveat, many Black activists, and local Black leaders at the time and even now believed that the killing of James Chaney would have gone unnoticed, unreported, and even uninvestigated like the killings of many other Black people before him, had two white men, one of them Andrew Goodman, not died as well, thus putting a spotlight on the murders in the media, ultimately resulting in government action. Indeed, Rita Schwerner, the wife of Michael Schwerner, pointed this out to the press that, "The only reason they (the press) noted James Chaney's death was because he was murdered with two white men."[39]

* * *

Not only were QC students on the front line of the activist movement of the 1960s, but some of them also recorded what they witnessed for generations to come.[40] A close examination of archival records in the Special Collections section at Queens College Rosenthal Library suggests that there were no obvious far-reaching efforts at collecting, retaining, and preserving information and insights about the activism of the Freedom Summer 1964 Project at QC Special Collections Library save for the efforts from Mark Levy and Betty (Bollinger) Levy (now deceased). From their written records, newspaper articles, opinions, letters to friends and family, correspondence, written interviews, newsletters, press releases, and letters to the press, Mark and Betty—perhaps more than any other participants from QC in the Freedom Summer Project— told us more of what it was like to work and live in Mississippi in the summer of 1964 and about the entire project. They left behind their honest and intricate accounts of life in the South for Blacks; the White volunteers; Black schools, Black school administrators and teachers; the Freedom Schools; the students; the CORE staffers; SNCC; the locals; the Black hosts; intimidation by White supremacists; the lukewarm attitude of the rest of the country toward the plight of Black people in Mississippi; and the entrenched system of oppression, disenfranchisement, and exploitation under which Blacks lived in Mississippi. They told us about the strong and positive Black society they saw in Meridian and throughout Mississippi which included Black churches, businesses, schools, colleges, professionals, social organizations, and the NAACP; they also told us about the strength and talents in the Black community and how and why some people in the Black community survived and prospered in spite of the odds stacked against them. They left behind eyewitness accounts of what they saw and heard during that summer and the emblematic and horrible intertwining of democracy, White supremacy, and state-supported violence. The documentations left behind by Mark and Betty inform us about the significance of their work that summer and reveal the deplorable state of democracy in Mississippi: intimidation, deprivation, oppression, and even violence against Blacks that needed urgent changes.

Both Mark and Betty (Bollinger) Levy attended Queens College and volunteered for the Freedom Summer 1964 Project. Mark was born in 1939 in New York City. His parents were Harry and Leona Levy. Betty was the daughter of Carl and Ruth Bollinger of Forest Hills, New York. Mark's family was middle class, Jewish, and apolitical, while Betty's family was working class, nonreligious, and had a history of social activism. Mark came to QC from Antioch College in Yellow Springs, Ohio in 1960. Both Mark and Betty were Student Association leaders at QC in the 1960s. Indeed, Mark was the Student Association President from 1962 to 1963, and Betty was the National Student Association QC chapter chair. Betty also participated in the Student Help Project.[41] Throughout his stay at QC, Mark was involved in campus politics ranging from student governance to students' rights and free speech. Betty was a "red-diaper baby"[42] whose mother was a union leader affiliated with the Congress of Industrial Organizations.[43] Betty's mother was subpoenaed when her union was invited to testify before Congress.[44] Mark and Betty were both recruited as volunteers for the Mississippi Freedom Summer Project by Dorothy (Dottie) M. Zellner. Mark's experience in student politics and advocacy and Betty's history of social activism and status as a "red-diaper baby" made them a natural fit for Freedom Summer activism. During the first week of orientation, Mark and Betty were chosen to join Michael Schwerner's Area (CORE) project. As a result, they, together with Rita Schwerner, were required to stay in Ohio for the second week of the orientation "to help put together and train a staff for the Freedom School Project."[45]

During the orientation, the Levys met Michael and Rita Schwerner, James Chaney, and Andrew Goodman.[46] Mark, Betty, Rita, and Andrew were all recent QC students. At the conclusion of the orientation, Mark and Betty were assigned as co-directors of the Meridian's Freedom School, which was in a large Baptist school building. The duo taught an innovative "counter curriculum" in the Freedom School and supported voter registration and the Mississippi Freedom Democratic Party (MFDP) projects.[47] The Meridian school in which Mark and Betty taught was selected as the site for "an inspiring and energy-charge, statewide, student meeting."[48] During their stay in Meridian, Mark and Betty went through periods of triumph and adversity, sorrow, and joy. These were communicated to their friends and families in personal letters and newsletters. Being a versatile letter writer, Betty wrote to friends and family, announcing their mission and what they hoped to accomplish in Mississippi. This letter, dated June 9, 1964, had this to say:

> Next week, my husband and I are going to Mississippi for the summer. We are taking part in a coordinated civil rights project involving 1,000 students, teachers, lawyers, and others in a major effort to break the cycle of discrimination in perhaps the most depressed and terror-ridden state of the deep South. The project focuses upon Mississippi, birthplace of the White Citizens' Council and breeding ground of the Klan, because it is here that human rights are most brutally and willfully abandoned and where the system of segregation is most strongly maintained and defended. It is hoped that once conditions in Mississippi are improved, the rest of the South, and indeed, the rest of the nation, will follow.[49]

The couple understood quite clearly that education and leadership development were the centerpieces of their mission; thus, they hoped that their students would learn from them, just as they too hoped to learn from their students. "The teaching, of course," wrote Betty, "will proceed in two directions—we will learn much from our students. We feel that we will be contributing our professional skills to a socially relevant and meaningful project and will be better qualified when we return in September to continue our teaching in the Harlem public schools."[50]

Teachers in the Freedom Schools used innovative instructional techniques that allowed students to participate in community, critical thinking, and political activism using progressive democratic instructional methods. The techniques used by teachers in the Freedom Schools included discussion of art, social action, creative writing, drama, newspaper commentaries, projects, and role-playing in class. Students were allowed to examine public policies critically so that they could participate in civic transformation effectively. The students explored forms of systematic oppression, inequality, and social hierarchy. The curriculum set for itself the task of uncovering how power was used to either frame or distort processes and interactions. It unraveled, unmasked, and critiqued domination and discrimination. Students were required to confront, contradict, and contest inequality and unequal power relations, particularly when differences were used to justify systemic inequalities in society. The Freedom Schools provided political education and taught African American history and literature, which segregated schools in the South did not teach.[51] The Freedom School teachers helped their students to develop intellectually and socially so that they could build up the skills they needed to make meaningful and transformative contributions to their society. Mark and Betty promised to allow their students freedom in the classroom as well as offer them self-respect.

The couple, however, had no illusion about the dangers involved in their mission and wanted friends and family members to do something to minimize their risks. They asked friends and relatives to write to President Lyndon B. Johnson, Robert Kennedy (the Attorney General), and US senators and members of Congress asking for federal protection while they and the other volunteers were in Mississippi. Betty wrote:

> Mark and I are both well aware of the risks involved in this project. We are also aware that our own safety and the safety of other civil rights workers depends greatly upon the degree of concern and active support of those up North. We are calling upon you to help us and to help in the struggle for human rights by writing to President Johnson, Attorney General Kennedy, and your own US Senators and Congressmen, urging Federal protection for civil rights workers who are fighting to obtain exactly what our nation claims to stand for: equality of opportunity for all citizens and freedom for all to take part in the democratic political process.[52]

She enclosed a sample form letter to help friends and family members reproduce similar copies for distribution.[53] She also enclosed a brochure that explained the aims, objectives, and *modus operandi* of the Freedom Summer Project in great details. Betty promised to "write…again shortly to give… more information about what friends and family members could do to help during the summer."[54] She concluded by reemphasizing the need to initiate action through letter writing to federal officials for their protection.

Sy Safransky, Long Island journalist announced the departure of Mark and Betty Levy to Meridian, Mississippi, advising, "When a mob starts beating you, drop to the ground, pull your knees up close to your chest, and cover your head with your hands. But always meet violence with nonviolence."[55] Mark and Betty told Sy Safransky, journalist, "We're trying to make the twentieth century relevant to democracy. We're going a little scared, but with fantastic determination."[56] They went on to say, "We intend to dedicate the rest of our lives to the cause of civil rights. This summer is just a start."[57] During their training in Oxford, Ohio, Mark, Betty, and the other volunteers were apprised of nonviolent strategies, the role of nonviolence in civil rights activism, the economic and political structure of Mississippi, and the objectives and techniques of voter registration in Mississippi. They were also instructed on how to control themselves in trouble spots and how to step in and assist in a nonviolent manner someone receiving a worse beating than they were. Participants were involved in role-play, and Mark said they felt they could do it. "While we were being kicked, we felt the determination to keep going."[58] Asked about their concerns, Mark responded, "We all know what may happen, but I feel most of us are thinking more about doing something than worrying about the risk."[59] The couple's parents had mixed feelings about their children's decision to go to Mississippi. Leona Levy, who broke down in tears when asked about her thoughts, answered that the project was vital to the nation and she approved of it 100 percent but was terrified for her [son's] life.[60] Likewise, although Carl and Ruth Bollinger had "deep concern" about the dangers involved, they felt it was something that needed to be done for the good of the country.[61] In a letter to her daughter, Ruth Bollinger wrote, "If we read between the lines the picture is heartbreaking and the dangers as great as ever."[62] The apparent danger associated with this undertaking compelled Mark Levy's mother to write to President Lyndon B. Johnson asking for protection for the volunteers. Hereunder is her heartfelt letter to President Johnson, which I consider worth reproducing here at length with her son's permission:

27 West 96th Street
New York 25, New York
June 5, 1964
President Lyndon B. Johnson
The White House
Washington, D. C.
Dear President Johnson:
My son Mark is going to Mississippi this summer with his wife, Betty. If he were going to war to protect our country from a common enemy, I would not worry so much. But he is going to Mississippi, within our country,

where he will face equal physical danger. This is not a civil war, but these students and teachers face brutality and humiliation because they want to spread the ideals and prerogatives of our Constitution to all citizens.

These young men and women are not radicals; they want to conserve the constitutional right to vote. They are not disenchanted with their government; they want to strengthen it at home. These people are not irresponsible: they are our future teachers and leaders; they are dedicated to preserving the ideals of the American way of life. They are volunteering their vacation time to fight against poverty, injustice, ignorance, and fear and to fight for equal human rights for all.

It is vital to the self-respect of our government that steps be taken now to assure that our national laws are upheld in Mississippi, that these devoted Americans are protected from physical injury while pursuing a constitutional objective.

Not only are the eyes of the 49 other states watching to see if the Federal government is really supreme over one segment, but the eyes of the world will be watching to see if Americans practice what they preach. The image of the United States to the whole world is at stake.

Very respectfully,

Mrs. Leona Levy[63]

On June 30, 1964, in a discussion with Ted Knap of *New York World Telegram and Sun*, Mark said that their mission in Mississippi "struck a responsive chord because young people these days want to do something, something meaningful."[64] And his wife, Betty responded, "All my life, I had a feeling against social injustice. This project fits in with everything I had done before."[65] The couple admitted that coming to Mississippi had its fearful moments, but their fear was not paralyzing.

* * *

Mark and Betty taught reading, art, mathematics, and Black history at the Freedom School. The pair left, perhaps, the most concise and lasting accounts of the workings of the Freedom Schools in the Queens College Archives. As stated above, they started their school in a former Baptist Seminary on July 6, 1964. According to the couple, the response from the students was tremendous. The enrollment went from a very humble beginning on July 6, 1964, to more than double that number by the end of the week. The tremendous increase had been despite threats from the principal of the local high school that those students who attended the freedom schools would not be allowed to graduate.[66] According to the Levys, the students kept enrolling despite these threats. Mark offered some explanation as to why: "They come despite threats and intimidation. They come because, as one thirteen-year-old expressed it: 'The white man thinks that he has pushed the [Black] people back so far that we are going to stay back. But the day has come when we know that we are not going to stay pushed down any longer. We want our rights, not in a minute, a day, or a year, but NOW'."[67] Toward the end of their project in August, Mark and Betty were proud to say, "We have set up an atmosphere in our classrooms where free discussion is possible."[68] They were delighted to hear a thirteen-year-old student say, "We learn about things that are not taught in the regular school.... We are learning things I've wanted to know for a long time.... We get a chance to express ourselves.... We have freedom to speak what we want..."[69] Mark was happy to say, "In fact, our students do not misbehave in class,"[70] and he noted with pride that because of the conducive learning atmosphere they created in their classrooms, students came to school because they wanted to, not because they had to. Additionally, rather than learning how to adjust to society, their students learned how to work to change society and to understand that freedom consists of one's capacity to choose his or her ends. Mark concluded, "Seeing our students grow in their sense of dignity and purpose and in their recognition that what they had to say was important, that people really listened, has made all the difficulties of this summer more than worthwhile for us."[71]

However, Mark and Betty reported that the principal and the teachers in the segregated local high school refused to support their efforts and were corrupt and depraved in dealing with students. The couple gave the example of one Black teacher who volunteered to help in the Freedom School in Meridian but couldn't continue because of reprisals (although some students thought that the teacher was a spy sent in to see who was attending).[72] There was also the case of a young Black man who worked as a scoreboard operator in the local ballpark and lost his job for coming to classes in the Freedom School. As a matter of fact, the mother of a student in the Freedom School got fired, which led to the removal of other children from the school by parents for fear of losing their own jobs after receiving warnings that, "they were getting out of place."[73] In spite of all the intimidation and harassment, Mark and Betty reported that their school registered 200 students, out of which at least 125 of them were in regular attendance daily. They commended the students for their fine minds, and Mark was proud to say, "Many of them (the students) who can't read or write decently at age twelve have native intelligence that is as fine as you'll find anywhere."[74] David Levine described the Mississippi Freedom Schools as an informal setting, with an idealistic college student who had no teaching experience, teaching an animated group of Black adolescents using a pedagogy which nurtured student voices with a discussion in literature that sparked consideration of daily oppression.[75]

* * *

Appeals for help were an essential part of the volunteer work. In a letter sent to the press and published in *Long Island Press* on July 19, 1964, Mark and Betty appealed for help for their school. They specifically requested books on Black literature—James Baldwin, Richard Wright, Langston Hughes, and others, books on Black history and more. "These books are crucial, as they are basic to our whole curriculum,"[76] they wrote. They informed their benefactors that it was preferable to send them books on Black history and literature rather than money because it was nearly impossible to find such materials in any Mississippi bookstore. Even exceedingly small quantities of two or three items would be good enough, they explained. There was also an appeal for funds. "IF, IN ADDITION, you could send funds, this too would be welcomed," they said, because "the day-by-day running expenses of the school add up, much more the big chunks of money needed for major supplies."[77] The best way to ensure that the money and books got to them was by sending the items directly to 2505 1/2 Fifth Street, Meridian, Mississippi.[78] This letter was met with an enthusiastic response and had a ripple effect in the community, particularly among those who donated objects and cash to the cause, according to Betty's mother.[79] In response to the appeal, Betty's mother wrote, "I am sending a few more books tomorrow— Minnie found some in her library, also Frank and Lil and others have [Black] history material which you should be getting."[80] The following day she wrote, "We are sending what you suggested to the Meridian Community Center, in your name, as enclosed. OK?"[81] Overall, public reactions to the appeals from Mark and Betty were mixed. There were those who subscribed to and defended their efforts, but others were not so supportive.

* * *

Mark and Betty wrote home that toward the end of the summer, the Council of Federated Organizations (COFO) organized and held a statewide Freedom School convention in their school in Meridian wherein delegates from all the freedom schools in the state came to assemble to draw up plans for the following year. The reason COFO selected the Meridian school for this convention was that it had the largest single school facility. It was also an act of defiance to the KKK and was designed to give honor to the memories of Goodman, Schwerner, and Chaney.[82] One hundred Freedom School delegates and their teachers attended this two-day conference. The conference was a reflection on the great lessons the students had learned from their Freedom School Citizenship Curriculum.[83] There were many speakers at the convention, including Robert Moses, A. Philip Randolph, and James Forman. There was a performance by the Free Southern Theater.[84] During the two-day workshop, "the student delegates prepared an impressive and wide-ranging list of demands that reflected the political awareness they had gained from the Freedom School Citizenship Curriculum."[85] As it is often said, activism is "the conscious fight for improved conditions for marginalized groups of individuals,"[86] the Freedom School students pointed out fundamental paradoxes in American democracy and made numerous demands from the state as remedies. According to Sandra Adickes, the students demanded from the state:

> [A]ccess to public accommodations. They demanded a building code that provided each home with, as minimum requirements, a complete bathroom unit, a kitchen sink, insulated walls and ceilings, a basement and attic, an adequate wiring system, and at least a quarter of an acre of land per building lot. They demanded better schools, including air conditioning, heating, laboratories, textbooks, and lunchrooms. They demanded integrated schools and better-paid, qualified teachers who were free 'to join any political organization to fight for Civil Rights without being fired.'[87]

The students concluded their demands with a request for the provision of "wider, well-lighted streets and regular garbage collection,"[88] in the Black communities. From the federal government, they wanted the "abolition of the House Un-American Activities Committee, an end to support for dictators in other countries, and imposition of economic sanctions against South Africa because of its policy of apartheid."[89]

* * *

In their last newsletter, Mark and Betty reminisced about their work in Meridian, Mississippi during that summer. They explored, analyzed, and gave eyewitness accounts of the conditions of Black people in Mississippi as they themselves witnessed it. They narrated their ordeals, fears, and tribulations and pondered, albeit loudly, the plight of the local Black activists who lived in Mississippi and would continue their struggle without the protection that came with the national spotlight, media attention, and national political officials paying attention because Mississippi was a state that supported violence against Blacks and even against the volunteer activists. They complained that New York City was filled with comfort and splendor which were denied to Blacks in Mississippi, but despite the material wealth in New York, these temporary possessions do not compare with the warmth, closeness, and true sense of community experienced among Blacks in Mississippi. They explained that with the loss of community in New York, there is an acute sense of dislocation. "There is a greater inner drive and spiritual freedom there which is missing among sophisticated New Yorkers, black or white, who take their external freedoms for granted,"[90] they argued. They were terribly upset about the system of terror under which Blacks in Mississippi lived. This, they explained, was the main reason most Blacks found it difficult to accept and trust Whites—because of the White privilege of being able to opt in and opt out places at will, privileges that Blacks did not have in Mississippi. They were also at a loss about how the nation had forgotten so soon the three men who were murdered in Neshoba County and wondered what would become of those volunteers and Blacks who were still in Mississippi registering voters and working on Freedom School projects, as the nation had turned its attention elsewhere. However, the larger question to them was whether the Black Mississippians left behind to face the wrath of anti-democratic forces would be forgotten as well? They also recollected their experience attending a memorial service for James Chaney where James' 11-year-old brother, Ben—who had himself been arrested twice for taking part in Civil Rights activism—told the audience to "stand up and be counted."[91] The couple attributed their own safety in Mississippi mainly to the publicity given to the killing of their three colleagues and noted, "In a very real sense, they died for us, they died so that we all may live and continue our work."[92] The couple insisted on retelling the story of their murdered colleagues over and over again, "so that you may come to understand, in a small way, what the Black people of Mississippi have lived with all summer, and in many ways, all their lives."[93] This last newsletter, it appears, was intended to spark a candid conversation about the plight of Blacks in Mississippi with a view to constructing an acceptable countervailing platform of struggle. The couple also used this as an opportunity to present the Freedom School as the epitome of change where topics such as segregation and discrimination were freely discussed and where political decolonization was central to their teachings. Importantly, Mark and Betty were elated with the progress of their students in the Freedom School, particularly in their students' ability to enact political dialogue, discourse, and counteroffensive against White domination and oppression. Yes, one of their students, a seventeen-year-old, told them how happy he was when he heard of the efforts to desegregate schools in Mississippi and concluded: "Boy, I can't wait to register for that white school."[94]

In a previous letter to the press, The Levys had sadly lamented that since they had been in Mississippi, unconsciously the outside world had become quite unreal to them in the same way that Mississippi was probably unreal to others—the onlookers. The couple tried to conjure up a picture of what living in Mississippi was really like, but unable to find the proper words, they simply concluded,

> It's hard to describe what it's like to live in a closed society where fear and terror are part of one's daily existence. For us it means being suspect wherever we go: the [Whites] hate our guts; the [Blacks] accept us only partially—people who they cannot help feeling somewhat ambivalent towards. For the [Blacks], it means starting each day not knowing whether they will live through the end of it.[95]

The couple also shared their firsthand knowledge of living in a police state like Mississippi with the public: that is, being considered suspects wherever they went. Although for Blacks, this was simply the normal trend of events or what it meant to be Black in Mississippi. Mark and Betty expressed their amazement at the seriousness of purpose that some of the Black activists had. "PERHAPS the most amazing and beautiful thing for us has been to see that even within this sick environment, people can manage to escape with a spiritual freedom that gives them the inner strength to live and to fight,"[96] they said. They particularly praised the hard work and dedication of Polly Heidelberg, the head of the local food pool, and commended the efforts of the other invisible hands they found in Mississippi in these glowing words: "These people have a vision and a hope greater than we've ever seen before."[97] Not only did the couple thank the Black community for the unforgettable experience they had while in Mississippi, but they focused on the kind and friendly gestures shown to them by the many locals who had opened their homes and their hearts to them, the outsiders. They were particularly grateful for the remarkable and momentous kindness, steadfastness, and heroism of Mrs. Dessie Turner-Collins and her husband who accommodated them. Indeed, Mrs. Turner-Collins, their host, once told Mark and Betty, "Some people are scared, but I'm not."[98]

In the press publication titled, *Fear Stalks LI Couple in Mississippi* published in the *Long Island Press* on July 30, 1964, Mark and Betty talked about their fears, tribulations, and run-ins with jungle justice in Mississippi. Mark said, "You feel the fear all the time. This phone we're talking on is tapped."[99] Although the couple had not been in any real danger except for a few minor encounters, Mark pointed out that they could not forget for a second about what had happened to their colleagues in Philadelphia, Mississippi. He told his audience that they lived "with the minute-to-minute ugliness of the White population fighting to keep [Blacks] from their rights."[100] And indeed, on many occasions, they saw volunteers who were "trying to register Freedom voters racing back, with hoodlums carrying chains and pipes chasing their cars."[101] But of course, it should be no surprise that Mark and his wife had a few unfriendly run-ins with White supremacist groups themselves in the town where they resided.

* * *

At the end of their assignment, Mark and Betty traveled to Atlantic City to attend the nominating convention where the Mississippi Freedom Democratic Party (MFDP) demanded to be seated instead of the regular, all-White Mississippi Democratic Party delegation. This was an affront to the White Democratic power structure in Mississippi. During the credentials hearing on August 22, 1964, MFDP delegates argued that their members should be seated because Blacks were shut out of the Democratic Party and its nominating process in Mississippi. In the end, MFDP was granted only two "at-large" delegates; all others were allowed as honored non-voting guests as a compromise by the White power structure. This was a "proposed" compromise that the MFDP rejected. The MFDP went back home to Mississippi empty-handed, and according to Mark Levy, "President Johnson had twisted so many arms and his political operatives pressured the MFDP supporters on the Credentials Committee to reject the MFDP proposal—that there was not enough support even for a minority report to get to the floor of the convention and be discussed."[102]

Being the activists they were, Mark and Betty returned to Mississippi in the summer of 1965 to continue their work where they were assigned to a school desegregation project in Jackson, Mississippi. While on their social justice journey, Mark and Betty contributed to fiery political activism and pioneering initiatives in the Freedom Schools in Mississippi. They were dissatisfied and disillusioned with democracy in the United States, particularly regarding the deafening silence of the nation to anti-democratic forces in Mississippi. However, Mark noted that he was grateful to have served as a 1964 Freedom Summer volunteer activist in Mississippi because he learned much from his participation in the movement, perhaps more so than he learned from his classes in college. He concluded that what he learned in Oxford, Ohio, during their training did not only shape his teaching during Freedom Summer but has guided his entire career ever since.[103]

* * *

Upon his return from the Freedom Summer Project, Mark Levy went back to New York City where he taught social studies at a junior high school in Harlem. He also taught in the SEEK program at Queens College (1968–1973). He received his MS in Social Studies Education in 1973 and in the same year took up an appointment as a union organizer and representative at United Electrical, Radio, and Machine Workers of America (UE). He also worked for Local 1199/NY (United Drug, Hospital, and Healthcare Workers Union), and later at the Committee of Interns and Residents (CIR/SEIU). As he put it, "Work in unions continued much of the effort of the (activist) movement and presented the opportunity for me to combine issues of class, race, gender, age, ethnicity, and nationality within a practical framework of fighting discrimination and struggling with working people to improve their lives."[104] Mark retired as the Executive Director of the Committee of Interns and Residents in 2008. He now delivers lectures on civil and human rights and activism in the United States and in the United Kingdom, specifically in England, Scotland, and Wales. In his lectures, Mark focuses on stories of local unsung heroes and heroines. He describes the involvement of young men and women, emphasizes grassroots organizing, and discusses how individuals make choices. At the national convention of the American Federation of Teachers (AFT) on July 12, 2014, Mark told his audience that, "The Civil Rights Movement is Not Over." According to him, there is an important connection between unemployment and freedom, and concluded that, "Freedom Summer should be remembered as one moment in a long—and still ongoing—struggle."[105]

Mark has published on Freedom Summer. His works have appeared in *Jewish Currents*, in books, teacher magazines, and on websites. He has been interviewed about Freedom Summer and Freedom Schools numerous times and has appeared in video clips. He was instrumental in the establishment of the Civil Rights and Activist Archive at the Queens College Rosenthal Library and created a Roll Call of Queens College Civil Rights alumni, faculty, and activists who served in the Southern Civil Rights Movement. He worked with activists in Meridian, Mississippi, to preserve their civil rights stories for posterity.[106] Mark Levy continues to be active in social justice activist struggles.

* * *

Betty Bollinger Levy (deceased) graduated from Queens College with a BA in psychology in 1963 before going to Mississippi in 1964 with her husband. They were assigned to serve as co-directors and teachers at the Meridian Freedom School in Neshoba County. She returned to work in Mississippi in the summer of 1965. Betty received a Master of Education in Elementary Teaching degree from Harvard University and a Ph.D. in Psychology—Combined TC and CU degree. She taught in an elementary school in Harlem for some years. After earning her doctorate, she joined the Women's Studies Department at the State University of New York College at Old Westbury as a full-time faculty. She died in 1974.

* * *

Mark and Betty (Bollinger) Levy were of course not the only QC activists who saw the contradictions that Mississippi presented to the ideals of American democracy. I turn now to another QC student, Robert Masters, who spent seven weeks in Greenwood, Mississippi, as a volunteer activist during the Mississippi Freedom Summer 1964 Project. Masters was born in 1944 and grew up in Huntington Station on Long Island. He attended Queens College from 1963 to 1966 and graduated from QC at the age of twenty-two with a degree in psychology. Masters started his intense activism in his freshman year at Queens College. In the Spring of 1964, he volunteered for the Mississippi Freedom Summer Project to help with voter registration in Mississippi.[107] He worked under the aegis of the Student Nonviolent Coordinating Committee (SNCC) while in Greenwood as a civil rights volunteer and student activist soliciting and trying to register voters at first, but later, recruiting delegates for the new Mississippi Freedom Democratic Party (MFDP).[108] Part of Masters' assignment was to canvass from door to door to enlist support among the African American community for MFDP's challenge to the established all-White Democratic Party delegation to the Democratic National Convention in Atlantic City in August 1964.[109]

As with the Levys, Masters told journalists that he participated in "sessions of role playing; how to lie on your side with your knees drawn up and your arms over your head, so as to receive the least amount of physical damage from clubs,"[110] during his orientation at Oxford, Ohio. He recounted how during training, they also "learned what to do when stopped by the police."[111] They were instructed in canvassing procedures, and a Justice Department lawyer warned the activists that "the FBI wouldn't be able to help them."[112] Although their colleagues, Michael Schwerner, Andrew Goodman, and James Chaney were murdered by White supremacists, their immediate reaction was not that of fear, but anger. "We just felt this tremendous anger, but no one left at any time because of fear,"[113] he told journalists. He noted, however, that the situation in Greenwood got worse by the day, and that "[t]he climate was changing from bad to worse."[114] He gave his listeners numerous accounts of police brutality and noted that Blacks began boycotting a grocery store after a policeman dragged a pregnant girl through the streets. Similarly, a Black youth had his beard pulled out hair by hair and was beaten up against a concrete wall. "The worst thing about it," Masters said, "was the failure of the FBI to come in and give any protection, which they should have done."[115]

As a result of this brutality, Blacks in Greenwood boycotted about five White-owned stores in the Black community. Masters was concerned that although Greenwood was the county seat of Leflore County with a Black population of about thirteen thousand (which amounted to roughly two-thirds of the adult population), Blacks had only 268 registered voters.[116]

The county was divided into sections and each volunteer was given a section to canvass. The volunteers lived with local families, and Robert was accommodated in Rev. and Mrs. Allen's home along with a Harvard student from New York, Bill Hodes. The two volunteers shared a mattress in their new residence.

In his early weeks in Greenwood, Robert was given responsibility for about five hundred eligible Black voters. Unfortunately, after canvassing and getting about fifteen people to come to the courthouse, only one would be registered successfully.[117] Indeed, through a series of personal letters, Robert gave insights into his assignments, objectives of the voter registration, organization, and *modus operandi* of the voter registration exercises in both Greenwood and Mississippi as a whole. In a handwritten letter to Mrs. Goldberg (a neighbor from Long Island), dated Friday 24, 1964, Masters explained in detail his assignments in Greenwood, his joys and tribulations, and the successes and failures of the exercise. First, he thanked Mrs. Goldberg for her compliments and kind words, which he thought he did not deserve but noted, "One of the things that keeps us going down here is the belief that we have the support of the majority of the people in the United States. Receiving a letter like yours is very reassuring to me,"[118] he wrote. Masters told Mrs. Goldberg that he was jailed for five days and while he was in jail, he met some poor Mississippi Whites, and he believed that "when they understood the true nature of the civil rights movement (as opposed to the views of our purpose as described by local politicians) they even went along with it."[119] He went on to tell her that if there were ways for people like herself "to open up the minds and hearts of the average segregationist, they would want to do our jobs for us because that is the only way for a full realization of the resources of the South."[120] Robert described his assignment and daily routines in Greenwood in these words, "My daily work consists of canvassing from door to door. Right now, there is an emphasis on organizing the Freedom Democratic Party (FDP), so when I canvass, it is to get people to fill out Freedom Registration Forms."[121] He described the FDP as a "new party designed to lay the groundwork in politically organizing the [Black] community."[122] Masters reminded Mrs. Goldberg that the Freedom Democratic Party is different from the old Democratic Party because it is run completely by the local people and is one example of grassroots mobilization of political forces. As a manifestation of their work, he stated, "Last night we had a countywide convention for the FDP completely run by the local people. It was exciting to see real grass roots politicking going on."[123] He hoped that in a few years, Blacks would be the most politically sophisticated group in the state of Mississippi and maybe in the country. "Not only will they be extremely aware of what is happening, but when they get full voting rights, they will probably control the state."[124] In his letter, Masters also spoke warmly about the hospitality of their Black hosts. "In general, the [Black] community has been very warm to us. Many of us have developed strong personal relations with the families with whom we are staying."[125]

In the same way that Mark and Betty appealed for books and funds for their school, Masters solicited funds for the project and requested new ideas for raising money or suggestions to help his parents raise funds for the project. "Support for the project has been coming in from many parts of the country. I've been working with my parents to get them to raise funds for the project. If you have any ideas on fundraising perhaps you could help my parents."[126] Masters ended his letter with "P.S. Here's a Student Voice!" On the same day, Masters wrote to his parents as well, explaining the nature of his tasks and the way forward. "I guess you've read something about the Freedom Democratic Party and understand the basis of our challenge of the regular Democratic Party,"[127] he wrote. With his characteristic candor, he explained that the reason for starting a new party was to open the process to everyone and to get the complete support of every Black person in Mississippi, but he regretted that at that point, they had only twenty thousand forms filled out of an estimated 450,000 Black electorates in their ambitious expansion program. This, in essence, he explained, is why he and others had to stay back physically in Mississippi to help the people with completing the forms, in the hope that the Black community would support their efforts. "The form we are using is simplicity itself. There's nothing to it, but there are many people who can't even fill it out."[128]

During his stay in Mississippi, Masters was arrested twice, first on July 16, 1964, when they mounted picket lines in front of the courthouse where voter registration was being held, and he was arrested again later, on a "trumped-up" charge of assault against a Mississippi White man. In both instances, Masters said he was scared because he saw some people being clubbed and saw a police officer beating up a girl, and during that incident there were about thirty police officers with steel helmets and their clubs drawn.[129] This is how the press reported one of the arrests:

The police arrested 111 civil rights workers and local (Blacks) here today for picketing during a mass voter-registration attempt. The 106 persons age 15 and over among the demonstrators were charged with violating a recently enacted anti-picketing law. They were held in the city jail, the Leflore County jail, at the county prison farm in lieu of $200 bond each. Five demonstrators 14 or under were turned over to their parents.[130]

In his letter to his parents, Masters mentioned his improved state of health after leaving jail, which he described as the "cage": "I've been eating a lot since getting out of the 'cage' and have put most of my weight back."[131]

While the Levys bore witness to and were recipients of hateful and violent comments, Masters' experience in Mississippi was much more physically violent. During his seven-week stay, he was beaten, manhandled, stepped on, threatened, cursed, and thrown into jail twice. Despite police brutality, back on Long Island, Masters counted the gains and blessings of the summer project to include the fact that the Black community was being awakened, and he believed that Blacks in Mississippi would someday be much more politically aware than the average White. As the students learned and gained critical awareness in the Freedom School, Masters believed that the community was becoming more knowledgeable—and, more importantly, vocal in that knowledge. According to him, "This awareness would shatter efforts by the state politicians to keep [Blacks] ignorant."[132] Masters used his time on Long Island to garner support for the Mississippi Freedom Democratic Party (MFDP).

* * *

In 1965, as the president of QC's Mississippi Freedom Project, Masters and five other student activists spent twelve days during winter intersession rebuilding four burned Black Baptist churches in Tougaloo, Mississippi. The team completed 560 hours of work coordinated by the Committee of Concern, an interracial group of Mississippi clergymen of all faiths. However, the technical aspects of the work were handled by the Society of Friends. The students did different types of work including hanging ceilings, landscaping, and completely shingling a roof. They did some construction work with concrete and spent two days painting church pews.[133]

From 1966 to 1970, Masters joined the Peace Corps and was posted to West Africa after graduating from QC in 1966. On his return, he read law at New York University Law School. He received his JD in 1973.

He served as Senior Vice President, General Counsel, Chief Compliance Officer, and Corporate Secretary at Acadia Realty Trust in New York, starting from 1998. Before joining Acadia, he had worked for private real estate companies, banks, a law firm, and the Department of Justice. He is retired from Acadia Realty Trust but now serves as a legal consultant to the company.

* * *

I'm tired of reading history, now I want to make it.

—Mario Savio

Unlike both the Levys and Masters, it appears that extraordinarily little is known about Mario Savio's Queens College activism connection.[134] Savio was born on December 8, 1942, in New York City into an Italian American family. His parents were Joseph and Dora Savio. His father immigrated from Sicily to the United States in 1928, and his mother's family came from northern Italy. Savio's father, Joseph moved his family from lower Manhattan to Queens, and Mario spent his childhood in Floral Park, Queens. He attended Martin Van Buren High School. Not only did Savio obtain very high grades, but he was also elected president of his class. Savio was a very brilliant student and, according to Robert Cohen, his biographer, he took "only the most difficult courses, competing with the strongest students, and…earned the numerical equivalent of an A in every course."[135] He was "one of only two Martin Van Buren High School students—out of five thousand—selected for a National Science Foundation (NSF) Summer Science - Math Institute at Manhattan College in 1959…"[136] Savio was also selected as one of the forty national finalists in the prestigious Westinghouse Science Talent Search in high school. Savio graduated from Martin Van Buren High School with a sterling academic record and was the valedictorian in his class. Because of his excellent academic achievement, he was readily admitted to Manhattan College in the Bronx with a full academic scholarship. Savio transferred from Manhattan College to Queens College in his sophomore year because Queens had "a more cosmopolitan intellectual and social milieu."[137] Robert Cohen argues that Queens College "with its predominantly Jewish student body and secular character…was an extension of the stimulating social and educational environment in which he

(Savio) had excelled at Van Buren."[138] In the oral interview conducted by Bret Eynon for Columbia University in 1985, Savio admitted that interacting with Jewish culture helped him to break away from what he increasingly perceived as the narrow Italian Catholic culture that he was born into.[139] He described the Jewish culture as one that had "much more respect for critical thinking than there was in the Catholic culture that I was born into."[140] It's not surprising, then, that QC became the place where Mario "took his first steps toward student activism."[141] At Queens, he traveled with a group of other students to Albany, New York, to protest the state imposition of fees in the City Colleges.[142] This protest revealed to Mario the power that students could have if only they decided to use it. When Dr. Stoke, the president of Queens College, banned some speakers from speaking at Queens College, Savio worked as a picket captain in the student strike organized by Kenneth (Kenny) Warner, president of the Student Association on November 16, 1961.[143] He also joined in the antidiscrimination demonstration outside the Woolworth's store in New York. He later said that he picketed outside the Woolworth's store because he "felt an immediate rapport based on the justice of it."[144] Relatedly, Savio joined a group of forty volunteers organized by Queens College's Newman House under the auspices of the Queens College Mexico Volunteers and spent the summer of 1963 in the town of Taxco in Central Mexico constructing a laundry facility for the poor. Mario later described this experience as "a private Peace Corps effort."[145] According to Robert Cohen,

> The Taxco project added to his (Savio's) understanding of class conflict and inequality. Even though Taxco was 'a center of tourism, a fabulously wealthy town,' in 'the hills up above surrounding the town' he observed desperate poverty, unlike any he had ever experienced. Savio saw 'whole families (one with seven children) sleeping in one filthy bed...starved children, widespread dysentery.'[146]

Savio's stay at Queens College did not last long, though he did take his burgeoning activism to his next college. He transferred from Queens College to the University of California at Berkeley in the fall of 1963. Midsemester during his first year at Berkeley, he joined the campus activist group, University Friends of SNCC, and the CORE chapter on campus, where he and some SNCC and CORE members picketed the Sheraton Palace Hotel. In a speech at Queens College some years later, he stated,

"I joined the campus group of the Student Nonviolent Coordinating Committee and picketed at a hotel with a group of CORE demonstrators. I was arrested when we staged a sit-in protest against discriminatory hiring practices. But I was exonerated at my trial."[147] In the interview with Bret Eynon, Mario explained that getting arrested for an activist cause was an accomplishment and a badge of honor because, "it proved that you were really committed, that it wasn't just words." He went on to conclude that "it was sort of the initiation into really being part of the movement in the strongest sense."[148]

It was at the University of California that Savio joined the Freedom Summer Project to register Blacks in Mississippi to vote. Though he joined the project at a different university, he developed much of his critical and activist consciousness at QC and took his first steps toward activism at QC.[149] Savio was informed of the Freedom Summer project by his cellmate, John King while they were both in jail following their Sheraton Palace Hotel arrest. Savio was immediately attracted to the work done by SNCC because of his burning desire for social justice and because, "they (SNCC) seemed to be waging the most admirable struggle for social justice in America, unsullied by self-interest, risking their lives for racial equality, and doing so without the ideological baggage of the Old Left."[150] He particularly admired the movement because of its "radicalism without ideology."[151] He wanted to work in Mississippi despite the sacrifices required because it afforded him the opportunity to help those who were very obviously oppressed, and it "represented a historic opportunity to change America."[152] As he emphasized, such acts of kindness "just appeal to human beings,"[153] and he wanted to be part of that community. He recollected his experience while working with the poor in Mexico and assured himself that he could handle the registration of Black voters in Mississippi:

> I believe I could be successful in convincing [Black] citizens of the importance of registering to vote, again on the basis of my work in Mexico last summer where I had to persuade the poor farmers in Taxco of the importance of helping us to help themselves; several of them expressed the belief that nothing could improve their situation, so desperate had become their situation.[154]

Despite all the dangers involved and in spite of the murder of Andrew Goodman, his friend from Queens College,[155] Savio volunteered to go to McComb, even though this was one of the most violent Ku Klux Klan areas because, as Savio saw it, "Somebody's got to do it." "Somebody had to go to McComb"[156] And he told Bret Eynon, "Finally, it came down to this: Okay. Here we are…This is going on. Am I going to be part of it or not? If I'm not part of that, I might as well not be here."[157] Due to insecurity, Savio and his group were not allowed to go to McComb immediately, so he spent the first few weeks in Holmes County registering voters before going to McComb later. Unfortunately, even in Holmes County, Savio and his colleagues were still at the receiving end of bomb threats from White supremacists, among other violence. Although Savio's experiences differed from Robert Masters' in Greenwood, but it was just as life-threatening. As Savio succinctly remembered years later, "Perhaps the worst night was the first night in Holmes County once we began living at the Freedom House. It was a night of veritable paranoia. We crawled about on hands and knees fearing to be caught before a window. We kept watch all night."[158] But Savio and his colleagues pressed ahead with their mission to reverse generations of racial oppression in Mississippi because, as they saw it, their adventure was worth the risk. This is what Savio said about their pursuit, "This is the only game in town. This is it. This is real thing going on at this moment in my country. Either I'm part of it, so I can at least feel that I've lived my own life, or else I'm not part of it, and just watch it."[159] A resounding connection between all volunteers of the Freedom Summer Project was, though dangerous, the work they did was irrevocably worth it to pursue change. In his first letter home from Holmes County, Savio said he was glad "to be part of such a change for good that's sweeping across our country." He went on to state, "The history of the world is pivoting on the internal changes that are going on today in America—and we are in part the agent of that change. A breath of freedom."[160] Savio's assignment in Holmes County centered on voter registration. The assignment was not easy sailing at first because many Blacks were afraid of reprisals. Here is one example where Savio lamented lack of cooperation, "I have had the agonizing experience of… talking with a family for fully an hour without convincing them they should go down to the courthouse to…register to vote."[161] He, however, did not blame Blacks for their reluctance to register to vote because even the willing participants, he came to realise, stood the risk of losing their jobs or their welfare checks; and in most cases Blacks were not even allowed to pass the literacy test irrespective of their reading or writing abilities because, as Elizabeth Martinez noted, there were many reasons the registrar could find to flunk a Black applicant, from not dotting an "i" to misspelling a word.[162]

But there were a few bright spots and success stories such as when Savio was given a warm and exciting welcome by a Black family during his first week of canvassing for votes. "Yesterday," Mario reported, "I spoke w/one man who said he had been 'uplifted' by our visit. He gladly welcomed the coming freedom, and would work to hasten it. I too was 'uplifted.'"[163] A few weeks later, Savio was happy to report that he was making slow but remarkable progress with his voter registration assignment. "With each person with whom I talk my desire to remain here past August increases. I'm ever more feeling this as a personal fight."[164] With time the responses Savio received from Blacks went from "If I go down and register to vote I'm gonna lose my work… They'll kick me off this land…I'm not going to be able to feed my family. May get beaten up," to "okay, where do I go [to register]?"[165] Savio wrote that some of those who went out to register to vote were elderly, and some even went to the White areas to register. He was so delighted with the turn of events that he reported, "It was very impressive and inspiring to see them marching down to the courthouse. The movement that had moved us so much had also been a kind of awakening for people who had been under the heel of an oppressive society for very long."[166] Despite overwhelming odds, the dramatic persistence of an old Black farmer to register to vote made Savio's faith in the rightness of their cause unshakable. This is Savio's recollection of the event:

> So, I remember, on this particular day—there was another white worker with me, another one of the volunteers—we came with this farmer. We're talking about an old man; he may have been sixty or seventy. He had a hat…He came in, and we all went into the courthouse, the three of us, and then he walked forward to the desk. He took his hat off, and he stood there. Then she (the registrar) started in on him: 'What do you want, boy?' 'I want to reddish, ma'am…' 'What's that you say, boy?'… 'I want to reddish, ma'am.' 'What's reddish? What are you talking about, boy?' And on and on and on. He never gave up. She finally had to give him the form.[167]

As Savio noted later, "That man's courage changed my life. Until then, I was still sort of an observer in a certain way. Less and less so, okay?" Savio went on to add, "But here's somebody, who because of something I had done, was maybe risking his family, facing that kind of humiliation...Yet he stood his ground...That was the point at which it all came real for me. That is, I'd chosen sides for the rest of my life."[168]

Aside from registering Blacks to vote in Mississippi, Savio was also involved in registration work for the Mississippi Freedom Democratic Party (MFDP). Indeed, as Savio discovered, registering voters for MFDP proved to be a much easier task than the work they had earlier done in getting people to the courthouse to register to vote, and he commented, "I've spoken to so many frightened, weary, nearly broken people who still had enough spirit left to light up when I explained the convention challenge to the party of the White Citizens' Council."[169] Registration for MFDP was easier because it was conducted by COFO and not by the state or county officials, and because there had been a similar mock election and mock registration campaign called Freedom Vote[170] that was conducted by COFO and SNCC in some areas of Mississippi. After his initial assignment registering Blacks to vote in Holmes County and in Jackson, Mississippi, Savio was sent to his original posting in McComb. Consequently, he left Holmes County for his new place of volunteer work. In McComb, Savio's Freedom House was guarded round the clock because there was always danger of night riders. However, as Savio reasoned, "Somebody had to go to McComb. Somebody's got to do it, so I'd guess you'd better do it,"[171] because if not Savio, who? In a 1985 interview, Savio told Bret Eynon emphatically, "Somebody had to go to McComb. I mean, there weren't millions of people saying, hey, take me!."[172] Savio's assignment in McComb changed from voter registration to teaching in a Freedom School where he proved to be an effective teacher. He taught Spanish, biology, English, remedial arithmetic, and citizenship at the McComb Freedom School.[173] Just as with Mark and Betty Levy, Savio noted the positive reception the students had for his class: "They love it and I love it. They're really learning. In two and a half weeks the class will end—damn! So much to do, so little time."[174] Savio "credited the Mississippi crusade with helping to break down the racial, regional, and class barriers that for almost a century had kept white America from opposing racist violence and segregation in the South."[175] As he saw it, Freedom Summer tore down the walls of racial essentialism and isolation created by White privilege. He praised the creative instincts of SNCC for bringing together, "privileged upper-and middle-class youths from northern campuses with the disenfranchised [Black] community of Mississippi, since it raised awareness about the hateful, violent, segregationist regime in a country that prided itself on its democratic values."[176] He saw this situation as a noticeably big change that could show young White Americans that racism had to go. In his final analysis, Savio regarded the Mississippi Freedom Summer as the most creative political endeavor he had ever experienced or heard about which certainly "will be seen as a key event in the twentieth century history of the United States, [which] was the trigger for very deep change."[177]

* * *

Savio returned to the University of California, Berkeley after his time in Mississippi, and from lessons learned and inspiration received during the Freedom Summer and activism at Queens College, he went back to Berkeley to fire up and lead the Free Speech Movement (FSM) of the 1960s.[178] Savio led a group of students to boycott classes in mid-September, 1964 after the university administration sent a letter to student political groups telling them that they could no longer use the plaza at Bancroft and Telegraph to solicit support for "off campus political and social action," in order for the institution to preserve its political neutrality. This directive was, however, modified wherein the university wrote that "the students were allowed to solicit funds and engage in recruiting members, provided they didn't join organizations which engaged in illegal activities such as sit-ins, picketing, and the like."[179] As an ardent activist, Savio opposed these directives because, as he pointed out at Queens College later, "We who are interested in the Civil Rights Movement couldn't go along with this directive. We felt that the courts were responsible for handling illegal actions and not the university."[180] Savio went on to explain, "I myself spent last summer in Mississippi participating in voter registration drives and teaching in Freedom Schools."[181] He continued by stating in the Bret Eynon interview that there should be no university regulation of the content of speech or advocacy because only the courts are charged with that responsibility.

Savio's argument and that of the Free Speech Movement was "that the University could exercise no authority over the content of speech or advocacy, and could regulate its time, place, or manner only to the extent necessary to protect the normal functioning of the University."[182] During the Free Speech demonstrations, more than seven hundred students were arrested and prosecuted during sit-ins at the university. On this front, Savio admitted that the Free Speech Movement adopted the methods and leadership style of SNCC in its *modus operandi*,[183] and in an unequivocal show of support for Savio and the Free Speech Movement, John Lewis, Chairman of SNCC, issued the following statements: "We wish to express our support for our brothers and sisters at the University of California in their fight for full free speech on the university campus."[184] Lewis saw the attack on free speech at the University of California as "attempts to curtail the activity of the Friends of SNCC…,"[185] He drew a moral equivalency between the events at Berkeley and the brutality against Blacks in the South and noted, "We are shocked at the brutality used by police against the students who sat in at the University's administration building. Police brutality in the South is nothing new to us—but what is happening in the so-called liberal community of Berkeley?"[186] Lewis made it absolutely clear that, "Students have the right to participate in political activity on and off the campus,"[187] and lamented, "We know well the attempts by administrators on the campuses of Southern [Black] colleges to break the civil rights movement by not allowing students to meet and advocate ideas on the campus. Now university administrators in the North are borrowing these same tactics."[188] "Such denial of students' rights— North or South—," he continued, "is an affront to the ideals of American democracy."[189] Savio explained many years later that at Berkeley, he "was part of a political group that was trying to prevent the University from taking back the freedoms that we'd won in the fall of 1964."[190]

Michael Harrington,[191] author of *The Other America* and Chairman, Board of Directors, League for Industrial Democracy, took a similar view on the ban on free speech at Berkeley. He weighed in on the controversy and lent his voice to the Free Speech Movement. In a press release on December 11, Mr. Harrington stated:

> The attacks on the democratic rights of Berkeley students are bred in the same atmosphere which produces the largest rightwing movement in any single state across our land. By denying the freedom of political expression to University of California students, President Kerr has unwittingly strengthened the hand of the ultra-right in its attacks on our liberties. Free speech *must* triumph—on the Berkeley campus.[192]

Mr. Harrington concluded that it was a mark of hypocrisy for the university to favor Civil Rights everywhere except at its doorsteps and cautioned that the "use of strong-arm methods by University police apes the methods of Southern racists in suppressing [Black] rights."[193] Robert

Cohen surmises that Savio's roles in the Civil Rights Movement and the Free Speech Movement were hedged on the side of social justice, ethical, and moral principles, and not for a career in politics. In a speech at Queens College, his alma mater, Savio explained the reasons for the sit-ins by stating how the Free Speech Movement did not want his university to dictate laws which rightly came under the jurisdiction of the courts.[194] He argued that the President of the University of California, Berkeley, Dr. Clark Kerr, was running a "Berkeley Knowledge Factory," because he had issued a series of directives that prohibited student governments on the campuses of the university from taking positions on off-campus political, religious, economic, intellectual, or other issues of the time.[195] In effect, students from the university were forbidden from raising money or recruiting members for off-campus organizations. Savio noted that Dr. Kerr ran the university like the manager of a big business [where] the administrators were the board of directors, the faculty served as the employees, and the students were the raw materials.[196] He went on to conclude that at Berkeley, "Nobody out there gives a damn for the undergraduate student, because there is a higher price for the graduate student."[197] He proposed that "the Queens College regulation requiring student organizations to register speakers with the college two weeks before they are scheduled to talk be broken...and broken...and broken."[198] He justified the protest at Berkeley by noting that the university should be a community of scholars and students that is completely free to inquire and to profess all points of view, whether intellectual points of view or political points of view because the academic community is best served when it has such freedom.[199] Savio was of the opinion that a university should not be in the business of censoring free speech because if that happens, all civil rights activities on campuses everywhere would be crippled if students could not advocate sit-ins; where people are often arrested and where civil rights demonstrations are often looked upon as criminal action by the police.[200] Mario worked as a picket captain at Queens College during the student strike organized by Kenneth (Kenny) Warner in 1961, and in 1963 he joined a group of protesters in Albany, New York against the imposition of tuition on the City University of New York students. The extent to which these protests at QC prepared Savio for the Free Speech Movement demonstrations at Berkeley is speculative at best. One thing is sure however, and there is ample evidence to support this from his friends and associates, Savio was perplexed when he went with the Queens College Mexico Volunteers to Taxco in Mexico to provide technical help to the poor. During this trip, Savio saw the sharp class divisions in Mexican society and the unwillingness of the Mexican authorities to ameliorate the conditions of the poor. It was this sharp division in Mexican society that strengthened Mario's social consciousness.[201] The influence of the Mexico trip as the forerunner to the Student Free Speech Movement at Berkeley is not in dispute because Robert Cohen, Savio's biographer reported that, "The Taxco project added to his understanding of class conflict and inequality."[202] "Why," Savio asked, "was there all this wealth side-by-side with all this shameful poverty?"[203] Indeed, in many of his FSM speeches and orations, Savio effectively documented the arrogance of power both at Berkeley and elsewhere. And according to Robert Cohen, Savio's Queens College speech on December 11, 1964, was a "homecoming event for Mario[because] it was at the Queens campus that Mario took his first steps towards political activism, travelling with a student group to do antipoverty work in Mexico in the summer of 1963."[204] In Mario's biography, Cohen goes on to explain that Savio's indignation over Mexico's extreme inequality not only affected his social consciousness but also pushed him toward a new eloquence as an assertive and powerful speaker.[205] The Mexico experience, according to Cohen, helped Savio to shed his bad stammer, to stand up for a group of Indian peasants and talk to them freely about liberation, democracy, and civil rights.[206] And indeed, Cohen concludes that it was because of his anger at the extreme inequality in Mexico, that Savio "emerged, chrysalis-like, and seemingly overnight into an assertive and powerful speaker-organizer,"[207] to the great surprise of his fellow volunteers. During the Free Speech Movement (FSM), Mario Savio emerged as a very compelling speaker, a trait he developed in Mexico.

* * *

After the Free Speech Movement, Savio was suspended from Berkeley for his activism. However, in the 1980s Savio went back to college. He obtained his BS in 1984 and a master's degree in physics from San Francisco State University in 1989.[208] He went on to teach physics at San Francisco State and later taught at Modesto Community College. In 1990, Mario was employed at Sonoma State University. He opposed and worked against California Proposition 187 which was to make immigrants residing in the state without legal permission ineligible for public benefits. He also criticized and challenged Proposition 209 in California, which, among other things, outlawed the use of affirmative action in admissions in the University of California system. In another fight, Savio opposed a fee hike at Sonoma State University because "it made the university too expensive for low-income students."[209] Mario died in 1996.

In 1998, Mario Savio and the Free Speech Movement he pioneered were honored by the University of California, Berkeley with an endowment for books, a university library café, and a digitized archive at the Bancroft Library of the University.[210]

* * *

"THE THUNDERING SILENCE of the good people is disturbing.... This is a family problem, and there are no outsiders."[211] These were the words of Aaron Henry at Queens College in April 1964 that compelled Nancy Cooper (now Nancy Cooper Samstein) to action. Nancy also listened to a speech by Allard Lowenstein in which he "outlined a bold strategy for breaking the civil rights deadlock in Mississippi."[212] Nancy, a friend and anthropology classmate of Andrew Goodman, had a few months earlier opted to join the *Mexico Volunteers*, "a student group that worked in a barrio outside Mexico City, a kind of summer Peace Corps project to build a school and thus further the cause of Mexican-American friendship and world peace."[213] But when Nancy listened to Allard Lowenstein, Aaron Henry, Barbara Jones, and Prathia Hall, an SNCC field secretary, she decided not to go to Mexico but to volunteer for the Freedom Summer instead because, as she saw it, what was happening in Mississippi was similar to what had taken place in Nazi Germany. Nancy, who "had grown up hearing firsthand accounts of the Holocaust from concentration camp survivors who were her family's neighbors in the Bronx,"[214] did not believe that such atrocities could happen in the United States. As an activist, Nancy was moved to action when Allard Lowenstein told the students at Queens College that "what happened in the South was their business, too. [That] they were not exempt from responsibility simply because they did not live in that section of the country."[215] Lowenstein told the students that it was time to "sit in rather than sit out."[216] Also very troubling to Nancy was the anticommunist witch-hunt her father and her father's friends had to endure as officers of the postal workers union in America—in a country that is supposed to be the land of the free.[217] Nancy and Andrew Goodman were referred by Barbara (Jones) Omolade to the Manhattan office of

SNCC for an in-person interview and both were accepted as Freedom Summer volunteers.[218] After the orientation in Oxford, Ohio, Goodman was sent to Meridian, and Nancy was posted to Canton where she taught in Freedom Schools. Nancy also worked for SNCC in the Washington, DC, office including working on the Mississippi Freedom Democratic Party Congressional seating challenge to the Mississippi all-White Democratic Party delegation at the Democratic National Convention in Atlantic City. To show how integral Queens College and its students were in social activism and in the fight for social justice in the 1960s, Nancy Cooper, a Queens College student gave up her graduate fellowship in anthropology to continue the struggle because, as Nancy said, "Everything accomplished over the summer in education and voter registration could disappear if someone doesn't stick around."[219] Nancy was part of the staff in the national SNCC office in Atlanta, Georgia for some years after her volunteer assignment was over.[220] She was married to Mendy Samstein, a civil rights activist, and a White organizer for SNCC. One of Nancy's most enduring contributions to SNCC and to the memory of Freedom Summer was her assignment to collect freedom school students' poetry which she put into a pamphlet that was later published in the revised edition of the book, *Letters from Mississippi: Reports from Civil Rights Volunteers & Poetry of the 1964 Freedom Summer.*[221]

After her SNCC volunteer work, Nancy established a "community-based, movement-oriented coffee shop in Atlanta, GA."[222] Nancy received a Master of Arts degree from New York University in 1984. Currently, she is an artist and serves as an adjunct instructor at the State University of New York College at Oneonta. Her work can be viewed at the Black Sheep Gallery in New Lisbon, New York where she resides, although her paintings, drawings, and constructs have been exhibited extensively in the United States and abroad. Her works "address a dimension of landscape and its anthropology."[223] Apart from teaching, she lives and raises sheep in New Lisbon, New York.

* * *

Joseph Liesner was born in the French Hospital in New York City on December 28, 1942. He attended Queens College from 1960 to 1964 and was a split biology/chemistry major. According to him, he was a real science nerd until his senior year when he started hanging out with some philosophy majors.[224] Though he may have had a hint or two about civil rights, it did not influence his decision to go South, until "he heard about the murder of Emmett Till and others in the South which so incensed him that he decided that the only moral thing to do was to respond to Bob Moses and SNCC and put his white body on the line to end racist murders in Mississippi."[225] In order to go to Oxford, Ohio, for the Mississippi Freedom Summer orientation, Liesner went through very difficult emotional struggles with his mother who "was obsessed with the dangers I [Joseph Liesner] faced in Mississippi."[226] As he recollected later, "It was partly for that reason, and greatly for my own wish to remain alive, that in Oxford I switched my volunteer assignment from Greenwood to Moss Point (Moss Point was the location where Queens College professor, Tony O'Brien was the coordinator) upon hearing about the disappearance of Schwerner, Chaney, and Goodman."[227] Joseph Liesner did voter registration in Moss Point and Pascagoula. Most of his "vivid memories revolve around his walking the dusty roads, talking to folks, training and escorting people to take the test for registering to vote."[228] "One of my most poignant memories of that summer," he recollected,

> is of the time I knocked at the screen door of an exceedingly small shack and as I heard footsteps shuffling towards the door, I began to make out a hunched-over man slowly approach the door using a cane to make his way. When he opened the door and took a long look at me, he exclaimed, 'Come here, Momma, it's one of them Jew boys from New York.' He and his wife were incredibly open to talking about their lives and registering to vote. The single-room shack had one entire wall covered with large colored pictures of roast hams, cakes, pies, and all kinds of food from the Sunday paper...[229]

In addition to "asking people to commit to attempting to register to vote,"[230] Liesner and his teammates spent a good deal of the summer teaching people how to explain the meaning of different parts of the US Constitution, because such interpretations were exceedingly difficult for illiterate sharecroppers to make, and without any doubt, those interpretations were certainly placed as obstacles to prevent Black Mississippians from voting.[231]

Liesner and his other colleague stayed with Mr. and Mrs. Smith in Moss Point, whom he commended as wonderful hosts.[232] Mr. Smith was retired from the International Shipyard in Moss Point, which at that time was the largest employer in the city.[233] Liesner was delighted to say that the Smiths and the other people they "met and worked with on the project were open, dedicated, and very courageous; facing threats to their jobs and lives for daring to attempt to register to vote."[234] He maintained that one day about twelve of them (activists) were arrested at the Holiday Inn. They were packed in a regular size station wagon and kept in the hot sun for over one hour with a cop pointing a shotgun at them and joking about how easily the trigger of the shotgun could be pulled. Liesner was able to read the inscription on the shotgun which stated, "Walk tall and carry me proudly for I make you any man's equal."[235]

When the project was finally over, Liesner was among the Freedom Summer activists who went to Atlantic City with the Mississippi Freedom Democratic Party delegation whose purpose was to attempt to unseat the regular Mississippi Democratic Party delegation at the Democratic National Convention. During this sojourn, Liesner "had some very memorable experiences hanging out with memorable people like Dick Gregory even though [they] were not successful in their attempt to get the Freedom delegation seated."[236] "We were," he was happy to say, "greatly successful in bringing the racist practices of the state of Mississippi to the forefront of America's conscience."[237] However, he lamented that some of the gains they made during that summer are being eroded today. But the most joyful lesson Liesner learned from the Freedom Summer experience was that several years later, in one of the reunions organized by Robert (Bob) Moses to see how the Mississippi Freedom Summer volunteers were doing, Professor Hardy T. Frye told them that "even though some of the electoral gains that followed the summer of 1964 were being undone or eroded, he goes back to Mississippi often and could attest to our impact by the fact that as he drives across the state there is a black sheriff in some counties, and that was good to hear."[238]

After graduating from Queens College in 1964, Joseph Liesner took a job as a caseworker in the Welfare Department of the New York City Department of Social Services. Later, he was employed as a science teacher in Williamsburg, New York. He moved to California to become a dance therapist before changing his profession to building construction/carpentry.[239] He is today working in television production, video editing, and videography. He is a government producer and an activist and lives in Berkeley, California.[240]

* * *

> Rita Schwerner had been working in Meridian for six months when her husband disappeared. History has seen Rita Schwerner as the widow of a martyr. Women's history demands that we see her fully embodied in time, a woman whose activism preceded and continued after the terrible summer of 1964. Rita Schwerner Bender is but one of many Jewish women activists whose less dramatic stories have yet to be told.
>
> —Debra L. Schultz

While violence against White activists in the South was certainly not unheard of as we have seen thus far, nothing quite perplexed those who worked with the Freedom Summer project like the death of Michael (Mickey) Schwerner, Andrew Goodman, and James Chaney. In fact, the deaths of Michael, Andrew, and James are a constellation of which the other activists orbited around. The beginnings of both Rita's and Michael's work in Mississippi echo the beginnings of other QC activists we have met thus far, although Michael and Rita Schwerner were posted to Meridian by CORE six months before the other activists came.

Rita (Levant) Schwerner Bender was born in 1942, a native of Mount Vernon, New York. Rita started her university education at the University of Michigan in the Department of Education. She was introduced to Michael by a friend.[241] Rita transferred to Queens College in 1962, where, in addition to her studies, she participated in volunteer work, tutoring disadvantaged youths in Jamaica, Queens.[242] Rita, together with her husband, Michael, joined the CORE chapter in New York City, and on July 11, 1963, they took part in a picket line at a construction site in Manhattan because of discrimination against the employment of minorities in the building industry. Rita, Michael, and four others were arrested for disorderly conduct for stepping in front of a cement truck. They both received suspended sentences. This was barely a week after Michael had spent two days in jail in Gwynn Oaks, Maryland, where he was arrested during a sit-in that was sponsored by CORE at a segregated amusement park on the outskirts of Baltimore.

In August 1963, Michael and Rita sponsored ninety representatives from the Hamilton-Madison Settlement House to attend the March on Washington. In mid-September, Rita and Michael were moved into action after they had seen on television the bombing of the Sixteenth Street Baptist Church in Birmingham, Alabama that killed four young girls. Michael applied to the CORE national office for employment asking for deployment in the South beginning in January 1964 after his wife would have graduated from QC. In his applications for the CORE position, Michael stated that he had chosen service to the poor and the disenfranchised as his life's work: "I am now so thoroughly identified with the civil rights struggle, that I have an emotional need to offer my services in the South,"[243] he stated. He went on to add that his profession of social work has been oblivious to the most cantankerous of the social diseases afflicting America, which is discrimination. "As a social worker, I have dedicated my life to social ills; however, my profession, except in isolated instances, as yet has not become directly involved in the most devastating social disease at the present time—discrimination."[244] Speaking bluntly and forcefully on this point, he stated, "I also feel that [Blacks] in the South have an even more bitter fight ahead of (them) than in the North, and I wish to be a part of that fight. In essence, I would feel guilty and almost hypocritical if I do not give full time for an extended period."[245] Though Michael had planned to do some part of his work in New York City, he felt it important to "have a first-hand understanding of how people in other sections of the country specifically are affected by prejudice and how discrimination is being dealt with... Therefore, I see working for CORE in the South as an educational experience that can be obtained in very few other ways."[246]

Sharing similar beliefs as her husband, and wanting to work near him, Rita wrote in her application to be employed by CORE, "My hope is to someday pass on to the children we may have a world containing more respect for the dignity and worth of all men than that world which was willed to us."[247] Rita's desire, as we can see, was to someday pass on to their children a better world than that which was handed over to them.[248] Rita was highly recommended to CORE by her friends for her "character, commitment, discipline, and understanding."[249] She was indeed quite excited about her new role because it afforded her an opportunity where she would use her skills to do good. Before they left for Mississippi, Rita wrote:

> Since I have become active in CORE here in New York, I have become increasingly aware of the problems which exist in the Southern states. I have a strong desire to contribute in some small way, by the utilization of those skills which I possess, to the redress of the many grievances occurring daily. I wish to become an active participant rather than a passive onlooker. Realizing that northern newspaper and radio accounts are often

distorted...I wish to acquire firsthand knowledge of existing conditions in the South.[250]

The couple left New York City for Mississippi on January 15, 1964, and they arrived in Meridian on January 21, 1964. Michael, working with James Chaney and other volunteers, immediately began to fix up the Community Center while Rita wrote letters to friends and family requesting funds, books, and office supplies. She also painted, decorated, and provided the rooms at the Community Center with drapes. In fact, Rita and Michael were the first White civil rights workers to be permanently stationed outside Jackson, the state capital.[251]

At the end of February, the Community Center at Meridian, which Rita described in her original contact letter as "five cold, empty, dirty and decaying rooms,"[252] was ready for use by Black youths and shortly thereafter, Rita was able to show off about ten thousand books in the library, mostly donated by New York publishers at her request. Not surprisingly, Rita was able to report exceptionally good news about the Community Center shortly thereafter: "We only saw the rooms as we hoped to make them: colorful, filled with books and the sounds of music and happy people working to become better and more useful citizens of Mississippi and the United States."[253] Rita anticipated teaching a sewing class as soon as she received the donation of fabric and a sewing machine promised by the International Ladies' Garments Workers' Union.[254] By mid-March, the sewing program was up and running and Rita wrote in her weekly report to the CORE head office on March 23, 1964, "I believe that we have found one of the programs which we were searching for, an entrance into the [Black] community."[255]

On March 28, 1964, Michael also gave his report about the remarkable progress of the Community Center in which he stated that, "classes to help people prepare for civil service jobs and clerical jobs have started and take place two nights a week. People are shown what kind of tests they will have to take and any difficulty they have is gone over on a more intensive basis...."[256] He was happy to report that the center served as a place where people could come for a variety of purposes: reading, talking, or playing games. The center was open seven days a week, and they tried to keep it open until the late evening.[257] With time Blacks began to trust Michael and Rita:

At first there was some suspicion of us as whites, but we believe that most of this has passed. Before we came there had been other workers in and out of Meridian, and the people are anxious to know that we intend to stay. They feel important to have workers assigned to their city. We believe that [Blacks] will accept more white workers in the summer program, though the white community is already jumpy—but this is to be expected and does not bother us.[258]

Because of their activism, Michael and Rita became the Klansmen's sworn enemies in Mississippi, and a plot was hatched to kill Michael.[259] During a meeting in May 1964, Sam Bowers, the Imperial Wizard of the White Knights of the Ku Klux Klan of Mississippi, remarked that Michael Schwerner was a "thorn in the side of everyone living, especially white people, and he should be taken care of."[260] Threats became more consistent after Michael and Rita had integrated a White church on the first Sunday in March.[261] They were cursed at and insulted on the street. Michael was called "'Jew-boy,' or 'nigger-lover' or 'race mixer' or nigger-loving Jew Communist."[262] He was arrested a couple of times and taken for questioning by the police. Rita received cards with the inscription, "With Deepest Sympathy." Telephone calls were made to Michael reporting that his wife was dead or would soon be dead and vice versa.[263] Various members of the White community had warned Michael many times to stop his activism or face the consequences. Some of the ugly encounters for Michael and Rita in Meridian included harassment, intimidation, and obscene phone calls that were so persistent and menacing that they had to take their phone off the hook at times. Indeed, Michael himself once said, "As promising as things look, one must keep in mind that Neshoba is a very 'tough' county, indicated by the fact that no [Black] has been registered since 1955."[264]

As prophetic as Michael's words sound today, on June 21, 1964, Michael Schwerner, Andrew Goodman, and James Chaney were kidnapped and murdered on their way to investigate the burning of the Mount Zion Methodist Church, in Neshoba County, Mississippi. Their bodies were found buried deep under an earthen dam located some six miles Southwest of Philadelphia, Mississippi on August 4, 1964. Earlier in the summer, Michael Schwerner had obtained permission from the Black parishioners to use the Mount Zion Church building for a Freedom School by telling them, "We can help you help yourselves...Meet us here, and we'll train you so you can qualify to vote."[265] Indeed, Michael told the same parishioners to take the very first steps toward racial equality by registering to vote.[266]

* * *

After Michael's death, Rita was not only an activist but a social justice crusader in her own right and devoted most of her life's work to activist causes. What follows is a story of courage, perseverance, and care for others. First, on Monday, June 22, 1964, Rita announced in Oxford, Ohio the disappearance in Philadelphia, Mississippi, of her husband Michael, James Chaney, and Andrew Goodman, and asked the volunteers to call or wire their congress members to ask for federal investigation and to request federal protection for civil rights workers. As one volunteer noted, "Rita asked us to form in groups by home areas and wire our congressmen that the federal government, though begged to investigate, had refused to act, and that if the government did not act, none of us was safe."[267] Rita was remarkable for her uncommon courage as she told the second group of volunteers at Oxford that the disappearance of the three Civil Rights workers only made it more important that the project must go on. And barely three days after her husband was reported missing, Rita had the courage to travel with Bob Zellner to Mississippi where she encountered Governor Paul B. Johnson of Mississippi in the company of a visiting Alabama governor, George Wallace on June 25, 1964. Unbeknownst to Johnson that Rita was at the press conference he gave in the company of George Wallace, where Johnson made a joke about the missing persons. Johnson's response provoked Rita's moral indignation in the crowd and she retorted, "We feel it's reprehensible for you to joke about this situation."[268]

Next, Rita and Bob Zellner met with Allen Dulles, the former CIA director who was sent by President Lyndon Johnson to go to Mississippi to investigate the disappearance. Rita used every opportunity she had to tell the government officials that they were not doing enough to investigate the disappearance. In an open and matter-of-fact way, she told Mr. Dulles that no serious search was going on in Neshoba County. Further, Rita and Bob Zellner boldly and aggressively confronted Lawrence Rainey, the Neshoba County sheriff about the disappearance of Michael, Andrew, and James. This was a great act of courage indeed because Rita and Bob Zellner were in a very hostile territory and were pursued by hostile Klansmen. Rainey, in his infinite wisdom, asked Rita and Bob to leave Neshoba County for their safety but Rita responded, "I'm not leaving until I see Mickey's car, and I don't care how many pickup trucks show up to intimidate me."[269] Upon further prodding, Rita told Rainey, "I'm not leaving here until I learn what happened to my husband," and exclaimed, "I'm going to keep drawing attention here until I find out, and if you don't like it you'll just have to have me killed too."[270] This was no small feat and was quite an act of courage. At this juncture, out of necessity rather than virtue, Rainey knew it was time to take Rita and Bob to the garage where her husband's burned-out car was stored. On June 29, 1964, during a meeting with US Deputy Attorney General Nicholas Katzenbach, Rita boldly proclaimed that no serious efforts were being made to unearth the disappearance of her husband and the other missing activists, "It's only a P.R. job, and not a very good one at that," she told Katzenbach, and Katzenbach responded, "What makes you qualified to say whether or not an investigation is under way?" Rita told Katzenbach in a noticeably clear language, because "I haven't been bought off like you by southern politicians...."[271] Earlier on, Rita had told an FBI officer who refused to wake up President Johnson to take her call that she was going to hold him personally responsible for the consequences of her husband's disappearance and the disappearance of the others. When Rita and Bob Zellner finally met with President Lyndon Johnson on June 29, 1964, and as LBJ was trying to exchange pleasantries, Rita told him, "I'm sorry, Mr. President, this is not a social call. We've come to talk about three missing people in Mississippi. We've come to talk about a search that we don't think is being done seriously."[272] And the president responded, "I'm sorry you feel that way, Miss."[273] Apprehensive that the federal government was not doing enough, Rita told the president that the two hundred naval cadets assigned for the search were barely a scratch on the surface; and that the President needed to send at least five thousand men to conduct a thorough search. The president expressed his deep sympathy and said the federal government was doing everything in its power, but he could not assure her of sending thousands of men to do the search as she requested. When the president left, Pierre Salinger, the president's press secretary, told Rita, "One does not talk to the president of the United States that way," and Rita responded, "We do."[274] At a press conference following the meeting with the president, Rita remarked, "The statements seemed somewhat contradictory to me.... When the federal authorities pull out of Meridian, Mississippi, I tremble at what is going to happen to the [Blacks] in the area."[275] Rita appealed to all men and women of goodwill to go to Meridian to search for the missing volunteers since the federal government had failed in its obligation to do so. Unfortunately, the bodies of the three civil rights workers were uncovered under an earthen dam six miles southwest of Philadelphia, Mississippi on August 4, 1964. As the disappearance of Michael, Andrew, and James became national news, and reporters were milling around her for answers about her husband's disappearance, Rita expressed her concern about White attitudes toward Black civil rights causes:

> It's tragic as far as I am concerned that White Northerners have to be caught up in the machinery of injustice and indifference in the South before the American people register concern. I personally suspect that if Mr. Chaney [...] had been alone at the time of his disappearance, that this case, like so many others that have come before it, it would have gone completely unnoticed.[276]

Nowhere was Rita's statement truer than in what Bob Moses, the director of SNCC's Mississippi Summer Project told the volunteers during the second week of the orientation. "When you come South," he told them, "you bring with you the concern of the country—because the people of the country don't identify with [Blacks]."[277] He continued by saying, "The guerrilla war in Mississippi is not much different from that in Vietnam. But when we tried to see President Johnson, his secretary said that Vietnam was popping up all over his calendar, and he hadn't time to talk to us."[278] Moses went on to add that because Whites were involved in the Summer Project, "a crack team of FBI men was going down to Mississippi to investigate,"[279] and lamented, "We have been asking for them for three years. Now the federal government is concerned; there will be more protection for us, and hopefully for the [Blacks] who live there."[280] Indeed, Rita's words were as true as they were prophetic because during the search for Goodman, Chaney, and Schwerner, the remains of eight Black Mississippians were unearthed, including Charles Eddie Moore, Henry Hezekiah Dee, and fourteen-year-old Herbert Orsby who was rumored to have been wearing a CORE t-shirt. These killings attracted no national attention, and those who killed them were never prosecuted.[281] Michael Wenger wrote in his book, *My Black Family, My White Privilege: A White Man's Journey Through the Nation's Racial Minefield* that, the lynching of thousands of Black men and women, the bombing of four girls in a Birmingham church, and the murder of Emmett Till including the killing of Medgar Evers, the Mississippi NAACP Field Secretary, and many other Black people in the South "had yielded little more than a tepid peep from a complacent nation." But the killing of "two White men had evoked a collective national scream."[282]

On December 4, 1964, the FBI arrested twenty-one White men and charged eighteen of them for conspiracy to violate the civil rights of the three volunteers. In the trial, seven of the conspirators were convicted including the Deputy Sheriff, Cecil Price, but Edgar Ray Killen (the mastermind) was only convicted forty-one years later for orchestrating the crime.[283] Could we now say that Rita Schwerner and others who were in the fight for justice won a little glimmer of victory for humanity? A glimmer of victory? The answer to this question, I think, should be left to the judgment of history and to future historians. But suffice it to say that among those arrested were Sheriff Lawrence Rainey and his deputy, Cecil Price. However, the twenty-one White men arrested were never tried for murder because it was believed that a Mississippi jury would never convict them. Of the number arrested, only seven of them, including Deputy Sheriff Cecil Price, were convicted for other offenses.[284] But Sheriff Lawrence Rainey was not one of those convicted.

In the case of Edgar Ray Killen, the Ku Klux Klan organizer and part-time minister of a small Baptist Evangelical Church who instigated the murders of Michael Schwerner, Andrew Goodman, and James Chaney, the jury was unable to reach a verdict in his first trial in 1967 because one of the jurors said she could never convict a preacher, a man of God. Killen was found guilty on three counts of manslaughter by a Mississippi state court in 2005. The verdict was confirmed by the Mississippi State Supreme Court in 2007. He was sentenced to sixty years in prison. He died in prison in 2018.

* * *

At the "National Conference: Crimes of the Civil Rights Era,"[285] held on April 28, 2007, at Northeastern University in Boston, Rita gave an eyewitness, firsthand account of the courage and sacrifices of those who participated in the struggle for social justice during Freedom Summer 1964 against a background of enormous barbarity perpetrated against the volunteers and the Black community. More than forty years after the murder of her late husband and others, she shared her thoughts about how she went about her business, often thinking that these evildoers would perhaps never see justice. Although she was relieved about the opening of the Civil Rights case in an American court many years later, she still wondered if this case would provide any measure of restorative justice, because "the crimes had been permitted to go unacknowledged for so long, that most of the killers were dead, and that of the eight direct participants still alive, only one was indicted and brought to trial."[286] And even then, the indictment of Edgar Ray Killen was brought on the narrowest of the issues.[287] Even more perplexing, she wondered, "was Edgar Ray Killen responsible for the deaths of three men?"[288] She worried like most of us that even though "a criminal trial is in at least one sense, an affirmation of the values that make civil society possible," in the case of some of the killers of the Civil Rights workers where there was no trial or punishment for forty-one years, it meant that these crimes went unacknowledged.[289] Rita argued that "knowledge of the crime and the failure of the community to impose consequences on the actors was a denial of the seriousness of the event, a diminishment of civil society."[290] She wondered if the trial of one individual would matter if the state did not acknowledge its own responsibility and culpability in the murders? She reasoned aloud that it was only through the acknowledgment of such culpability by the state that we can move forward because such an admission would allow society to build on "those experiences to construct for the first time, a commonality of purpose to confront the legacy of slavery, a confrontation and acknowledgment which this country has yet to experience."[291]

However, to determine if restorative justice had been achieved for the crimes that were committed in Neshoba County, Rita argued that one had to be present in the courtroom to assess individual and community reactions during the trial of Edgar Ray Killen. For instance, in her personal journey in search of restorative justice, she met an African American woman in the courthouse who told her that "sitting through the trial and hearing the verdict was her opportunity to bear witness in the face of her community's fear."[292] She also met a man who had been a seventeen-year-old student and a civil rights activist during Freedom Summer who told her, "Rita, today we got a little justice."[293] There was also the case of a White observer, Florence Mars who sat through the entire trial in spite of her ill health because she suffered serious harassment in her efforts to cooperate with investigators over the disappearance of the three civil rights workers. Florence Mars had written a tell-all book in 1977 titled *Witness in Philadelphia*. The book spoke of her predicament in her efforts to cooperate with the authorities in the investigation and noted the "failure of local people to acknowledge responsibility for the crimes which occurred in their midst."[294] Rita told the public that she saw in the courtroom Stanley Dearman, the former editor and publisher of the *Neshoba Democrat* who wrote about the importance of the trial long before it was popular to do so. Also, in the courtroom was a Mississippi Highway patrolman who told Rita about the bad men and the bad things he witnessed and heard while serving in the police department in the county, although many of those bad people had eventually left or retired. As Rita saw it, for many in the courthouse, the trial was like a confession of truth. But there were also some unrepentant people who were in total denial that anything bad at all had or could have happened in Neshoba County. While Rita commended the efforts of the state attorney general and the Neshoba County prosecutor for their courage in prosecuting the case at great political risks to themselves, she condemned other state government functionaries and actors like Governor Haley Barbour for their nonchalance to the cause of social justice in Mississippi. In fact, many in government circles in Mississippi and throughout the South fell into this category. In Rita's view, justice in Mississippi had been served only partially by the single trial of Edgar Ray Killen because the participation of the government itself in actions that created, encouraged, and perpetuated the violence had not been discussed. She asked, "So, are the trials of old men, generations after the crimes, relevant to restorative justice?"[295] "Possibly," she answered. However, "without an honest accounting for our history, we cannot move forward,"[296] Rita maintained. The subtext in this argument is the complicity of the state government in spying and perpetuating crimes against American citizens. She explained that no sooner had she and her husband arrived in Meridian, than "a state legislator requested that the Sovereignty Commission investigate us."[297] It is important to point out that as early as 1956, the state of Mississippi had established the Sovereignty Commission for the purpose of maintaining racial segregation and White supremacy and to "spy on its citizens and keep a handle on anyone, Black or White, who challenged Jim Crow segregation."[298] W. Ralph Eubanks argued that the Sovereignty Commission was "empowered to do and perform any and all acts and things deemed necessary and proper to protect the sovereignty of the state of Mississippi, and her sister states, from encroachment thereon by the Federal Government."[299] Accordingly, the Sovereignty Commission, "recruited informers, harassed Civil Rights workers, and accumulated files about individuals that violated their privacy and could be used to destroy them, and perhaps even kill them."[300] Rita believes strongly in the complicity of the government in the murder of the three civil rights workers because a few days before the murders of the Civil Rights activists in Neshoba County, the Sovereignty Commission passed on information about the church that would host the training for the voter registration. Indeed, it was a Sovereignty Commission informant who "passed on intelligence revealing when Mickey and James planned to visit the burned-out church to check on the injured members."[301] And by all known accounts, it was state agents, the sheriff's deputy, the Philadelphia and Meridian police, and the state highway patrol officers who conspired and facilitated the arrest and the murders of Michael Schwerner, Andrew Goodman, and James Chaney. Rita was emphatic in making the statement that "The Sovereignty Commission, an official arm of the State, was directly involved in providing the intelligence that led to James, Mickey, and Andy's murders."[302] She was blunt and clear about the fact that we can only move forward with an honest accounting for our history: government complicity and our common heritage derived from slavery, racism, and poverty. She concluded that, "To the extent that this opportunity for truth-telling has been lost, the trials have been inadequate in establishing restorative justice."[303]

After the Freedom Summer 1964 Project, Rita stayed in Washington, DC, to work on the MFDP challenge through June 1965. She graduated from Rutgers Law School in 1968 and now lives in Seattle, WA. She is a principal in the legal firm of Skellenger Bender, P. S. in Seattle, Washington State. She has practiced law in Seattle, WA since 1975 and has published, written, and lectured extensively on civil rights and restorative justice issues throughout the United States. Rita served as the Seattle Regional Director of the Legal Services Corporation from 1977 to 1982. She is a fellow of the American Academy of Adoption Attorneys and a fellow of the American Academy of Assisted Reproductive Technology Attorneys. She has taught law at various universities over the years.

One of the most unique discoveries in the Queens College archives was a short note from Rita inviting Mark and Betty (Bollinger) Levy to occupy her apartment when the Levys first arrived in Meridian because her husband, Michael, was presumed dead. Rita made this kind gesture even though she was going to remain in Meridian herself. This shows a moment of Rita's profound caring for others and the project even while she was grieving. This act of kindness is heartwarming and serves as an essential testament to the caring person Rita is. Also, this document is reminiscent of the unique nature of QC archival resources and serves as a discovered treasure.

* * *

Finally, an important point to note is that the *Price of freedom* and *activism* in Mississippi during Freedom Summer 1964 was enormous. Apart from the amount of money that the Freedom Summer activists were required to bring with them to Mississippi, the many restrictions imposed on them, and the constant harassment they encountered, by the end of the ten weeks, four people had been murdered (including Andrew, Michael, and James), about 80 civil rights volunteers were severely beaten, over 1000 people were arrested, and 67 churches, homes and businesses were burned or bombed including 37 Black Churches during that summer.[304] However, I wish to point out that participation in Freedom Summer is often attributed to students mostly from "the elite universities," or to "Northerners from the best schools" in the United States: Harvard, Columbia, Stanford, Princeton, Yale, Antioch, Chicago, Kent State, Wisconsin, Oberlin, Reed, Swarthmore, Ohio State, UC, Berkeley, the University of Virginia, etc.[305] In this chapter, I tell the story of eight dedicated and brave Queens College students who participated in righting the wrongs of the past. The chapter provides QC students' narratives and analytical overview of their response to SNCC and COFO's request for Civil Rights activism and the quest for racial equality in Mississippi. This is the story of eight QC activists who risked their lives in search of equality for others. It is also the story of students who risked their futures to make a difference. As Frances Moore Lappe, a writer and activist once said, these [QC]volunteers refused to be "bystanders or victims of history."[306] It is clear from the activities of these integral players that the fervor for social activism and change was just as intense on the QC campus, as it was for students who worked and volunteered in the campuses of the elite universities in the United States. Indeed, many of the QC volunteers I interviewed told me that Freedom Summer constituted a serious effort at rectifying a great wrong for which they are grateful to have participated, working on the principles of democracy, freedom, and social justice, for which, I think, their stories should be told.

Mark Levy and Betty (Bollinger) Levy, Co-Directors of the Meridian Freedom School with their students outside during Freedom Summer (Photograph, Courtesy of Mark Levy)

Mark Levy, Betty (Bollinger) Levy, and Ronnie de Sousa during Freedom Summer orientation in Oxford, Ohio, 1964 (Photograph, Courtesy of Mark Levy)

Notes

1. Steven M. Buechler, *Social Movements in Advanced Capitalism: The Political Economy and Cultural Construction of Social Activism*. New York: Oxford University Press, 2000, p. 17.
2. Jerusha O. Conner, *The New Student Activists: The Rise of Neoactivism on College Campuses*. Baltimore, MD: Johns Hopkins University Press, 2020, p. 44.
3. Belinda Robnett, *How Long? How Long? African-American Women in the Struggle for Civil Rights*. New York: Oxford University Press, 1999, p. 7.
4. See the wide range of explanations given even by these three authors: Doug McAdam, *Freedom Summer*. New York, NY: Oxford University Press, 1988; Doug McAdam, "Gender as a Mediator of the Activist Experience: The Case of Freedom Summer." *American Journal of Sociology*, Vol. 97, No. 5, 1992; Doug McAdam, "Recruitment to High-Risk Activism: The Case of Freedom Summer." *American Journal of Sociology*, Vol. 92, No. 1, 1986; Doug McAdam and Ronnelle Paulsen, "Specifying the Relationship Between Social Ties and Activism." *American Journal of Sociology*, Vol. 99, No. 3, 1993; Belinda Robnett, "African-American Women in the Civil Rights Movement, 1954–1965: Gender, Leadership, and Micromobilization." *American Journal of Sociology*, Vol. 101, No. 6, 1996. Belinda Robnett, *How Long? How Long?*
5. It is important to point out that African American struggle for social justice did not begin with Freedom Summer. African Americans had fought for liberation from slavery, the Ku Klux Klan, lynching, Klan violence, the White Citizens' Council, the Mississippi Sovereignty Commission, and other racist groups. They picketed, conducted boycotts, marched, and formed associations. Fathers, mothers, sons, and daughters were gunned down, tear gassed, whipped, water hosed by city police, state police, and the National Guard. Many fought and died in trying to exercise their rights.
6. Chude Allen, "My Parents Said Yes!" In Jacqueline Johnson, ed. *Finding Freedom: Memorializing the Voices of Freedom Summer*. Oxford, OH: Miami University Press, 2013, p. 27.

7. Seth Cagin and Philip Dray, *We Are Not Afraid: The Story of Goodman, Schwerner, and Chaney and the Civil Rights Campaign for Mississippi*. New York: Nation Books, 2006, pp. 234–235.
8. Barbara (Jones) Omolade's collection at Queens College archives has Queens College student activist sign-in sheets with Andrew Goodman as the 7th signatory. See Box 1, folder 8, Barbara (Jones) Omolade Collection.
9. See Andrew Goodman, *Wikipedia, the free encyclopedia*, p. 1. http://en.wikipedia.org/wiki/walden_School_(New_York_City) (Accessed 8/19/2013).
10. Bruce Watson, *Freedom Summer: The Savage Season of 1964 That Made Mississippi Burn and Made America a Democracy*. New York: Penguin Books, 2010, p. 83.
11. Cagin and Dray, *We Are Not Afraid*, pp. 47–48 and 234.
12. Cited in Bruce Watson. *Freedom Summer: The Savage Season of 1964 That Made Mississippi Burn and Made America a Democracy*. New York: Penguin Books, 2010, p. 83.
13. Ibid.
14. Leo Hershkowitz, "Andrew Goodman on Freedom's Walk." In Stephen Stepanchev, ed. *The People's College on the Hill: Fifty Years at Queens College, 1937–1987*, Queens College of the City University of New York: Shirley Strum Kenny, President, p. 68.
15. Watson, *Freedom Summer*, p. 83.
16. Hershkowitz, "Andrew Goodman on Freedom's Walk," p. 68.
17. Cagin and Dray, *We Are Not Afraid*, p. 235.
18. Jane Strippel, "Friends of the Mississippi Summer Project." In Jacqueline Johnson, ed. *Finding Freedom: Memorializing the Voices of Freedom Summer*. Oxford, OH: Miami University Press, 2013, p. 20.
19. Cited in Watson. *Freedom Summer*, p. 84.
20. Ibid.
21. John Dittmer, *Local People: The Struggle for Civil Rights in Mississippi*. Urbana, IL: University of Illinois Press, 1994, p. 247.
22. Ibid., p. 283.
23. Manning Marable, "Introduction, Searching for Restorative Justice: The Trial of Edgar Ray Killen." *Souls*, Vol. 10, No. 2, 2008, p. 155.
24. Hershkowitz, "Andrew Goodman on Freedom's Walk," p. 68.
25. Ibid.

26. Ibid.
27. Ibid.
28. "A Classmate Tells About Andy Goodman." Box 1, folder 15, Michael Wenger Collection, Department of Special Collections and Archives, Queens College, City University of New York.
29. Cited in Cagin and Dray, *We Are Not Afraid*, p. 241.
30. "Families of Rights Workers Voice Grief and Hope." Box 1, folder 2, Robert Masters Collection, Department of Special Collections and Archives, Queens College, City University of New York.
31. Ibid.
32. Ibid.
33. Mark Levy, "About Freedom Summer '64 and Q.C." (n.d).
34. "A Classmate Talks About Andy Goodman." Box 2 folder 15, Michael Wenger Collection, Department of Special Collections and Archives, Queens College, City University of New York.
35. Shomial Ahmad, "Queens College and Civil Rights: Alumni Reflect on Activism 50 Years Ago." *PSC CUNY*, May 2014 (Clarion/May/2014).
36. "No More Dying Over Me." Box 1, folder 5, Arthur Gatti Collection, Department of Special Collections and Archives, Queens College, City University of New York.
37. Ibid.
38. Ibid.
39. Debra L. Schultz, "Why I Tracked Them Down: Our Unsung Civil Rights Movement Heroines." *Lilith Magazine*, Fall, 1999, p. 11.
40. Some of the documents they left behind include "QC 50s–70s activist student narrative."
41. Mark Levy, "A Monumental Dissent." In Jacqueline Johnson, ed. *Finding Freedom: Memorializing the Voices of Freedom Summer*. Oxford, OH: Miami University Press, 2013, p. 59. Betty was also a volunteer for the Jamaica Student Help Project. See Box 1 folder 7, Michal Wenger Collection, Department of Special Collections and Archives, Queens College, City University of New York.
42. These were sons and daughters of intellectuals or labor unionists whose parents or relatives had joined revolutionary and activist movements and communicated to their children and wards radical political values that made activism an attractive option. See also

Jon N. Hale, *The Freedom Schools: Student Activists in the Mississippi Civil Rights Movement*. New York: Columbia University Press, 2018, p. 89.
43. Jon N. Hale, *The Freedom Schools: Student Activists in the Mississippi Civil Rights Movement*. New York, NY: Columbia University Press, 2018, p. 89.
44. Ibid.
45. Mark Levy, "About Freedom Summer '64 and Q.C." p. 2.
46. Levy, "A Monumental Dissent," p. 59.
47. Levy, "About Freedom Summer," p. 2.
48. Ibid.
49. "Next Week We Are Going." Box 1 folder 6, Mark Levy Collection, Department of Special Collections and Archives, Queens College, City University of New York. Betty Bollinger Levy's Unpublished letter to Friends and Supporters.
50. Ibid.
51. George W. Chilcoat and Jerry A. Ligon, "Developing Democratic Citizens: The Mississippi Freedom Schools as a Model for Social Studies Instruction." *Theory and Research in Social Education*, Vol. 22, No. 2, 1994, pp. 128–175. Daniel Perlstein, "Teaching Freedom: SNCC and the Creation of the Mississippi Freedom Schools." *History of Education Quarterly*, Vol. 30, No. 3, 1990, pp. 297–324. Jon N. Hale, *The Freedom Schools*. Mark Levy, "A Monumental Dissent."
52. Next Week We are Going. Box 1 folder 6, Mark Levy Collection.
53. Ibid.
54. Ibid.
55. "Long Island Press Article." Box 10, folder 5, Mark Levy Collection, Department of Special Collections and Archives, Queens College, City University of New York. Sy Safransky, "L I Couple Mississippi-Bound to the Battlefields of Racial Bias." *Long Island Press*, June 28, 1964.
56. Ibid.
57. Ibid.
58. Ibid.
59. Ibid.
60. Ibid.
61. Ibid.

62. "Dear Betty." Box 1, folder 1004, Mark Levy Collection, Department of Special Collections and Archives, Queens College, City University of New York.
63. "President Lyndon B. Johnson." Box 1, folder 2001, Mark Levy Collection, Department of Special Collections and Archives, Queens College, City University of New York (Reproduced with permission).
64. "New York World Telegram and Sun." Box 5, folder 10, Mark Levy Collection, Department of Special Collections and Archives, Queens College, City University of New York. Ted Knap, "Rights Worker Talks: I Felt I Was Needed." *New York World Telegram and Sun*, June 30, 1964. See Mark Levy Collection, Selected Letters and Articles, p. 7.
65. Ibid.
66. "Long Island Press Article." Box 11, folder 1, Mark Levy Collection, Department of Special Collection and Archives, Queens College, City University of New York, p. 10. *A Letter from Mississippi: Ugly Face of Racism Seen Each Day, LIers Report*. Letter sent to press by Mark and Betty Levy, *Long Island Press*, July 19, 1964, p. 9.
67. Ibid.
68. "Our Last Summer Newsletter." Box 1, folder 2, Mark Levy Collection, Department of Special Collections and Archives, Queens College, City University of New York. *Our Last Summer Newsletter* by Mark and Betty Levy to Many Friends and Project Supporters at the end of the Summer, September 1, 1964, p. 13.
69. Ibid.
70. Ibid.
71. Ibid.
72. Mark Levy's correspondence with the author 12/11/2019.
73. "Long Island Press Article." Box 11, folder 2, Mark Levy Collection, Department of Special Collections and Archives, Queens College, City University of New York. Leonard Victor, "Fear Stalks LI Couple in Mississippi." *Long Island Press*, July 30, 1964, p. 10.
74. "Long Island Press Article." Box 11, folder 2, Mark Levy Collection, Department of Special Collections and Archives, Queens College, City University of New York. pp. 10–11.

75. David Levine, "Mississippi Freedom Schools." Unpublished Manuscript, 2012, p. 2.
76. "Long Island Press Article." Box 11, folder 1, Mark Levy Collection, Department of Special Collections and Archives, Queens College, City University of New York. *A Letter from Mississippi: Ugly Face of Racism Seen Each Day, LIers Report*. Letter sent to the press by Mark and Betty Levy, *Long Island Press*, July 19, 1964, p. 9.
77. Ibid.
78. Ibid.
79. "Dear Betty." Box 1 folder 1004, Mark Levy Collection, Department of Special Collections and Archives, Queens College, City University of New York.
80. Betty Dear." Box 1 folder 1003, Mark Levy Collection, Department of Special Collections and Archives, Queens College, City University of New York.
81. "Dear Betty." Box 1 folder 1004, Mark Levy Collection, Department of Special Collections and Archives, Queens College, City University of New York.
82. These were the three Civil Rights workers killed by the KKK. See correspondence between the author and Mark Levy, November 26, 2019.
83. Sandra E. Adickes, *The Legacy of a Freedom School*. New York, NY: Palgrave Macmillan, 2005, p. 86.
84. Aug. 8, Freedom Schools Convention: Zinn Education Project. https://www.zinnedproject.org/news/tdih/freedom-schools/ (Accessed 10/17/2019).
85. Adickes, *The Legacy of a Freedom School*, p. 86.
86. Jerusha O. Conner, *The New Student Activists: The Rise of Neoactivism on College Campuses*. Baltimore, MD: Johns Hopkins University Press, 2020, p. 37.
87. Adickes, *The Legacy*, pp. 86–87. The students also requested: [H]ealth care facilities with integrated staffs and qualified doctors who addressed patients "properly," chest X-rays, annual checkups, and the abolition of sterilization used as punishment for any offense. They demanded a public works program and equal distribution of federal aid under Title VI of the Civil Rights Act, along with the enforcement of the Fair Employment provision of that same section. They demanded enforcement of Section Two of

the Fourteenth Amendment in order to eliminate discriminatory voter registration practices and the poll tax. They demanded the appointment of "qualified Negroes" to the police force and police protection from hate groups such as the Klan.

88. Adickes, *The Legacy of Freedom Schools*, p. 87.
89. Ibid.
90. "To all Our Friends: Our Last Summer Newsletter." Box 1, Folder 2, Mark Levy Collection, Department of Special Collections and Archives, Queens College, City University of New York. Mark and Betty Levy, "To all Our Friends: Our Last Summer Newsletter," written by Mark and Betty Levy, Unpublished Letter, September 1, 1964.
91. Ibid.
92. Ibid.
93. Ibid.
94. Ibid.
95. "Long Island Press Article." Box 11, folder 1, Mark Levy Collection, Department of Special Collections and Archives, Queens College, City University of New York. *A Letter from Mississippi: Ugly Face of Racism Seen Each Day, LIers Report*. Letter sent to the press by Mark and Betty Levy, *Long Island Press*, July 19, 1964, p. 8.
96. Ibid.
97. Ibid.
98. "Long Island Press Article." Box 11, folder 1, Mark Levy Collection, Department of Special Collections and Archives, Queens College, City University of New York. *A Letter from Mississippi: Ugly Face of Racism Seen Each Day, LIers Report* by Mark and Betty Levy, *Long Island Press*, July 19, 1964, p. 9.
99. "Long Island Press Article." Box 11 folder 2, Mark Levy Collection, Department of Special Collections and Archives, Queens College, City University of New York. *Fear Stalks LI Couple in Mississippi* by Leonard Victor, *Long Island Press*, July 30, 1964, p. 10.
100. Ibid.
101. Ibid.
102. Correspondence between Mr. Levy and the author 12/11/2019.
103. Levy, "A Monumental Dissent," p. 64.

104. Mark Levy, "Veterans of the Civil Rights Movement." webspinner@crmvet.org (Accessed 6/2/2019).
105. Mark Levy, "Teaching for Change." https://www.teachingforchange.org/mark-levy-speech-at-aft, p. 2 (Accessed 12/20/2018).
106. Levy, "Veterans of the Civil Rights Movement." webspinner@crmvet.org (Accessed 6/2/2019).
107. "Station Youth Talks About His Seven Weeks in Mississippi." Box 1, folder 2, Robert Masters Collection, Department of Special Collections and Archives, Queens College, City University of New York.
108. Ibid.
109. "Robert Masters' Mail to Mrs. Goldberg and His Parents, 1964." Box 1, folder 1, Robert Masters Collection, Department of Special Collections and Archives, Queens College, City University of New York.
110. "Station Youth Tells About His Seven Weeks in Mississippi." Box 1, folder 2, Robert Masters Collection, Department of Special Collections and Archives, Queens College, City University of New York.
111. Ibid.
112. Ibid.
113. Ibid.
114. Ibid.
115. Ibid.
116. Ibid.
117. "Ller Back from Miss., Sure of Gains." Box 1, folder 2, Robert Masters Collection, Department of Special Collections and Archives, Queens College, City University of New York.
118. "Dear Mrs Goldberg: Robert Masters' Mail to Mrs. Goldberg." Box 1, folder 1, Robert Masters Collection, Department of Special Collections and Archives, Queens College, City University of New York.
119. Ibid.
120. Ibid.
121. Ibid.
122. Ibid.
123. Ibid.
124. Ibid.

125. "Robert Masters' Mail to Mrs. Goldberg." Box 1, folder 2, Robert Masters Collection, Department of Special Collections and Archives, Queens College, City University of New York.
126. Ibid.
127. "Robert Masters' Mail to His Parents." Box 1, folder 1, Robert Masters Collection, Department of Special Collections and Archives, Queens College, City University of New York.
128. Ibid.
129. "Ller Back from Miss., Sure of Gains, Printed Material." Box 1, folder 2, Robert Masters Collection, Department of Special Collections and Archives, Queens College, City University of New York.
130. "Mississippi Jails 106 Court Pickets." Box 1, folder 2, Robert Masters Collection, Department of Special Collections and Archives, Queens College, City University of New York.
131. Ibid.
132. "Ller Back from Miss., Sure of Gains, Printed Material." Box 1, folder 2, Robert Masters Collection, Department of Special Collections and Archives, Queens College, City University of New York.
133. "College Mississippi Project Rebuilds Tougaloo Churches." Box 1, folder 2, Robert Masters Collection, Department of Special Collections and Archives, Queens College, City University of New York.
134. Mario Savio was the leader of the Free Speech Movement at the University of California, Berkeley. Before then he studied at Queens College from September 1961 to January 1963. At QC, he took part in numerous demonstrations including working as a picket captain during the student strike on campus on November 16, 1961. Mario also went to Albany along with other Queens students to protest the proposal to introduce fees into CUNY colleges. While at QC Savio participated in other demonstrations such as joining the picket outside the Woolworth's store in Manhattan, New York.
135. Robert Cohen, *Freedom's Orator: Mario Savio and the Radical Legacy of the 1960s*. New York: Oxford University Press, 2009, p. 22. See also, "Rebel Leader's Goal: To Make History." Box 2,

folder 1, Arthur Gatti Collection, Department of Special Collections and Archives, Queens College, City University of New York.
136. Ibid., p. 22.
137. Ibid., p. 37.
138. Ibid.
139. "Student Movements of the 1960s Project: The Reminiscences of Mario Savio." Interview conducted by Bret Eynon. Box 2, folder 7, Arthur Gatti Collection, Department of Special Collections and Archives, Queens College, City University of New York, p. 6.
140. Ibid.
141. Cohen, *Freedom's Orator*, p. 37.
142. Ibid.
143. See Cagin and Dray, *We Are Not Afraid*, p. 103.
144. Cited in Cohen, *Freedom's Orator*, p. 37.
145. Cohen, *Freedom's Orator*, p. 37.
146. Ibid.
147. "Cheers for Savio at Queens College." Box 2, folder 1, Arthur Gatti Collection, Department of Special Collections and Archives, Queens College, City University of New York.
148. "Student Movements of the 1960s Project." p. 21.
149. See Cohen, *Freedom's Orator*, p. 37.
150. Ibid., p. 50.
151. Ibid.
152. Ibid.
153. Ibid. Mario saw events in the South as America's greatest dilemma and a paradox, the government of a free people denying fundamental rights to some of her citizens. See also, Bret Eynon interview, p. 23.
154. Cited in Cohen, *Freedom's Orator*, p. 51. It is important to point out here that Mario went to Mexico from Queens College.
155. "Rebel Leader's Goal: To Make History." Box 2, folder 1, Arthur Gatti Collection, Department of Special Collections and Archives, Queens College, City University of New York.
156. See "Student Movements of the 1960s Project: The Reminiscences of Mario Savio." Box 2, folder 7, Arthur Gatti Collection, Department of Special Collections and Archives, Queens College, City University of New York, p. 30.
157. Ibid, p. 23.

158. Cohen, *Freedom's Orator*, p. 54. A similar incident is narrated about Jackson in, "Student Movements of the 1960s Project" p. 36.
159. "Student Movements of the 1960s Project," pp. 23–24.
160. Cohen, *Freedom's Orator*, p. 55.
161. Ibid p. 56.
162. Elizabeth Martinez ed., *Letters from Mississippi: Reports from Civil Rights Volunteers & Poetry of the 1964 Freedom Summer*. Brookline, MA: Zephyr Press, 2007, p. 78.
163. Cohen, *Freedom's Orator*, p. 56.
164. Ibid.
165. Ibid., p. 57. See also "Student Movements of the 1960s Project: The Reminiscences of Mario Savio." Box 2, folder 7, Arthur Gatti Collection, Department of Special Collections and Archives, Queens College, City University of New York, p. 42.
166. Cited in Cohen, *Freedom's Orator*, p. 57.
167. "Student Movements of the 1960s Project: The Reminiscences of Mario Savio." Interview by Bret Eynon. Box 2, folder 7, Arthur Gatti Collection, Department of Special Collections and Archives, Queens College, City University of New York, pp. 42 and 43. See also Cohen, *Freedom Orator*, pp. 57 and 58.
168. Ibid., p. 43.
169. Cited in Cohen, *Freedom's Orator*, p. 58.
170. Freedom Vote was a mock election conducted by COFO and SNCC officials in some parts of Mississippi to demonstrate to Americans that Blacks in Mississippi would vote if they were allowed to register free from intimidation and discrimination.
171. "Student Movements of the 1960s Project: The Reminiscences of Mario Savio." Box 2, folder 7, Arthur Gatti Collection, Department of Special Collections and Archives, Queens College, City University of New York, p. 30.
172. Ibid.
173. According to Robert Cohen, Savio taught an activist-tinged version of civics p. 62.
174. Cohen, *Freedom's Orator*, p. 62.
175. Ibid, p. 64.
176. Ibid.

177. "Student Movements of the 1960s Project: The Reminiscences of Mario Savio." Box 2, folder 7, Arthur Gatti Collection, Department of Special Collections and Archives, Queens College, City University of New York, p. 44.
178. Savio went from QC and Freedom Summer to lead the Free Speech Movement which is regarded as one of the most unforgettable examples of student activism because it led the way for a national movement.
179. "Cheers for Savio at Queens College." Box 2, folder 1, Arthur Gatti collection, Department of Special Collections and Archives, Queens College, City University of New York.
180. Ibid.
181. Ibid.
182. "Student Movements of the 1960s Project: The Reminiscences of Mario Savio." Box 2, folder 1, Arthur Gatti Collection, Department of Special Collections and Archives, Queens College, City University of New York, p. 49.
183. Ibid., p. 57.
184. "For Immediate Release." Box 1, folder 15, Arthur Gatti Collection, Department of Special Collections and Archives, Queens College, City University of New York.
185. Ibid.
186. Ibid.
187. "For Immediate Release." Box 1, folder 15, Arthur Gatti Collection, Department of Special Collections and Archives, Queens College, City University of New York.
188. Ibid.
189. Ibid.
190. "Student Movements of the 1960s Project: The Reminiscences of Mario Savio." Box 2, folder 7, Arthur Gatti Collection, Department of Special Collections and Archives, Queens College, City University of New York, p. 32.
191. It should be noted that Michael Harrington later became a professor at Queens College.
192. "For Release." Box 1, folder 15, Arthur Gatti Collection, Department of Special Collections and Archives, Queens College, City University of New York.
193. Ibid.

194. "Cheers for Savio at Queens College." Box 2, folder 1, Arthur Gatti Collection, Department of Special Collections and Archives, Queens College, City University of New York.
195. Ibid.
196. Ibid.
197. Ibid.
198. Ibid.
199. "Overflow Crowd Hears 'Rebel with a Cause.'" Box 2, folder 1, Arthur Gatti Collection, Department of Special Collections and Archives, Queens College, City University of New York.
200. Ibid.
201. Cohen, *Freedom's Orator*; Arthur Gatti, "Mario Savio's Religious Influences & Origins." Box 2, folder 11, Arthur Gatti Collection, Department of Special Collections and Archives, Queens College, City University of New York; Gil Fagiani, "Mario Savio (1942–1996): Resurrecting a Modern Radical." Box 2, folder 11, Arthur Gatti Collection, Department of Special Collections and Archives, Queens College, City University of New York 1997; Robert Cohen, "Introduction to Mario Savio Speech." *History, Theory, Culture*, Summer, 2005, pp. 71–74.
202. Cohen, *Freedom's Orator*, p. 37.
203. Arthur Gatti, "Mario Savio's Religious Influences & Origins." Box 2, folder 11, Arthur Gatti Collection, Department of Special Collections and Archives, Queens College, City University of New York 1997, p. 14.
204. Robert Cohen, "Introduction to Mario Savio Speech." *History, Theory, Culture*, Summer, 2005, p. 74. Box 2, folder 11, Arthur Gatti Collection, Department of Special Collections and Archives, Queens College, City University of New York 1997, p. 74.
205. Cohen, *Freedom's Orator*, p. 38.
206. Ibid.
207. Ibid.
208. Ibid., p. 278.
209. Ibid., p. 299.
210. Jesus Mena and Jose Rodriguez, "UC Berkeley to Honor Mario Savio, Free Speech Movement with Library Gift, Café." https://www.berkeley.edu/news/media/releases/98legacy/04_29_98a.html (Accessed 10/25/2019). See also, "The Cover." *Libraries & Culture*, Vol. 37, No. 3, 2002, pp. 269–271.

211. Cited in Cagin and Dray, *We Are Not Afraid*, p. 47.
212. Ibid.
213. Ibid., p. 48.
214. Ibid., p. 49.
215. Ibid., p. 104.
216. Ibid.
217. See ibid., p. 50.
218. Ibid., p. 235.
219. "No More Dying Over Me." Box 1, folder 5, Arthur Gatti Collection, Department of Special Collections and Archives, Queens College, City University of New York.
220. See Montgomery—Freedom School Workshop Correspondence 1964–1965 (Lucile Montgomery papers, 1963–1967; Historical Society Library Microforms Room, Micro 44, Reel 1, Segment 8a). https://content.wisconsinhistory.org/digital/collection/p15932coll2/id/32942/ (Accessed 7/10/2021).
221. I received this information through correspondence with Mark Levy.
222. Levy, "Additions to the Q.C. Roll Call Appendix 1" (n.d.).
223. ART at SUNY Oneonta/Faculty http://www.oneonta.edu/academics/art/faculty.html (Accessed 7/13/2012).
224. E-mail correspondence with Mr. Joseph Liesner, October 20, 2012.
225. Ibid.
226. Ibid.
227. Ibid.
228. Ibid.
229. Ibid.
230. Ibid.
231. Ibid.
232. Ibid.
233. Ibid.
234. Ibid.
235. Ibid.
236. Ibid.
237. Ibid.
238. Ibid.
239. See Elizabeth Martinez ed., *Letters from Mississippi*, p. 359.

240. "Joseph Liesner-Business Profile: Berkeley Community Media." Zoominfo.com https://www.zoominfo.com/p/Joseph-Liesner/53225549. (Accessed 9/20/2019).
241. Cagin and Dray, *We Are Not Afraid*, p. 257.
242. Ibid., p. 258.
243. Ibid., p. 259.
244. Ibid.
245. Ibid.
246. Ibid.
247. Cited in Debra L. Schultz, *Going South: Jewish Women in the Civil Rights Movement*. New York, NY: New York University Press, 2001, p. 63. See also Cagin and Dray, *We Are Not Afraid*, p. 259.
248. Cagin and Dray, *We Are Not Afraid*, p. 259.
249. Ibid., pp. 259–260.
250. Cited in Schultz, *Going South*, p. 63.
251. Cagin and Dray, *We Are Not Afraid*, p. 12.
252. Cited in Schultz, *Going South*, p. 63.
253. Ibid.
254. Cagin and Dray, *We Are Not Afraid*, p. 262.
255. Ibid., p. 269.
256. Ibid.
257. Ibid.
258. Ibid., pp. 269–270.
259. Ibid., pp. 266 and 272.
260. Ibid., p. 266.
261. Ibid., p. 267.
262. Ibid., p. 268. See also Schultz, *Going South*, p. 64.
263. Schultz, *Going South*, p. 64.
264. Cagin and Dray, *We Are Not Afraid*, p. 271.
265. Ibid., p. 2.
266. Ibid.
267. Sally Belfrage, *Freedom Summer*. Charlottesville, VA: University Press of Virginia, 1990, p. 12.
268. Schultz, *Going South*, p. 67.
269. Ibid., p. 69.
270. Ibid.
271. Ibid.
272. Cited in Watson, *Freedom Summer*, p. 111.
273. Ibid.

274. Ibid., pp. 111–112.
275. Schultz, *Going South*, p. 70.
276. Episode 5, "Mississippi: Is This America?" (1962–1964), *Eyes on the Prize: America's Civil Rights Years*, Produced by Henry Hampton. Boston, MA: Blackside, 1986, p. 75.
277. Belfrage, *Freedom Summer*, p. 10.
278. Ibid.
279. Ibid.
280. Ibid.
281. See Shomial Ahmad, "Queens College and Civil Rights: Alumni Reflect on Activism 50 Years Ago." *Clarion*, May 2014, p. 4.
282. Michael R. Wenger, *My Black Family, My White Privilege: A White Man's Journey Through the Nation's Racial Minefield*. Bloomington, IN: iUniverse, Inc. 2012, p. 44.
283. Douglas O. Linder, "The Mississippi Burning Trial (U. S. vs. Price et al.)." http://law2.umkc.edu/faculty/projects/ftrials/price&bowers/acount.html (Accessed 9/29/2012).
284. Ibid.
285. The proceedings of this conference was published in *Souls*, Vol. 10, No. 2, 2008 with the title, *Searching for Restorative Justice: The Trial of Edgar Ray Killen*.
286. Rita L. Bender, "Searching for Restorative Justice: The Trial of Edgar Ray Killen." *Souls*, Vol. 10, No. 2, 2008, p. 156.
287. Ibid.
288. Bender, "Searching for Restorative Justice: The Trial of Edgar Ray Killen," p. 156.
289. Ibid., p. 157.
290. Ibid.
291. Bender, "Searching for Restorative Justice," p. 156.
292. Ibid., p. 158.
293. Ibid.
294. Ibid.
295. Ibid., p. 164.
296. Ibid.
297. Ibid., p. 162.
298. W. Ralph Eubanks, *Ever Is a Long Time: A Journey into Mississippi's Dark Past, A Memoir*. New York: Basic Books, 2003, p. xiv.
299. Ibid.

300. Ibid.
301. Bender, "Searching for Restorative Justice," p. 162.
302. Ibid.
303. Ibid., 163.
304. See Doug McAdam, *Freedom Summer*. New York, NY: Oxford University Press, 1988. See also Manning Marable, "Searching for Restorative Justice: The Trial of Edgar Ray Killen." *Souls*, Vol. 10, No. 2, 2008, p. 156.
305. John Dittmer, for example maintains that "The typical volunteer was white, affluent, politically liberal, and enrolled at a prestigious university." P. 244. See also, Doug McAdam, *Freedom Summer*. New York, NY: Oxford University Press, 1988, p. 5; Bruce Watson, *Freedom Summer, The Savage Season of 1964 That Made Mississippi Burn and Made America a Democracy*. New York, NY: Penguin Books, 2010, p. 15; Gwendolyn Zoharah Simmons, "Reflections on the Orientation and My Participation in the 1964 Mississippi Freedom Summer Project." In Jacqueline Johnson, ed. *Finding Freedom: Memorializing the Voices of Freedom Summer* (pp. 49–56). Oxford, OH: Miami University Press, 2013, p. 54.
306. Cited in Jane Strippel, "Friends of the Mississippi Summer Project." In Jacqueline Johnson, ed. *Finding Freedom: Memorializing the Voices of Freedom Summer* (pp. 13–22). Oxford, OH: Miami University Press, 2013, p. 20.

CHAPTER 5

The Bridge Leaders

Riots in Florida. Economic reprisals in Tennessee. Senseless killings in Mississippi. Police brutality and open indifference to segregation right here in New York. These are some of the recent results of the battle for racial equality. How long will we let these things continue before we in the college community become distressed enough to take action?
—Barbara (Jones) Omolade

Pervasiveness and virulence of racism in the South animated Queens College students into activism, as we have seen so far. The volunteers and activists we have studied made it clear why they, specifically, became involved in social justice and change. But, as we explored in the first few chapters of this book, how does one's feelings of unease or discomfort translate to activism? What makes people come together to form an activist group or movement? In other words, what propels a person to activism? Doug McAdam in a good number of his studies has summarized various theoretical explanations for participation in activism.[1] Consistent with these findings, some scholars have identified institutional and interpersonal networks, and proper conceptualization of social movement leadership as necessary for successful social movement mobilization.[2] It has also been argued that college and university environments provide perfect opportunities for recruitment of students with similar interests

© The Author(s), under exclusive license to Springer Nature
Switzerland AG 2024
M. O. Bassey, *Student Activism in 1960s America*, Palgrave Studies in the History of Social Movements,
https://doi.org/10.1007/978-3-031-54794-2_5

into activist groups. Indeed, Nick Crossley made the point that, "University campuses facilitate the formation of a critical and connected mass of previously politicized actors who then use their further networks to recruit political novices into activism."[3] Such recruitment tools include important connections and interpersonal relationships mediated through the framework of existing community associations, systems, institutions, and organizations.[4] As Belinda Robnett has pointed out, social movements do not occur in a vacuum, indeed, individuals must be persuaded to participate in a movement by intermediate players who act as bridge leaders.[5] Bridge leaders use specific recruitment tools and methods to persuade the public to buy into the organization's objectives. These leaders initiate positive relationships, "(1) between the social movement organization(s) and potential adherents and constituents, (2) between prefigurative and strategic politics, and (3) between potential leaders and those already predisposed to movement activity."[6] Robnett maintained that during the Civil Rights movement, bridge leadership positions were held primarily by women who performed such functions through "frame bridging, amplification, extension, and transformation."[7] Bridge leaders carry out their functions by establishing and strengthening ties between the social movement and individuals, and by utilizing strategies aimed at changing individual consciousness, through tactics that interrogate, contextualize, and reconceptualize existing relationships between the individual, the state and other institutions.[8] Charles Payne affirmed that during the Civil Rights movement, "women operated as network centers, mobilizing existing social networks around the organizing goals, mediating conflicts, conveying information, [and] coordinating activity..."[9] He explained that women provided accommodation and places to eat and sleep for the Civil Rights workers; they agitated more than men; participated more at mass rallies and demonstrations than men; and most importantly, they attempted to register to vote in greater numbers than men. Women also created and sustained good relations and solidarity among co-workers.[10] Bridge leaders provided those who were already enthusiastic about the cause with the necessary information to convince them to join the movement; they employed moral suasion to persuade constituents to want to join; they extended the movement's goals to include the interests of would-be volunteers; and they changed the individual's perspective in congruence with the movement's objectives.[11] In essence, bridge leaders act as middle management, translating and transmitting the organization's mission, goals, objectives, and *modus operandi* to the rank and file.

Anthony Oberschall refers to bridge leaders as those who can stimulate rational individuals to take part in social movements and organizations.[12] In other words, bridge leadership is "the ability to influence others and to gain the loyalty of followers."[13] To emphasize the importance of bridge leadership to movement mobilization and participation, Oberschall points out that participation and talk "conducted in casual meetings and small groups for the most part and in which a diversity of points of view are expressed, is so characteristic of the early phases of social movements ..."[14] therefore, there is need for bridge leadership.

The exploration and analyses that follow reveal that the success of the recruitment efforts for Freedom Summer 1964 at Queens College depended greatly on the recruitment abilities of the organizers of the various campus activities. However, a careful examination of archival records in the Special Collections Department at the Queens College library informed me that there was no greater inspiration and organizational ability for the Freedom Summer 1964 recruitment efforts on QC campus than those credited to members of the Student Help Project (SHP), Congress of Racial Equality (CORE), and the Civil Rights Coordinating Council (CRCC). The contributions of these organizations were as interesting as they were fascinating. Indeed, their legacies are as powerful today as their insights were timely then. They saw injustice and tried to right it. Consequently, in this study, a significant amount of time and space have been devoted to the milieu and context within which these organizations operated jointly, severally, and/or individually.

* * *

During the Freedom Week organized by the Civil Rights Coordinating Council and sponsored by CORE, volunteers were recruited for the Freedom Summer 1964 Project at QC. Applicants were required to complete detailed and elaborate application forms including name, age, date of birth, race, school, school address, year in college, phone number, and home address among others. The organizations involved in Freedom Week events and recruitments at QC were Queens College chapter of CORE, the Student Help Project, and the Civil Rights Coordinating Council, chaired by Barbara Jones (later Barbara Jones Omolade) (now deceased). Barbara did a lot of campus recruiting of students for Freedom Summer 1964, and it is here that she truly showed her bridge leadership skills,[15] and exhibited her autonomous pioneering abilities.

Barbara begins the preface to her book, *The Rising Song of African American Women*, by defining herself as a "product of an intellectual tradition which until twenty-five years ago did not exist within the academy,"[16] and her custom, like the patchwork in a quilt that is assembled from meaningful bits and pieces.[17] According to Barbara, her tradition has no name "because it embraces more than womanism, Blackness or Africana studies..."[18] She calls herself a "griot historian and sociologist who primarily writes for, speaks to, and organizes with African American women and anyone else who finds meaning and significance in our lives."[19]

Barbara was born on October 29, 1942, in Brooklyn, New York, the daughter of an ambulance driver and a first-generation northerner who was the first in her family to receive a college degree. In 1954, she was chosen to integrate an all-White junior high school located just a few blocks away from her neighborhood. Barbara excelled in both junior high and high school and was equally skilled in math, writing, and the social sciences.[20] Furthermore, she was also very "popular and comfortable despite being in an overwhelmingly white school, primarily attended by Italian and German students who were the children of recent immigrants."[21] Barbara was not only academically very good in high school, but she was also a part of the tiny group of students who ran the student government and the student newspaper. She remembered her high school as a place of mutual support and respect with a heightened sense of confraternity among all the students, and noted, "As a Black woman I was different, but in many ways very similar to my white female school mates. We were a community of learners and school activists who spent more time talking about our schoolwork and ideas than boys and dating."[22]

Barbara was somewhat unsettled in college because there were no support systems. She was also amazed because there were so few Black students in the commuter college, she attended that it could well have been said that she was the only Black student at her college.[23] Barbara entered Queens College in 1960 and graduated in 1964. By all accounts, her college experience was boring and unstimulating because there were neither role models nor books about the Black experience. Indeed, there were no redeeming features at the college to sustain her, except for the training and encouragement she received from her family and her community.[24] College seemed to have dulled her brilliant mind and even caused her to cast some doubt about her self-worth. Here is her recollection: "College bored and disappointed me because it dulled my mind and made me doubt myself. I was not merely learning my subjects, I was attempting to be a subject, and my presence in the classroom as a learner directly contradicted my absence from the scholarship."[25] Barbara did not stand alone in her recollections. Indeed, bell hooks recounted a similar experience after she was sent to an integrated high school. She wrote, "When we entered ...desegregated white schools we left a world where teachers believed that to educate black children rightly would require a political commitment."[26] According to hooks, in her integrated high school, they were "mainly taught by white teachers whose lessons reinforced racist stereotypes,"[27] which made education no longer about the practice of freedom. She went on to say, "Realizing this, I lost my love of school. The classroom was no longer a place of pleasure or ecstasy."[28]

But, everything in Barbara's experience changed mid-way through her college career, "when the Civil Rights Movement imposed itself on [her] television screens."[29] According to Barbara, the Movement's "presence was felt in every sermon and in every place where we gathered."[30] The winds of the Civil Rights Movement blew intensely in Barbara's direction because as the daughter of Black southerners, she grew up reading "white only" signs on her family trips to the South and she saw her father's "silent rage at Jim Crow."[31] As a senior in college, Barbara joined and worked in the New York office of SNCC, perhaps because, "college seemed irrelevant in light of the revolution that was going on around [her]."[32] In 1964, during the spring semester, she chaired the Civil Rights Coordinating Council at QC. She had been sold on progressive politics after reading James Baldwin,[33] but as she recollected later, it was the movement (SNCC) that taught her how to think critically and intellectually. It was through this movement that she learned about social construction, political science, radical politics, and activism because she studied the perspectives and worldviews of people in SNCC as well as their practices and methods.[34] To Barbara, the benefits of belonging to SNCC were obvious. First, it opened new doors, provided new ways of thinking and looking at things, and she was delighted with the new vistas her membership in the organization had given her. Quoting Kwame Ture (formerly known as Stokely Carmichael), she said, "We learned more in the movement from the local people than from all the college professors we sat under."[35] She continued by saying that local people in the South, like Fannie Lou Hamer, taught them to read—not just books but to read the situation they were in.[36] This is perhaps why she said that she is "a worker and family woman who frankly looks down on folks who are not willing to be part of the necessary struggles of everyday life, or who think themselves too educated to learn from those around them."[37]

In the spring of 1964, as the Chair of the Civil Rights Coordinating Council, Barbara participated in organizing Freedom Week along with others from April 20–24, 1964, and served as an important bridge leader at Queens College. The Freedom week was sponsored by the Queens College Chapter of CORE, which also supported the Mississippi Freedom Project. In a memorandum on behalf of the Civil Rights Coordinating Council that was sent out to the college community announcing the Freedom Week, Barbara explained the purpose of the week in the following words:

> For too long, the college community has remained silent on many of the vital issues of our day. One of the most pressing [issues] today is the struggle for racial equality in the United States as a whole and particularly in New York City. Thus, we have designated the week of April 20–24 Freedom Week at Queens College.[38]

The memo noted that some of the primary objectives of the week would include, to identify the major local problems, make students aware of them, and encourage them to face the problems and also to find ways to make meaningful contributions toward the solution of the problems.[39] Other objectives of the week included raising money for the Mississippi Summer Project in support of "several Queens College students who will devote their time this summer to an all-out assault on Mississippi's racist policies."[40] The memo emphasized that racial equality was the most important issue facing Americans at that time; therefore, the college community should become an effective voice in aiding the elimination of injustices. To be sure, the memo requested Freedom Week to be the beginning of *protest* at Queens College against all forms of racial discrimination.[41]

In a different memo to all members of the faculty and students on behalf of her committee, Barbara pointed to events in other parts of the country as justification for Freedom Week and for students' actions and protests: "Riots in Florida. Economic reprisals in Tennessee. Senseless killings in Mississippi. Police brutality and open indifference to segregation right here in New York. These are some of the recent results of the battle for racial equality."[42] She then wondered, "How long will we let these things continue before we in the college community become distressed enough to take action?"[43] Speaking on behalf of her committee, Barbara alerted the college community to the fact that, there was an important Civil Rights bill pending in the US Senate, and that, a group of students from Columbia, Cornell, and other eastern universities were getting ready for a voter registration drive in [Mississippi] during the summer.[44] In light of these developments, the Civil Rights Coordinating Council made it clear that some students at QC had decided to take the bull by the horns, and in very specific terms announced that,

> Some Queens College students have decided that they cannot sit idly by in this era of revolution. Several will participate in the Mississippi Summer Project. A larger number is now in the process of organizing Queens College Freedom Week, a week dedicated to the education of Queens College students to the issues involved in the Civil Rights struggle and to the possibilities for local direct action.[45]

Freedom Week was also a period to raise money for Queens College students who wished to participate in the Mississippi Summer Project. This, indeed, according to the organizing committee, was a period for participation, action, and intellectual deliberation. It was a time for "lectures and rallies that informed faculty, students, and the Queens community about the Mississippi Freedom Summer Project and recent developments in the Civil Rights Movement."[46] One of the guests during Freedom Week was Rt. Rev. Monsignor Asip of the Society for the Propagation of the Faith. Monsignor Asip was engaged to speak on the topic, *Race and Religion*,[47] on April 23, 1964, at 5:30 p.m. in the College Memorial Center.

During Freedom Week, the Civil Rights Coordinating Council appealed for cooperation from all the faculty because members were aware that any such activity on a college campus cannot be fully successful without faculty support and participation.[48] The committee asked for faculty assistance in planning and carrying out the venture successfully, especially with reference to the planned seminars. Faculty were requested to act as resource people who would introduce each seminar. The committee thought it would be helpful if faculty added the Freedom Week programs to their schedules, and requested them to announce Freedom Week plans, seminar schedules, and statement of objectives in their classes throughout the week. Committee members were thankful to everyone in the college because they realized the enormity of the request but argued that given the magnitude and importance of the issues involved, a full-scale effort was necessary if anything was to be achieved. Members of other organizations on campus were requested by the Civil Rights Coordinating Council and the Queens College chapter of CORE to cancel their own activities, engagements, and meetings for the week so that their members could attend events organized during Freedom Week. It is important to note that the planning committee's responsibility during Freedom Week also included fundraising.

The organizing committee brought in speakers such as Allard Lowenstein, Aaron Henry, Travis Britt, and Prathia Hall to speak to students as part of the Freedom Week to enhance the recruitment of Freedom Summer activists.[49] As a series of lectures, marches, and rallies were organized at QC devoted to Civil Rights issues, the most successful recruitment efforts for the Freedom Summer Project at QC were undertaken. This is how Seth Cagin and Philip Dray described the personal initiative of one of the leaders in the recruitment efforts at Queens:

> That April, shortly after hearing Al Lowenstein describe the Summer Project in a Queens College address, Andy and Nancy Cooper contacted Barbara Jones, a black student at QC who was active with SNCC. Barbara, who had been radicalized by her reading of James Baldwin, campaigned to interest as many people as she could in the southern movement.[50]

Andrew Goodman and Nancy Cooper were referred to the Manhattan office of SNCC for their personal interviews by Barbara (Jones) Omolade.[51] This e-mail exchange between Mark Levy and Robert Masters, speaks to Barbara's quintessential bridge leadership credentials in particular, and her leadership skills in general:

> I heard about [the Mississippi Summer Project] on campus. There was an African American student named Barbara [Jones-Omolade] who organized something I went to. Then there were several follow up meetings. I guess I got to know Andy [Goodman] through those meetings. There was a group of us driving to Ohio from New York which included Andy and me. I stayed at his apt. the night before we left. I was in Greenwood for the summer working with Stokely Carmichael (later known as Kwame Ture). I remember Rita Schwerner because she was in our office a lot calling all over the country but didn't realize the connection [to Q.C]. The Greenwood office had a WATS [Wide Area Telephone Service] line.[52]

It was also during Freedom Week that the planned demonstrations at the 1964 World's Fair gathered steam among QC students. "At nearby Queens College," wrote Cagin and Dray, "the issue of how to greet the fair was hotly debated by Andy Goodman and his fellow students. Farmer had long been scheduled to deliver a speech at the college to kick off Freedom Week, but was called away to deal with the stall-in crisis."[53] Cagin and Dray noted that the "organizers of Freedom Week added to their program a plan for interested students to march to the fair site on opening day to join Farmer's inside-the-fair actions."[54] On her own part, Barbara wrote materials for the Freedom School curriculum and spent the summer of 1964 in SNCC's DC office challenging the government to find the bodies of Goodman, Schwerner, and Chaney. She could not participate in Freedom Summer because she was assigned to the Student Nonviolent Coordinating Committee's Offices in New York and Washington, D.C. during this period.[55]

After graduating from Queens College, Barbara left New York City to join SNCC in Atlanta in September 1964. Considering her parents' apprehension to her Civil Rights work and activism, she sent a letter to them explaining her reasons and the circumstances of her choice. "I decided to work for SNCC because I am [Black],"[56] she wrote, [and] "I've always been very conscious of the fact of my being [Black]."[57] Given her circumstances, she told her parents that she was not going to run away from her own reality because the reality for Black people in America comes with enormous responsibilities since there is no justice for Blacks in the United States. She argued that she felt particularly compelled to join the fight for social justice because even White people were beginning to acknowledge that the time had come for such a struggle to begin by joining the movement. She reminded her parents that the struggle for social justice was not reserved for extraordinary people like Rev. Martin Luther King, Jr., but was also for ordinary people like college kids and old people too.[58] She explained that she felt compelled to participate because, "there were also some older people like my Uncle Archie, my grandfather, and my aunt Estelle, telling how they were beaten, jailed, and fired because they dared to go down to register to vote."[59] Equally significant to her was the fact that there were still some Black people in the South who were being denied their very basic fundamental human right—the right to vote. Sarcastically, she agreed with her parents that she may have been brainwashed into acting against racism and discrimination as they thought, but she was only brainwashed to know that as a Black girl, she had "nothing to lose in this fight against the chains that bound me and my people."[60] Indeed, President Nelson Mandela of South Africa once made a similar statement. In his autobiography, *Long Walk to Freedom*, he stated:

> I slowly saw that not only was I not free, but my brothers and sisters were not free. I saw that it was not just my freedom that was curtailed, but the freedom of everyone who looked like I did…It was this desire for the freedom of my people to live their lives with dignity and self-respect that animated my life, that transformed a frightened young man into a bold one, that drove a law-abiding attorney to become a criminal, that turned a family-loving husband into a man without a home, that forced a life-loving man to live like a monk.[61]

Barbara wrote to her parents that, going to college, living in a comfortable house, having clothes, even being able to get a job in New York was not going to change the fact that she was a black girl in a white man's country and she had nothing to lose by fighting racism.[62] She went on to say that the school system in America was corrupt because it shortchanged Black and Puerto Rican children while privileging White children. In New York, she told her parents, she would be able to touch the lives of only a few children, but in SNCC she "can help to bring about more basic changes which can allow me to go back to the south that I love and live there with my friends, white and black, building a new world and living a life with meaning."[63] She was excited to tell her parents of SNCC's determination to end racial discrimination in housing, voting, employment, and education. Also, of no less importance in SNCC's work was the movement's mission to shine the searchlight on excessive violence and police brutality in the South. The SNCC, she argued, was holding the United States to its democratic ideals of equality of personhood. She reminded her parents of SNCC's goal of "seeking a community in which man [and woman] can realize the full meaning of self, which demands open relationships with others."[64]

Barbara was happy to tell her parents with obvious exuberance about the minor but significant changes that were taking place in the Deep South, which included the rise of indigenous political leaders who would emerge as the true representatives of the people. She could not hide her excitement about the founding of the Mississippi Freedom Democratic Party (MFDP) with all its attendant benefits for Black people in the

South. She spoke passionately and with pride about the Freedom Schools designed to teach Black children about their own history and heritage, a subject she did not have the good fortune of learning throughout her own public school education. In his book, *The Mis-Education of the Negro* (1933), Carter G. Woodson argued that the education given to Black children in America was uninstructive because it lacked the interplay between Black children and their environment. Woodson came to this conclusion because the "neglect of Afro-American History and distortion of the facts concerning [Blacks] in most history books, deprived the black child and his whole race of a heritage, and relegated [him/her] to nothingness and nobodyness."[65] This type of education, according to Molefi Asante, had created a split in the personality of Blacks typified by dual identities resulting in a profound identity crisis,[66] which has made African Americans "decry any such thing as race consciousness."[67] Indeed, as Barbara noted,

> Freedom in Mississippi, like freedom anywhere, means to have schools that teach you about the world, not just the white man's concept of the world. It means freedom to vote for people who will be responsive to you and your problems. We are simply working for change in the conditions of the life of [Blacks] in the Deep South. We have had some success, and we keep on pushing.[68]

Barbara stated with pride and delight the contributions of patriots like Ella Baker, Walter Tillow, Frank Smith, and her humble self, the secretary, staff of the Washington Freedom Democratic Party office who had worked so hard to put together the Mississippi Freedom Democratic Party challenge to the regular, lily-white Democratic Party delegation from Mississippi.[69] She concluded by telling her parents, "This is simply what this movement is about, liberating people so they can be people, not just white and black, not denying what you are, but looking for the qualities that count: integrity, honesty, and companionship."[70] Indeed, for Barbara, social activism was SNCC's hallmark, and its *modus operandi* was as Julian Bond said, taking the "message of freedom into areas where the bigger Civil Rights organizations feared to tread."[71]

* * *

After her work with SNCC, Barbara went on to pursue higher education with a focus on African American women's history and activism.

She received her master's degree from Goddard College and a Ph.D. from the City University of New York. Barbara had worked for women's and activist organizations including SNCC, The Center for the Elimination of Violence in the Family, Empire State College Center for Labor Studies, and the Women's Action Alliance. She taught a course on African American women at the College of New Rochelle, Co-Op City Evening Program in 1977. This was the first social science course of its kind on African American women's history in the country. In 1981, she joined the City College of New York Center for Worker Education and was admitted to its faculty shortly after. In 1983, with help from others, she founded *Friends of Women's Studies* at City University of New York. This organization was responsible for the establishment of the CUNY faculty development seminar on balancing the curriculum across gender, race, ethnicity, and class. Her landmark book, *The Rising Song of African American Women* was published in 1994. She left the City College Center for Worker Education to become the first dean of Multicultural Affairs at Calvin College (now Calvin University) in Grand Rapids, Michigan in 2004, a position she held until she finally retired from active service. She was one of the contributors to the book, *Hands on the Freedom Plow: Personal Accounts by Women in SNCC* (2010). In her contribution, "Building a New World," she shares the contents of a letter she sent to her parents explaining her decision to join the Civil Rights Movement and the SNCC office in Atlanta. Her other books include, *It's a Family Affair: The Real Lives of Black Single Mothers,* and *Faith Confronts Evil.* Barbara died in 2023.

* * *

It was a Mark of Honor to Resist
—Dorothy M. Zellner

As I carried out this research, it became clear to me that Dorothy (Dottie) M. Zellner was one of the profound leaders in the recruitment of students for Freedom Summer 1964 and was a towering figure in Civil Rights activism from Queens College in the 1960s. Dorothy Miller Zellner was born in 1938 in Manhattan, New York. She attended Queens College and served as the editor of the Queens College student newspaper, the *Crown*.[72] Dorothy worked for the liberal student newspaper for several years, first as a reporter and later becoming its editor in 1958. As a reporter and editor, Dorothy Zellner wrote about racism and discrimination and was well-connected to Queens College students who were activists at the time. As a recent graduate from Queens College, Dorothy read in *New York Times* how four young Black men from Greensboro, North Carolina sat down at a Woolworth's department lunch counter and ordered lunch at the whites-only counter but when they were refused service, they declined to leave and stayed until the store was closed. Dorothy thought those young men were inventive, clever, and brave.[73] This incident is often described as the 1960 Greensboro lunch-counter sit-in. The four university freshmen were from the Agricultural and Technical College of North Carolina (now North Carolina A&T State University). These students who were known as the Greensboro Four were: Joseph McNeil, Franklin McCain, Ezell Blair, Jr. (later known as Jibreel Khazan), and David Richmond. This singular event, it appears, catalyzed Dorothy into social activism because she stated, "Somehow, I knew that for me this was more than just an interesting news story about some heroic young people far away. Within a few weeks I applied to participate in a nonviolent direct-action workshop organized by CORE in Miami."[74] Dorothy narrated the story of what animated and shaped her worldview about social activism in this way:

> 'Equality for [Black] people' had been an axiom of my upbringing as the child of immigrant Jewish leftists; therefore, unlike most white Americans, I actually knew something of black history. I had even glimpsed both the great Paul Robeson and W. E. B. DuBois in person. And I had grown up with the heroic stories of resistance to fascism, particularly of the young Jewish fighters of the Warsaw Ghetto who fought the Nazis in a last spurt of defiance and despair[75]

Debra Schultz maintained that as an adolescent, Dorothy read "zillions of books about the war and about the Holocaust. 'She posed to herself the question,' If I had been alive in 1943 in Warsaw what would I have done? And I decided very early on that I would have had to fight."[76]

Dorothy applied to CORE to participate in a direct-action nonviolent workshop in Miami. Her application was accepted and in June 1960 she went to Miami for training along with thirty-five other participants. During a sit-in to challenge Miami's segregated eatery designed as part of the workshop, Dorothy and others were arrested and put in jail. At the end of the workshop, she traveled to New Orleans with the New Orleans contingent. In New Orleans, before the city's first sit-in at Woolworth's on Canal Street, Dorothy and some others acted as scouts and "cased" the store. On the day of the sit-in, she made and brought the picket signs and acted as a designated driver. A few of the demonstrators were arrested and Dorothy rushed to YMCA to work the phones for their bail money. During the period of her organizing in the South, Dorothy was arrested twice, pulled over, patted down by police for no good reason, and knocked on the head by a fanatical cop. In June 1961, she was offered a job as a research assistant with the Southern Regional Council (SRC) in Atlanta to work under James A. Moss, the research director who was her former professor at Queens College. Les Dunbar was the SRC executive director. Dorothy's first assignment with SRC was to research and write a white paper on behalf of the organization about the sit-in movement. The significance of Dorothy's assignment at the SRC lay in the fact that several newspaper reporters used the SRC archives in Atlanta for their reporting.[77] However, the greatest worry for Dorothy in Atlanta was how to confront the culture of segregation because everything in Atlanta at this time was segregated. As she described it, "This meant a schizoid existence for all of us at SRC. We worked in an interracial organization, but once we left the SRC offices on Forsyth Street, every single thing we chose to do – whether eating lunch, shopping, going to a movie – was determined by race."[78] As Debra Schultz stated, "Confronting the culture of segregation was one of many adaptations the southern movement required,"[79] because "even northern activists with impeccable civil rights credentials had to learn a whole new way of being when they crossed into the South."[80] Indeed, Dorothy herself confessed that although she grew up in a family with leftist views and radical political values, it was the first time she came face to face with Black culture, Black social environments, Black ministers and even Black religious people.[81]

Debra Schultz explained that "red-diaper babies like Dottie Miller Zellner... grew up in families that proudly communicated radical political values," and such "upbringing instilled a sense of community and purpose that made the call of the civil rights movement irresistible."[82] This is perhaps why Dorothy was so excited when she secured her dream job with the SNCC in 1962, which she described as the object of her journey to Atlanta that would enable her to do something needed; something that would help her to contribute and belong to a movement she considered so very important—an organization she loved.[83] Dorothy started working for SNCC as a volunteer in the fall of 1961, but worked as a staff member for the organization from 1962 to 1967. Her initial assignment at SNCC as a staff member was to work in the communications department with Julian Bond, the communications director on SNCC's newsletter, the *Student Voice*. The *Student Voice* was SNCC's mouthpiece as it orchestrated the needs, philosophy, and achievements of the organization to the outside world, perhaps setting Dorothy up as an effective bridge leader. The *Student Voice* was responsible for building "community and morale among the movement's widely dispersed field workers and supporters."[84] The *Student Voice* reported on the maltreatment of Blacks and SNCC volunteers in the South when very few national papers dared or had the courage to do so. It was indeed Dorothy through the *Student Voice* who "helped bring the reality of southern violence to national attention."[85] James (Jim) Forman, Executive Secretary of SNCC (1961–1966), stated that in the early days, the most serious weakness in SNCC was in the area of communications because, the "mass media of the country printed very little news at that time of what was happening to Black people,"[86] and Dorothy helped to bring the reality of Southern violence to national attention.[87] She brought to light the organization's message and reports on stories that were suppressed by the mainstream media. A true bridge leader, indeed. Julian Bond, Communications Director of the Student Nonviolent Coordinating Committee (1960–1965), once highlighted Dorothy's enormous contributions to the *Student Voice* as a mouthpiece for SNCC, which included the lines, "She gave us a presence, she broke through a blackout that hid what we did from the world. She courted reporters, she told them the news, and the SNCC story slowly unfurled."[88] The importance of Dorothy's work at SNCC was well understood and appreciated by the organization because the leadership understood that "National publicity, if correctly used and focused, is a powerful weapon in any move for change in Mississippi."[89]

Dorothy's other assignments included receiving reports from SNCC field secretaries, for example, from Sam Block, Hollis Watkins, Willie Peacock, Reggie Robinson, Curtis Hayes, Ruby Doris Smith-Robinson, and others.[90] She made press releases, sent telegrams to the White House, and sent requests to the US Department of Justice asking for protection for SNCC volunteers.[91] As Dorothy herself recollected, the reports she often sent "described in a matter-of-fact way what had happened at this or that courthouse when they accompanied disenfranchised black people, mostly sharecroppers or domestic workers, to register to vote in rural Mississippi or Georgia."[92] In a general sense, as Dorothy remembered,

> The story was always the same: after weeks of slow and patient urging by field secretaries, local black people agreed to go to the courthouse to register; stood online for hours, often in sizzling heat or damp cold; and endured heckling and abuse. The end was always the same: invariably someone was arrested, someone was beaten, someone was shot at, someone was fired, and nobody was registered.[93]

These reports were used for sending telegrams to the President; for press releases; for writing articles in the *Student Voice;* for garnering support and donations from Northern supporters or simply for publishing SNCC pamphlets. Indeed, brutal police activities as far away as Danville, Virginia were recorded and reported in the *Student Voice*. Dorothy boldly and forcefully documented the length and breadth of the efforts by Southern whites to deny African Americans the right to vote, thereby authenticating the work of the SNCC.[94] The *Student Voice* "built community and morale among the movement's widely dispersed field workers and supporters,"[95] and propelled SNCC to national prominence.

During her days at SNCC, Dorothy wore many hats, but her most important assignment was running the Northeast Regional Office of SNCC in Cambridge, Massachusetts in the fall of 1963. When the idea of Freedom Summer 1964 was orchestrated by SNCC, Dorothy was assigned the responsibility of recruiting volunteers from Northeastern colleges and universities. She was responsible for screening Freedom Summer applicants to disqualify those who were not cut out for the assignment, to boot out thrill seekers, and to eliminate those who did not foresee the seriousness and dangers of the assignments, or those with propensity to be disrespectful to people in the Black community.[96] Dorothy showed remarkable skills as a bridge leader in executing this assignment. In an interview with *Clarion*, PSC/CUNY news magazine, Dorothy said, "We were very concerned about divas and nutcases. We wanted people who had respect for the black community, who would not do something crazy like wearing shorts to church. We didn't want prima donnas who said, oh okay, I'll do this, but I won't do that."[97] In a series of discussions with me and from his written reports, Mark Levy confirmed that he and his late wife, Betty (Bollinger) Levy were recruited by Dorothy Zellner in Boston for Freedom Summer 1964.

Dorothy had been given a major role by SNCC in interviewing volunteers for Freedom Summer throughout the Northeast. She was charged with the responsibility of making recommendations for acceptance or rejection of "applicants." She first talked to Mark Levy about Freedom Summer while they were travelling on a commercial bus between Massachusetts and New York. As a testament to Dorothy's remarkable recruitment skills and as a bridge leader, Mark said that although he was reluctant to join other campaigns, the way Dorothy talked about Freedom Summer was different. He remarked, "She talked about it not as a bunch of white freedom riders going down South, but as a request by local Mississippians to 'come on down and help us.' So, we were not going down as missionaries. [That] was something that I could say 'yes' to."[98]

During Freedom Summer orientation at the Western College for Women in Oxford, Ohio, Julian Bond, the communications director, and Dorothy were put in charge of seminars and briefings for those volunteers who would be responsible for communications within the volunteer corps. In discharging these duties, Dorothy emphasized to the trainees that it was their responsibility to always track down volunteers. "If people go out and say they are coming back at three," she told them, "And if it's ten after and they're not back, start calling – the jails first, then hospitals, and so on,"[99] she emphasized. After the orientation, Dorothy relocated to Greenwood, Mississippi office, where SNCC had moved its operational headquarters because it was the only place that the Justice Department was able to provide some modicum of protection for the volunteers in Mississippi.[100] In Greenwood, Dorothy worked a shift on the WATS [Wide Area Telephone Service] line. She made and took calls and communicated with the press concerning people who had been abused and or arrested and gave incident reports to families of victims. Greenwood itself was engaged in cotton agriculture with all its racial ramifications. As a recent reviewer commented, "Greenwood, SNCC, and the Summer Project made for a volatile mix. The white volunteers boarded in black homes, and both they and their hosts were continually harassed, beaten, and jailed for minor or imaginary infractions of local laws."[101] Of Dorothy's contributions to SNCC and to activism, Jane Bond Moore, her former apartment mate commented, "I learned about politics and class warfare from Dottie. During the Cuban missile crisis, (Dorothy) picketed in a park, bringing the wrath of the SRC down on her."[102] Dorothy's moral suasion was her crusade for social equality.

* * *

After five years, Dorothy left SNCC in 1967 when SNCC was transitioning into an all-Black organization.[103] Dorothy joined the Southern Conference Educational Fund (SCEF) in New Orleans after many years of challenging but meritorious service to SNCC. In 1972, she qualified as a licensed practical nurse credited with organizing a union in the New Orleans Home for Incurables. In 1983, she returned to New York and was employed at the Center for Constitutional Rights in 1984. She worked there for about thirteen years. At the Center, Dorothy was responsible for managing the Center's publications as well as the group's Ella Baker Legal Internship program for students of color. She was later employed by the City University of New York School of Law as Director of Institutional Advancement and Publications in 1998. Dorothy's article, "Red Roadshow: Eastland in New Orleans," which was published in *Louisiana History,* was given a New York Foundation for the Arts award. She delivers talks and lectures about Civil Rights activism, SNCC, and on Blacks and Jews in the Civil Rights Movement. She is an activist and a writer. Her articles have appeared in *Jewish Currents,* and in other publications. She was featured in the book, *Going South: Jewish Women in the Civil Rights Movement* by Debra L. Schultz. Dorothy wrote a chapter in, and is one of the editors of the publication, *Hands on the Freedom Plow: Personal Accounts by Women in SNCC.* She has spoken and written on Palestinian issues as well.[104] In 2009, she signed a petition appealing to the Israeli Defense Forces to stop the atrocities in Gaza. Dorothy has been featured in many books and television programs and was featured in TNT's "Century of Women."[105] She is a founding member of *Jews Say No* and serves as a volunteer for the organization *Jewish Voice for Peace.* She is now retired from her employment at the City University of New York School of Law.

* * *

Another important player in recruiting for social justice causes at QC was Andrew Berman, particularly regarding translating and transmitting values and missions throughout the campus through alternative presses. Andrew was born in Brooklyn, New York in 1947. After attending Francis Lewis High School, he became a student at Queens College in 1963 at the age of 16. He graduated in 1967 with a degree in Mathematics. His early life was heavily influenced by his parents' Leftist politics. Although he was recruited for the Mississippi Freedom Summer Project, he could not participate because he did not meet the minimum age requirement. Unable to go to Mississippi as a volunteer, Andrew developed other interests by attending formal and informal meetings and discussion groups which helped him to discover a larger world of ideas and intellectual exploration and social activism. Because of his interest in socialism, peace, social justice, and Civil Rights causes, he joined organizations which were concerned with the exchange of ideas, particularly those that emphasized social change. In 1963, he joined the Queens College chapter of CORE. Andrew volunteered on campus passing out leaflets and recruiting students for activist causes. In 1964, he participated in a sit-in organized by CORE at the Government Pavilion at the New York World's Fair at Flushing Meadows Corona Park. The theme of the Fair was "Peace Through Understanding," and was dedicated to "Man's Achievement on a Shrinking Globe in an Expanding Universe." Berman and his fellow activists saw the fair as a symbol of American hypocrisy. "We contrast the **real world** of discrimination and brutality experienced by [Blacks], North and South, with the **fantasy world** of progress and abundance shown in the official pavilions,"[106] they queried. During the sit-in, Berman was arrested and jailed for one night at the Hart's Island jail.

Berman and Howard (Howie) Epstein co-founded the student group, "Independent Students for a New Left" (ISNL) in 1963 with Professor Bell Gale Chevigny and later Sol Resnick as faculty advisors respectively. As part of their campus activities, ISNL invited speakers to campus including three students who had visited Cuba in violation of the State Department's travel ban. In a letter to the editor of the student paper, *Phoenix,* Berman justified the invitation of "unorthodox and controversial" speakers as part of the educational function of an academic institution and on First Amendment grounds.[107] ISNL was transformed into the Queens College chapter of the radical Students for a Democratic Society (SDS) in 1964. In a memo to new members, the cofounders described SDS as:

> a national student coalition of radicals seeking to extend democracy in the university, to work for social and economic change through grass-roots organizing, to work within the struggles for peace, civil rights, and civil liberties. It is a non-doctrinaire organization and thrives on internal dissention.[108]

The organizers went on to state, "SDS is the student department of the League for Industrial Democracy...although SDS operates independent of the LID."[109] With previous demonstrations still fresh in their minds, Berman and Epstein, as cochairs of Queens College, Students for a Democratic Society, organized or participated in several other protests on campus: Vietnam-Teach-In, a Fast for Peace in Vietnam, the Chase Manhattan-South Africa Protest, the Vietnam-Santo-Domingo rally, University Reform, Getting SDS people and friends into Student Government, and the "banned" Cuba Speakers protest. Another demonstration of Andrew Berman's activism is that the SDS under his leadership at QC conducted a fifty-six-hour Fast for Peace in Vietnam, and more than sixty-three Queens College students took part in the fast.[110] Also, the organization under Andrew Berman's leadership brought speakers such as the outspoken activist, Herbert Aptheker, M/Sgt Donald Duncan, and Levi Laub to speak on campus with exceedingly large crowds in attendance.[111] In a memo issued to its members on June 1, 1965, SDS under Berman boasted that its greatest accomplishment of the year was "SDS becoming a fact of life on the WMCA (White, Middle Class, Apathetic) Queens College campus." Another one of its achievements was the close contacts SDS was able to forge with progressive faculty at QC.[112]

Since Queens College had banned two existing student newspapers, *Crown* and *Rampart*, in favor of one paper, *Phoenix* operating on campus, Andrew Berman waged an endless battle of words against the college administration. In support of Freedom of the Press and the First Amendment, SDS published a newsletter called *The Activist* without the approval of the college administration—a direct affront to the College Red Book[113] publications policy. The *Activist* emphasized the need for a greater student voice in college decision-making. *The Free Press*, an independent, off-campus newspaper, reported the publication of *The Activist* with the following caption, "SDS Publishes 'Illegal' Newsletter." *The Free Press* went on to state, "Students for a Democratic Society (SDS) made a direct challenge of the Red Book publications policy last Wednesday by distributing the *Activist*, a newsletter, without Administrative sanction."[114] SDS's action here clearly violated the provisions laid down by the Manual of Policies and Procedures for Student Activities, otherwise known as the Redbook. Berman, however, defended the *Activist* by stating in a front-page editorial that, "freedom of the press is not a privilege to be extended or restricted at the whim of any committee, but rather a right guaranteed in the First Amendment to the Constitution... We therefore regard all restrictions on the free expression and dissemination of ideas on the Queens College campus to be null and void."[115] In the same piece, Berman noted that there was no sign that students' rights on campus would be realized unless students asserted their rights plainly and openly.[116] He explained that publishing the *Activist* involved more than a desire to bring about an open publications policy to Queens College campus, but, for a very long time many members of SDS had wanted a newsletter that would reach not only their members but other students on the campus so as to present the SDS's point of view more fully and to start a dialogue on campus.[117] According to Berman, challenging the existing policies is only a means to this larger end.[118] He called on students to support the (SDS's) endeavor by either writing letters to President McMurray, Dean Kreuzer, the Faculty Committee on Student Activities and Services (FCSAS), and the Faculty Council in support of the position they had taken or by submitting articles to the *Activist* or by starting similar publications on their own.[119] To make the *Activist* truly independent, Berman appealed to friends and supporters for the sum of $175 to purchase a second-hand photo-offset press on behalf of SDS stating, "If we can acquire one we can make the ACTIVIST, our free-press crusading journal, entirely self-supporting. We can issue mass quantity, high quality leaflets. We can give the local anti-war movement added impetus by making the press freely available."[120]

The college administration reacted to the "illegal" publication of the *Activist* by placing SDS on probation. In his memo on the suspension letter, Berman wrote, "ambiguous nature of the power we are dealing with."[121] The SDS ignored the disciplinary injunction and continued to publish the *Activist* and the group was suspended as a student organization for its defiance, which meant loss of its office space and funding. However, the group continued to publish their newsletter, albeit underground. Other student groups protested the ban placed on SDS by the College Administration by establishing their own underground independent newspapers and newsletters such as *Graffiti, The Free Press*, and *Queens College Underground Press*. In its editorial, *The Free Press* explained why it started publication as an off-campus newspaper serving Queens College students. The editorial was emphatic in noting that, "Freedom of the press is one of the most basic rights that can be granted to students—and one that they must fight for when it is denied."[122] Under great pressure from the Student Association President, Harvey

Weiner, "SDS voted to temporarily and voluntarily suspend publication of the *Activist*."[123] However, SDS members promised to resume publication if they found out that the administration was not acting in good faith. The decision to suspend the publication of the *Activist* was a source of great displeasure and protests on campus. Students' displeasure against the administration's one-newspaper policy was widely felt throughout QC. It can be said that the establishment of alternative presses was the most important development in the struggle for First Amendment rights and freedom of the press at QC in the 1960s. As a result of the groundswell of student discontents and protests over encroachment on their First Amendment privileges, the College Administration decided to relax the policies guiding publication of student newspapers and newsletters. The Manual of Policies and Procedures for Student Activities was amended to reflect the new posture of the Administration. This was a great *Free Speech* victory for Students for a Democratic Society in which Berman was the co-chair.

* * *

After graduating from Queens College with a BA in Math in 1967, Berman joined the Peace Corps and was posted to teach Math in high school in Togo, West Africa for two years. He returned to the United States after his Peace Corps service and continued with his work in the antiwar movement, which included membership in the Committee of Returned Volunteers and the Liberation News Service. He was a member of the Venceremos Brigade that traveled with 215 other volunteers in 1969 to cut sugarcane in Cuba to protest the US economic blockade and subsequent ban on travel to the Island. Berman joined the US Army in 1971. During his stay in the army, he supported anti-Vietnam War soldiers and spoke against US imperialist foreign policy from within. Because of his antiwar position, he was transferred from Germany to Fort Polk in Louisiana. In 1973, he was given an honorable discharge from the US Army. After his discharge, he went back to college and obtained a degree in Engineering from the University of Illinois. He relocated to Chicago where he worked as a software developer for Bell Labs. In Chicago, Berman continued his activism, including working toward the impeachment of President Richard Nixon and protested President Reagan's Contra War. He organized with members of Veterans for Peace who denounced the United States' war in Afghanistan. He is now retired and lives in Minnesota but continues to volunteer to teach GED math classes to immigrant students.

* * *

We turn lastly to Elliot Linzer, who was born in 1946 in Brooklyn, New York but grew up in Rosedale, Queens. As a youth he was intrigued by the 1961 Freedom Rides and joined the War Resisters League when he was only fourteen years of age. In high school, he took great interest in pacifist and Civil Rights activism. Linzer entered Queens College in 1963. In his first semester in college, he joined the Queens College chapter of CORE because he had participated in various CORE activities, including attending lectures given by CORE officials and participated in a CORE benefit fundraiser selling tickets for a CORE concert at Carnegie Hall in New York even before coming to college. Because of his age, he could not be recruited for the Freedom Summer, but he was allowed to manage a Freedom School in St. Albans, Queens, New York, in one of CORE's sponsored school boycotts in 1964. Linzer participated in many CORE chapter activities, including many activities in South Jamaica. He was an active member of the Queens College CORE chapter just as he was a member of many other off-campus and on-campus activists' groups, such as the Young People's Socialist League (YPSL). During the summer of 1963, Linzer served as a staff member for the March on Washington for Jobs and Freedom organized by A. Philip Randolph, Bayard Rustin, and others.[124] In an e-mail to Mark Levy, Linzer gave this remarkable and interesting anecdote about that trip which I think is worth reproducing here at length:

> I went down [to the March in DC] on the staff bus, a very uncomfortable school bus. Our departure, from the March office on 130th Street in Harlem, was scheduled for something like 1:00 am, but was delayed by two bomb threats. When we got to Washington, I headed straight for the staff tent, even though I had a podium pass. I climbed under a table and fell asleep! I actually slept through Martin Luther King, Jr.'s speech! ... Political speeches made at rallies are not usually known for their historic value. I'd been to hundreds of rallies by 1963 and didn't expect King's speech to be as dramatic as it was. I had read the original text for John Lewis's speech a few days earlier and expected it to be the highlight of the March. Was I wrong about that![125]

As stated earlier, because he was unable to go for Freedom Summer due to his age, Linzer distributed flyers for CORE activities on campus. Some of the flyers he distributed read, "You are asked to give the equivalent cost of one meal to a fund being raised by Q.C. CORE, Student Christian Association, Hillel, and the Northern Student Movement for the people in Mississippi who are being denied the basic essentials of existence because they participated in voter registration drives."[126] Other flyers went further, stating, "A rally will be held on campus at 1:00 (free hour) to explain the Mississippi situation in greater detail, and to promote greater student awareness and personal commitment to the Civil Rights Movement. There will be both on-campus and off-campus speakers. Please inform your friends!"[127] By way of explanation of what was expected, some of the flyers went on to note, "We are asking the student body on this day to forgo lunch and /or snacks, and to donate the money usually spent on food to the people being denied government aid due to economic reprisals for working on voter registration in Mississippi."[128] Regarding where to drop the donations, the appeal stated, "Places for donations will be provided in the cafeteria and the CMC by Queens College CORE.... Please drop into the CORE office in the back of the lower lounge (in CMC)."[129] Linzer, along with other members of the QC chapter of CORE, participated in picketing the World's Fair on Wednesday April 22, 1964. In this instance the demonstrators demanded the following:

1. EMPLOYMENT close down all construction sites immediately until the work force in that industry is fully integrated.
2. SLUM HOUSING begin an immediate "rent strike" throughout the ghetto areas.
3. SCHOOLS produce immediately a plan with a timetable for total desegregation of all schools.
4. POLICE BRUTALITY create a Public Review Board, selected by civil liberties, civil rights, and church groups to investigate complaints of police brutality.[130]

In the flyer calling students out for the World's Fair demonstration, the QC chapter of CORE wrote, "All students and faculty members are welcome to participate in our peaceful protest."[131] Another flyer added, "This is a nonviolent demonstration and all participants are expected to abide by all the instructions."[132] Another flyer in Linzer's collection stated, "[Twenty-two thousand] [Blacks] are starving in Leflore County, Mississippi, the place where Emmett Till was murdered. Ross Barnett cut them off from federal surplus food because they tried to vote. Buy a few extra cans of food for the brave people of Mississippi."[133]

Archival material in Linzer's box at the Queens College Civil Rights Archives is indicative of the fact that there was another demonstration organized by SNCC, CORE, and SDS at the US Court house at Foley Square, in New York between Worth Street and Chambers Street. This demonstration was for the release of Dion Diamond—SNCC Field Secretary, Charles McDew—SNCC Chairman 1960–1963, Bob Zellner—SNCC Field secretary, and Ronnie Moore—CORE Field Secretary in the South. These people were arrested in Baton Rouge, Louisiana on trumped-up charges of criminal anarchy because of their participation in voter registration and the promotion of racial justice. The flyer announcing the demonstration stated, "We demonstrate to request the Department of Justice to use its influence to get these illegal charges dropped.... The movement cannot allow the charge of criminal anarchy to stand uncontested."[134] It should also be noted that Elliot was a draft resister during the Vietnam War. Key sections of the Selective Service Act of 1967 were declared unconstitutional in a lawsuit that Elliot and others filed (Linzer, et al., v. Selective Service Board 64, et al.).

* * *

In 1967, Linzer interrupted his studies at Queens College to enroll at the New School for Social Research in an Interdisciplinary program and obtained his B.A. degree in Social Sciences in 1969 from New School University. He obtained his M.A. in Sociology from Queens College, The City University of New York in 1980. He has worked in the publishing industry since 1964, as an indexer from 1969, and as a free-lance indexer from 1971 to present. He belongs to several professional organizations including: the Editorial Freelancers Association (EFA), the American Society for Indexing (ASI). Elliot was president of the New York Chapter of the American Society for Indexing for seven years. He was a co-executive of the Editorial Freelancers Association from 1990–1992 and had served on its board of governors on numerous occasions since 1977. He received the Civil Rights Movement Alumni Award from Queens College in 2009.[135] He lives in New York.

In this chapter we see those who worked behind the scenes for activist causes on and off QC campus. These were the recruiters for the various activist endeavors. They raised funds, gathered books and supplies, and recruited sponsors. They found innovative and imaginative ways to entice those who had the propensity to say yes to come to the cause. Importantly, through their organizing efforts, they provided the vision and the energy needed to center intending activists to charge forward. In some cases, they spearheaded and served as the catalysts that bonded the various interests together. They were involved in the planning and the execution of rallies, marches, sit-ins, demonstrations, seminars, panel discussions, and workshops, which in some cases resulted in higher-than-expected crowds that helped in the recruitment of adherents.

Notes

1. Doug McAdam, *Freedom Summer.* New York, NY: Oxford University Press, 1988; Doug McAdam, "Recruitment to High-Risk Activism: The case of Freedom Summer." *American Journal of Sociology,* Vol. 92, No. 1, 1986, pp. 64–90; Doug McAdam, "Gender as a Mediator of the Activist Experience: The Case of Freedom Summer." *American Journal of Sociology,* Vol. 97, No. 5, 1992, pp. 1211–1240; Doug McAdam and Ronnelle Paulsen, "Specifying the Relationship Between Social Ties and Activism." *American Journal of Sociology,* Vol. 99, No. 3, 1993, pp. 640–667.
2. See Belinda Robnett, "African-American Women in the Civil Rights Movement, 1954–1965: Gender, Leadership, and Micromobilization." *American Journal of Sociology,* Vol. 101, No. 6, 1996, pp. 1661–1693; Belinda Robnett, *How Long? How Long? African-American Women in the Struggle for Civil Rights.* New York, NY: Oxford University Press, 1999, Anthony Oberschall, *Social Conflict and Social Movements.* Englewood Cliffs, NJ: Prentice-Hall, 1973; Eric L. Hirsch, "Sacrifice for the Cause: Group Processes, Recruitment, and Commitment in a Student Social Movement." *American Sociological Review,* Vol. 55, No. 2, 1990, pp. 243–254.
3. Cited in Jerusha O. Conner. *The New Student Activists: The Rise of Neoactivism on College Campuses.* Baltimore, MD: Johns Hopkins University Press, 2020, p. 2.

4. Robnett, "African-American Women," pp. 1661–1667; Robnett, *How Long? How Long?* pp. 12–35.
5. Robnett, "African-American Women in the Civil Rights Movement," pp. 1661–1693; Robnett, *How Long? How Long?* (Intro & Ch.1).
6. Robnett, "African-American Women in the Civil Rights Movement," p. 1661.
7. Ibid., p. 1664.
8. Ibid.
9. Charles Payne, "Men Led, but Women Organized: Movement Participation of Women in the Mississippi Delta." In Vicki L. Crawford, Jaqueline Anne Rouse, and Barbara Woods, eds. *Women in the Civil Rights Movement: Trailblazers & Torchbearers, 1941–1965.* Bloomington, IN: Indiana University Press, 1993, p. 8.
10. Payne, "Men Led," pp. 8–9.
11. Robnett, "African-American Women in the Civil Rights Movement," p. 1664.
12. This is the second level of leadership. See Oberschall, *Social Conflict and Social Movements,* pp. 146.
13. Robnett, *How Long? How Long?* p. 18.
14. Oberschall. *Social Conflict and Social Movements.* p. 174.
15. See Mark Levy, "A Monumental Dissent." In Jacqueline Johnson, ed. *Finding Freedom: Memorializing the Voices of Freedom Summer.* Oxford, Ohio: Miami University Press, 2013, p. 59. See also Seth Cagin and Philip Dray, *We Are Not Afraid: The Story of Goodman, Schwerner, and Chaney, and the Civil Rights Campaign for Mississippi.* New York: Nation Books, 2006, pp. 234–235.
16. Barbara Omolade, *The Rising Song of African American Women.* New York: Routledge, 1994, p. ix.
17. Ibid.
18. Ibid.
19. Ibid.
20. Omolade, *The Rising Song,* p. x.
21. Ibid.
22. Ibid.
23. Omolade, *The Rising Song,* p. xi. Rosalyn Terborg-Penn encountered a similar situation particularly at George Washington University where she went to graduate school. See her essay, "A

Black History Journey: Encountering Aptheker along the Way." *Nature, Society, and Thought*, Vol. 10, Nos. 1 and 2, 1997. The same goes for bell hooks, *Teaching to Transgress: Education as the Practice of Freedom*. New York, Routledge, 1994, pp. 3–4.
24. Omolade, *The Rising Song*, p. xi.
25. Ibid.
26. bell hooks, *Teaching to Transgress*, p. 3.
27. Ibid.
28. Ibid., pp. 3–4. See also Marilyn Allman Maye et al., *Seven Sisters and a Brother: Friendship, Resistance, and Untold Truths Behind Black Student Activism in the 1960s*. Coral Gables, FL: Books & Books Press, 2021, p.166.
29. Omolade, *The Rising Song*, p. xi.
30. Ibid.
31. Ibid.
32. Ibid.
33. Seth Cagin and Philip Dray, *We are not Afraid: The Story of Goodman, Schwerner, and Chaney and the Civil Rights Campaign for Mississippi*. New York: Nation Books, 2006, p. 234.
34. Omolade, *The Rising Song*, pp. xi–xii.
35. See Omolade, *The Rising Song*, p. xii.
36. Ibid.
37. Ibid., p. ix.
38. "Freedom Week, Queens College, April 20–24, 1964. STATEMENT OF PURPOSE." Box 1 folder 9, Barbara (Jones) Omolade Collection, Department of Special Collections and Archives, Queens College, City University of New York.
39. Ibid.
40. Ibid.
41. "Freedom Week, April 20–24: To all Organization Presidents." Box 1, folder 9, Barbara (Jones) Omolade Collection, Department of Special Collections and Archives, Queens College, City University of New York.
42. "FREEDOM WEEK: APRIL 20–24th: TO ALL MEMBERS OF THE FACULTY." Box 1, folder 9, Barbara (Jones) Omolade Collection, Department of Special Collections and Archives, Queens College, City University of New York. Italics added.
43. Ibid.
44. Ibid.

45. Ibid.
46. Corinne Klee, "Barbara (Jones) Omolade: Biographical Note." Department of Special Collections and Archives, Queens College, City University of New York.
47. See Box 1, folder 9, Barbara (Jones) Omolade Collection, Department of Special Collections and Archives, Queens College, City University of New York.
48. "FREEDOM WEEK: APRIL 20–24th: TO ALL MEMBERS OF THE FACULTY." Box 1 folder 9, Barbara (Jones) Omolade Collection, Department of Special Collections and Archives, Queens College, City University of New York.
49. See Cagin and Dray. *We are not Afraid*, pp. 48–49.
50. Ibid., p. 234.
51. Ibid., p. 235. Andrew Goodman's name is listed as number 7 in Barbara's sign-in sheet. See Box 1, folder 8, Barbara (Jones) Omolade Collection, Department of Special Collections and Archives, Queens College, City University of New York.
52. Mark Levy, "Additions to the QC Roll Call Appendix1: The Search for Queens College – Mississippi Freedom Summer'64 Connections."
53. Cagin and Dray, *We are not Afraid*, p. 237.
54. Ibid.
55. Mark Levy, "A Monumental Dissent," p. 59.
56. Barbara Jones Omolade, "Building a New World." In Faith S. Holsaert et al., eds. *Hands on the Freedom Plow: Personal Accounts by Women in SNCC*. Urbana, IL: University of Illinois Press, 2010, p. 388.
57. Ibid.
58. Ibid. p. 389.
59. Ibid.
60. Ibid.
61. Nelson Mandela, *Long Walk to Freedom: The Autobiography of Nelson Mandela*. Boston, MA: Little, Brown and Company, 1995, p. 624.
62. Barbara, "Building a New World," p. 389.
63. Ibid., pp. 389–390.
64. Marion Barry, cited in Elizabeth Martinez, ed., *Letters from Mississippi: Reports from Civil Rights Volunteers & Poetry of the*

1964 Freedom Summer. Brookline, MA: Zephyr Press, 2007, p. iii.
65. Charles H. Wesley and Thelma D. Perry, *History Is A Weapon: The Mis-Education of the Negro*, 1969, pp. 1–2. http://www.historyisaweapon.com/defcon1/misedne.html (Accessed 8/25/ 2009).
66. See Molefi Kete Asante, *Kemet, Afrocentricity and Knowledge*, Trenton, NJ: Africa World Press, Inc., 1992, pp. 161–167.
67. Carter G. Woodson, *The Mis-Education of the Negro*. Trenton, NJ: Africa World Press, Inc., 1993, p. 7. Originally published in 1933.
68. Barbara Jones Omolade, "Building a New World," pp. 390–391.
69. Ibid., p. 391.
70. Ibid.
71. Julian Bond, "Introduction." In Elizabeth Martinez, ed. *Letters from Mississippi: Reports from Civil Rights Volunteers & Poetry of the 1964 Freedom Summer*. Brookline, MA: Zephyr Press, 2007, p. iv.
72. E-mail correspondence between Dorothy M. Zellner and Mark Levy, December 4, 2018. Debra L. Schultz, *Going South: Jewish Women in the Civil Rights Movement*. New York: New York University Press, 2001, p. 6.
73. Dorothy M. Zellner, "My Real Vocation." In Faith S. Holsaert et al., eds. *Hands on the Freedom Plow: Personal Accounts by Women in SNCC*. Urbana, IL: University of Illinois Press, 2010, p. 311.
74. Ibid., p. 312.
75. Ibid., p. 311.
76. Debra L. Schultz, "Why I tracked Them Down: Our Unsung Civil Rights Movement Heroines." *Lilith,* Fall, 1999, p. 12.
77. See Jane Bond Moore, "A SNCC Blue Book." In Faith S. Holsaert et al., eds. *Hands on the Freedom Plow: Personal Accounts by Women in SNCC*. Urbana, IL: University of Illinois Press, 2010, p. 328.
78. Zellner, "My Real Vocation," p. 314.
79. Schultz, *Going South*, p. 6.
80. Ibid.
81. Ibid.
82. Ibid., p. 146.
83. Zellner, "My Real Vocation," p. 315.

84. Schultz, *Going South*, p. 34.
85. Ibid., p. 35.
86. Ibid.
87. Ibid.
88. Ibid., p. 34.
89. Bob Moses cited in John Dittmer, *Local People: The Struggle for Civil Rights in Mississippi*. Urbana, IL: University of Illinois Press, 1994, p. 194.
90. Interview with Dorothy Zellner 8/21/2023.
91. Zellner, "My Real Vocation," p. 316.
92. Ibid.
93. Ibid.
94. Schultz, *Going South*.
95. Ibid., p. 34.
96. Zellner, "My Real Vocation," p. 322.
97. Shomial Ahmad, "Queens College and Civil Rights: Alumni Reflect on Activism 50 Years Ago" PSC CUNY May 2014 (clarion/may/2014).
98. Ibid.
99. Zellner, "My Real Vocation," p. 322.
100. Charles M. Payne, *I've Got the Light of Freedom: The Organizing Tradition and the Mississippi Freedom Struggle*. Berkeley, CA: University of California Press, 2007, p. 174.
101. G. Bestick, "Review" of *Freedom Summer* by Sally Belfrage. http://www.amazon.com/Freedom-Summer-Carter-Woodson-Institute/pd/0813912997/ref=s ... (Accessed 3/7/2013).
102. Moore, "A SNCC Blue Book," p. 328.
103. This was also at a time when the alliances that made up the COFO working arrangement had begun to unravel.
104. See for example, Dorothy M. Zellner, "King's words live in Palestinian City." *Dominican Life, USA*. http://www.domlife.org/2011Stories/mlk_zellner.htm (Accessed 6/16/2012).
105. Dorothy M. Zellner (Biographical Details). http://cosmos.ucc.ie/cs1064/jabowen/IPSC/php/authors.php?auid=25409.
106. See "How CORE Views the Fair: Symbol of American Hypocrisy." Box 1, folder 3, Arthur Gatti Collection, Department of Special Collections and Archives, Queens College, City University of New York.

107. Box 1, folder 3, Andrew Berman Collection, Department of Special Collections and Archives, Queens College, City University of New York.
108. "Letter to New Q.C. SDS Members." Box 1, folder 3, Andrew Berman Collection, Department of Special Collections and Archives, Queens College, City University of New York.
109. Ibid.
110. "SDS Fast: From Stupor to Involvement." Box 1, folder 12, Andrew Berman Collection, Department of Special Collections and Archives, Queens College, City University of New York.
111. "Fellow Democratic Radicals and Other Members of QCSDS. "Box 1, folder 2, Andrew Berman Collection, Department of Special Collections and Archives, Queens College, City University of New York.
112. "Dear Queens College, SDS member/friend." Box 1, folder 3, Andrew Berman Collection, Department of Special Collections and Archives, Queens College, City University of New York.
113. The Red Book was Queens College Manual of Policies and Procedures for Student Activities known on campus as the Red Book.
114. "SDS Publishes 'Illegal' Newsletter." Box 1, folder 12, Andrew Berman Collection, Department of Special Collections and Archives, Queens College, City University of New York.
115. *The Activist: Why We Publish.* Box 1, folder 12, Andrew Berman Collection, Department of Special Collections and Archives, Queens College, City University of New York.
116. "SDS Publishes 'Illegal' Newsletter." Box 1, folder 12, Andrew Berman Collection, Department of Special Collections and Archives, Queens College, City University of New York.
117. Ibid.
118. Ibid.
119. *The Activist: Why We Publish.* Box 1, folder 12, Andrew Berman Collection, Department of Special Collections and Archives, Queens College, City University of New York.
120. "The One Seventy-Five Fund: Students for a Democratic Society." Box 1, folder 3, Andrew Berman Collection, Department of Special Collections and Archives, Queens College, City University of New York.

121. "Office of the Dean of Students." Box 1, folder 12, Andrew Berman Collection, Department of Special Collections and Archives, Queens College, City University of New York.
122. "Renegade Newspaper Hits Queens Campus." Box 1, folder 12, Andrew Berman Collection, Department of Special Collections and Archives, Queens College, City University of New York.
123. See, "SDS's Illegal Paper Quits Under S. A. Pressure." Box 1, folder 12, Andrew Berman Collection, Department of Special Collections and Archives, Queens College, City University of New York.
124. See Levy, "QC 50s–70s Activist Student Narrative."
125. Ibid.
126. "Fast for Freedom." Box 1, folder 9, Elliot Linzer Collection, Department of Special Collections and Archives, Queens College, City University of New York.
127. Ibid.
128. Ibid.
129. Ibid.
130. "Our People Demand." Box 1, folder 9, Elliot Linzer Collection, Department of Special Collections and Archives, Queens College, City University of New York.
131. "The World's Fair Demonstration by Q.C. Students." Box 1, folder 9, Elliot Linzer Collection, Department of Special Collections and Archives, Queens College, City University of New York.
132. "Instructions for Pickets, World's Fair Project." Box 1, folder 9, Elliot Linzer Collection, Department of Special Collections and Archives, Queens College, City University of New York.
133. "[Blacks] are Starving in Leflore County." Box 1, folder 9, Elliot Linzer Collection, Department of Special Collections and Archives, Queens College, City University of New York.
134. "Picket Demonstration." Box 1, folder 9, Elliot Linzer Collection, Department of Special Collections and Archives, Queens College, City University of New York.
135. See Mr. Linzer's LinkedIn page.

CHAPTER 6

The Rebuilders

In this chapter, we meet the students that I call the rebuilders—those who, in many ways, helped shape and rebuild in their activist journeys. A key moment began during the January break of 1965, where a group of six Queens College students including Robert (Bob) Masters, Jonathan Alexander, Arthur Gatti, Walter Jarsky, Robert Madden, and Gus Peros went to Tougaloo, Mississippi, to repair churches that had been burned down during Freedom Summer. The team spent 560 work hours rebuilding Black churches that had been burned by White supremacists during the summer of 1964.[1] The program was sponsored by the Queens College Mississippi Freedom Project of which Robert Masters was the president.[2] The students and their faculty adviser, Professor Sidney B. Simon, spent twelve days in Tougaloo rebuilding four churches that had been burned down by the KKK because these churches had been used as Freedom Schools, and for voter registration during the summer of 1964.[3] The work was coordinated by the Committee of Concern, an interracial group composed of Mississippi clergies of all faiths. The technical aspect of the work was handled by the Society of Friends. The QC volunteer activists worked with local Mississippi College students. The students executed work such as hanging ceilings, landscaping, and putting up roof shingles,[4] and they spent two days painting church pews.[5] The refurbished churches were all built with brick.

© The Author(s), under exclusive license to Springer Nature Switzerland AG 2024
M. O. Bassey, *Student Activism in 1960s America*, Palgrave Studies in the History of Social Movements,
https://doi.org/10.1007/978-3-031-54794-2_6

* * *

While in Tougaloo, the students maintained that safety was a major issue. They "admitted that they experienced general tension and apprehension for their safety."[6] As a result, the coordinators always applied strict rules for the volunteers. For one, they could not drive at night. When traveling, they had to move in pairs, and according to Professor Simon, the group was watched at night by armed Black guards.[7] Professor Simon recounted how they were followed by two trucks with headlights pointed directly at them. To their surprise, in their apprehension that members of the Ku Klux Klan were following to mug them, they later discovered that the followers were the Black guards who were assigned to protect them.[8] An excellent report card was given to Professor Simon for the exemplary work done by the Queens College team in rebuilding churches in Tougaloo. The letter of commendation was written by William P. Davis, Chairman, Committee of Concern.[9]

* * *

At the written request of Arthur Gatti, a Queens College student activist, the Queens College team was permitted to return to Mississippi to participate in the rebuilding of Black churches during the Easter break of 1965, "because the group from Queens College had made a positive contribution in January,"[10] and the Queens College students fit in well with the community. The letter to Arthur Gatti reads inter alia:

> I accepted your offer of a group to help at Easter time, because the group from Queens College had made a positive contribution in January. You are aware of the tensions under which we work in Mississippi. We have plenty of trouble in the State without importing any more. Therefore, it is important that your group come with a motivation to help in the complex human relations problem as well as work on rebuilding a church.[11]

Interestingly, the invitation noted that Queens College students would be put to work in Meridian,[12] a city with increased potential for violence. Lawrence Scott of the committee of concern's letter to Gatti made this point very clearly: "I am placing the Queens group in Meridian which is one of the tougher spots in the state."[13] The letter noted that the committee wanted volunteers who would help rebuild churches in Mississippi and not Civil Rights workers because there was a higher likelihood that Civil Rights workers would trigger the KKK. Scott pointed out how easily rumors about Civil Rights volunteers could wind up provoking the KKK in Mississippi through this example of Notre Dame students:

> A group of ten from Notre Dame have just completed ten days of exemplary work on the three rural churches north of Meridian. The false rumor got out that they were a new civil rights group in town, and the Catholic hospital where they lived was harassed. The KKK was evidently activated and two days after the group left, attempts were made to burn two [Black] churches in Meridian. Since then, there have been news stories and favorable public interpretations of the church rebuilding program. Thus, we don't want to take a chance on any group who wants to run around all over town in either [Black] beer joints or civil rights circles. Such activity would be immediately interpreted as deception on the part of the Committee of Concern and Mennonites and Quakers who sponsor your appearance in Mississippi.[14]

To decrease the likelihood of violence, this group of Queens College volunteers lived with white families and had about eight students from Mississippi colleges working with them. QC students who led the second church rebuilding efforts in Mississippi included: Bob Madden, Marc Helman, Lewis Fein, Ronald (Ron) Pollack, Bob Morrissey, with Professor Steve Zeigfinger listed as the faculty adviser.[15]

* * *

One of the QC student activists who led the rebuilding efforts in Mississippi was Arthur Gatti. Arthur Gatti entered QC in the early 1960s and graduated in 1965 with a minor in poetry. He won the 1965 CUNY-wide Dwight Durling Award for a manuscript of poetry. Because of the Vietnam War, he entered the "world of 1960s activism." Gatti was an active member of the Queens College CORE and was a co-founder of Queens College Students for a Democratic Society (QCSDS). He collaborated extensively with Mario Savio, (who was his friend from QC), and the leader of the Free Speech Movement at the University of California, Berkeley. The two organizations that Gatti belonged to were at the forefront in the fight for social, racial, and economic justice, and throughout his sojourn at QC, he was highly involved in social and political activism. In the summer of 1963, he, along with a group of volunteers from QC, went to Mexico as members of the Queens College Mexico Volunteers organized by the Queens College's Newman House. The purpose of the trip was to help impoverished Mexicans with some development projects. While in Mexico, Gatti and his group were stationed in the city of Taxco in Guerrero state. In Taxco, Gatti's group helped in building a laundry facility for the poor.[16] Mario Savio participated in the Taxco development project, where he acted as the translator for the QC group. Unfortunately, Savio did not return to Mexico for the second trip, but his friend Arthur Gatti did.[17] In the second trip, Gatti and his group built a school.[18] This school is still in use in Mexico.[19]

Gatti was involved with other activist groups such as the Queens College Mississippi Freedom Project, the anti-Vietnam War movement, the Youth International Party, the War Resisters League, and the National Mobilization Committee to End the War in Vietnam. He participated in numerous protests both on and off campus, including protests in response to the disappearance and murder of Andrew Goodman, Michael Schwerner, and James Chaney in Mississippi in 1964. He was a co-community organizer with Tom Hayden (deceased) in Newark, New Jersey, working under the auspices of the Newark Community Union Project (NCUP), which was the Student for a Democratic Society-inspired effort to organize in poor communities as a means of combating inequality and disparity in Newark. Gatti was appalled by the aftermath of the deadly Newark uprising of 1967. He took part in the recovery efforts and documented the terrible damage done by the riots to people, goods, and property.

Gatti said that activism and political involvement led him to journalism.[20] He has written and published hundreds of articles and columns, published two books, written many downtown staged comedies, and sold a screenplay to Hollywood.[21] He now writes and teaches poetry. He has won numerous writing awards and is a member of the Producer-Writers Guild of America.[22] As a continuation of his activism, during the AIDS crises in the 1980s, Gatti was a founding sous chef at the West Village's St. Luke in the Fields Saturday Dinner for PWAs. This project provided Saturday dinners and weekend teas to thousands of AIDS patients. Gatti spent almost 10 years cooking on Saturdays for people with AIDS because of his concern at seeing so many of his friends and neighbors sick or dying from the disease.[23]

* * *

Professor Sidney (Sid) B. Simon (1927–2023) was in the department of education at Queens College and worked closely with the Student Help Project; the Jamaica-Virginia Tutorial Project and CORE. He was born in Pittsburgh, Pennsylvania in 1927. He attended Penn State University after WWII using the GI Bill and graduated in 1949. He joined the Department of Education at Queens College in 1959. Dr. Simon's involvement as faculty advisor for the Student Help Project and CORE was not his first attempt at activism. Earlier in his academic career, he joined both his colleagues and students to picket the New York World's Fair because they thought it was a wasteful exuberance of the money that could have been better used for education.[24] Also, they saw the fair as a "fantasy world of progress and abundance shown in the midst of poverty in the Northern urban cities and the horror of Southern legalized brutality."[25]

Dr. Sidney Simon was the faculty adviser to the QC students who went to Tougaloo, Mississippi in January 1965 to rebuild burned down Black churches. While in Mississippi, he and his group were deeply touched by the level of inhumanity that was apparent in the South. By all accounts, oppression and discrimination against Blacks constituted the most intractable problems that plagued southern society. But as bad as these were, the team was flabbergasted by the kindness, joyousness, and hospitality of their Black hosts.[26]

The contributions of the Queens College volunteers in rebuilding churches in Mississippi was very much appreciated. In a letter addressed to Dr. Simon by William P. Davis, Chairman, Committee of Concern, Davis expressed great appreciation for the good work done by Dr. Simon and his students in Mississippi. The letter reads:

Dear Dr. Simon:

Time alone will reveal the vast contribution you and Queens College students made to further good human relations in Mississippi.

I am grateful for the copy of the press release and for the fine work you did. I wish I had adequate words to express my appreciation.

Enclosed is a copy of the report I gave at the hearing of the Civil Rights Commission.

Please give my thanks to all the students.

With kindest personal regards,

Very sincerely yours,

Signed

William P. Davis, Chairman

Committee of Concern[27]

Dr. Simon left Queens College in 1965 after six years to assume the position of associate professor at Temple University. Four years later, in 1969, he left Temple for the University of Massachusetts as a full professor. He retired as Professor Emeritus from the University of Massachusetts. Dr. Simon had authored or coauthored about thirteen books, including renowned best sellers, *Values Clarification* and *Getting Unstuck: Breaking Through Your Barriers to Change*. He had published over one hundred articles. His articles had appeared in academic and self-help journals and magazines such as *Reader's Digest, Ladies Home Journal, Glamour,* and many others. "He was an internationally and nationally recognized authority in the areas of values clarification and values realization, self-esteem, and negative criticism."[28] Dr. Simon was nominated for the teacher of the year award twice and received the Golden Apple award and the National Self-Esteem Conference award. In correspondence with me, Dr. Simon said, "Thank YOU, for being willing to keep alive those memories."[29]

Dr. Simon led seminars and workshops for over fifty years. He was a renowned guest speaker who had addressed audiences at *The Betty Ford Center, Oprah,* and at *The Donahue Show*.[30] He died in 2023 at the age of 96.

* * *

You are here because history is being made here and this generation of students is found where history is being made.
—Dr. Martin Luther King, Jr.

Another initiative undertaken by some Queens College students and faculty was the Summer Community Organization and Political Education (SCOPE) Project. This was an undertaking of the Southern Christian Leadership Conference (SCLC) headed by Dr. Martin Luther King, Jr. The purpose of the SCOPE project was to begin the voter registration process for Blacks while the Voting Rights Act was pending before Congress. SCOPE was under the direction of SCLC's Voter Registration and Political Education Director, Rev. Hosea L. Williams, who was also a key aide to Dr. Martin Luther King, Jr. The volunteers were assigned to register African American voters in over 120 counties in about six Southern states.[31] The exercise resulted in the registration of 49,302 new Black voters in the South.[32] Some of the SCOPE activists who are affiliated with Queens College include: Dean Savage; Rabbi Moshe Mitchell (Mickey) Shur; Barbara Williams Emerson and Peter Geffen.

* * *

Dean Savage was born in Washington State. He went to Stanford University where he obtained his bachelor's degree in history in 1963. In 1965, as a graduate student at Columbia University, he was recruited by an acclaimed history professor, James P. Shenton, to join the SCOPE project. He volunteered for service in the South and was posted to Orangeburg, South Carolina. Savage spent the summer of 1965 registering Black people to vote. He was arrested for protesting a voter registration slowdown, and as he recollected the incident later, he said, "A number of us held a sit-in, and with the expected result, everybody got arrested."[33] He went on to say, "We got to see a part of America that many of us would have never imagined."[34] Dean participated in many Civil Rights demonstrations even before he came to Columbia including a demonstration outside Woolworth's in Palo Alto, California in the 1960s in support of the Greensboro Four.

Dean Savage obtained his master's degree from Columbia University in history and his PhD from the same institution in sociology in 1975. Professor Savage started his career at Queens College in 1971. He retired as professor emeritus in the Department of Sociology where he had served as the chair at different times. For many years he taught a senior seminar on "Inequality in Higher Education," and for decades his research focused on tracking the outcomes of CUNY PhD recipients in sociology as a way of improving data on PhD placements. In this study, all the students who completed their PhDs in sociology at CUNY Graduate Center were required to complete the Survey of Earned Doctorates (SED).[35] As of September 2013, Professor Savage had created a database of 471 people dating back to 1971.[36] Between 2013 and 2019, he also assembled tables of the number and share of Queens College baccalaureate graduates who pursued further education, by degrees sought and program level.[37] Although he has retired, he still works on projects concerning student outcomes and on QC Oral History collection relating to former faculty and staff.

* * *

Rabbi Moshe Mitchell (Mickey) Shur was born in New England in 1944. He attended Columbia University in New York and was also recruited for SCOPE by Professor James P. Shenton. Moshe Shur served in Orangeburg, South Carolina, principally registering Black people to vote.[38] His assignments included talking to locals in churches and conducting educational seminars on why Blacks should register to vote. As he stated in the SCOPE Chapter 33 Interview, "Our plan was just in political education."[39] He served as the chairman of the SCOPE project at Columbia University in 1965 and became the national chairman of the student committee of the organization (SCOPE) in 1966.[40] During their assignments in Orangeburg, SCOPE volunteers worked collaboratively with a Civil Rights attorney, who was their point person.[41] As Rabbi Shur told me in an interview, he went to South Carolina not with any agenda, but as a consistent advocate of Black equality, because he knew that was the right thing to do, and because of his desire to help people who had never been given a chance. In other words, by registering Blacks to vote, he hoped, they would be empowered to take their destinies in their own hands.[42] In a *Daily News* interview on February 13, 2006, Rabbi Shur said, "This was something of an injustice, and with my Jewish background, if you see an injustice, you have to do something about it. And Dr. King had taken a stand, and it was the right thing."[43] He admitted though, that he didn't realize the significance of what he was doing until many years later.[44]

In Orangeburg, Rabbi Shur and his other colleagues lived with people in the community and traveled the rough, rural, red clay roads for miles to get Black people to register to vote. The volunteers were often led by Black civil rights volunteers who were conversant with the topography of the area: they pointed out houses of potential voters.[45] Some Blacks were, for the most part, receptive to the call to register to vote. However, some disappointments were experienced when Blacks were disallowed from registering through White machinations such as closing the registration centers ahead of schedule.[46]

The volunteer experience for Rabbi Shur was exhilarating and must have opened the doors for him to begin to think about his present profession.[47] As he spent time registering voters, he developed a deep spiritual connection to the work he was doing. Indeed, Rabbi Shur later noted that volunteer work is a living memory that branded him and molded his future. He took great pride in his advocacy for the Black community, and in the SCOPE Chapter 33 interview, he explained in unambiguous terms why he held strongly to that position:

> Well, the poverty of the people down here. That really struck home. I came here just, you know, interested in helping people, and I've become a little bit louder, so to speak. I can show this by my speaking to churches. I used to speak quietly, but now I get up, and I yell...[48]

Rabbi Shur, of course, did not blame Blacks in the South for their lack of forcefulness about their living conditions, because he understood quite clearly that the people's apathy derived from the "intimidation that they've suffered all of their lives."[49] He argued that to understand the people's apathy fully was to understand their lack of exposure to the outside world. Equally important, he explained that the purpose of their volunteer work was to speak for those who had no influence and to convince Blacks of the supreme importance of creating a countervailing platform of struggle. He was jailed with thirty-four others in Orangeburg, South Carolina, for demonstrating against a voter registration slowdown.[50] Validation, universal acclaim, and acceptance of their volunteer work in the South, he stated, was more aligned with helping the people than where those who helped fell on the political spectrum:

> It's a desire...to help the people, you know. These people are basically one; they're poor people, and they've never had a chance, and they've been treated badly. I think that's the issue, and I know you might belong to some sort of group, either right or left... you're trying to help people.[51]

Rabbi Shur thought at the time that the actions of the volunteers were idealistic. "I don't think anybody has reached the political state where they think that anything they're doing is going to change the whole South."[52] But these volunteers were visionaries because on August 6, 1965, President Lyndon B. Johnson signed the Voting Rights Act into law and for this, the volunteers could claim a great victory. Rabbi Shur told me with great pride that during his volunteer service for two consecutive summers (1965 and1966) in the South, he had the great privilege of meeting important civil rights leaders like Dr. Martin Luther King Jr., Bayard Rustin, Hosea Williams, and Andrew Young.[53] Before volunteering for the SCOPE Project, Rabbi Shur had participated in other activist causes. For example, he participated in a march in Harlem where twenty thousand people participated, and he went to Washington in March 1965 to talk to his congressman and his senator about the passage of the Voting Rights bill.[54] He also worked at a youth center in Harlem, taking children out to the park once a month.[55]

Rabbi Shur completed a joint degree in History and Biblical Studies from Columbia University and the Jewish Theological Seminary respectively in 1966. He received his Juris Doctor (J.D.) from Wayne State University Law School in 1969, and a master's degree in Near Eastern Languages and Literature from the University of Michigan. He received his Rabbinic Ordination: Yeshiva Toras Yisroel, Jerusalem, Israel in 1976. He joined Queens College in 1979 and served as Rabbi, Executive Director, University Chaplain: Queens College Hillel from 1979 to 2011. Before joining Queens College, he was Rabbi, Executive Director: Hillel at the University of Virginia from 1977 to 1979. He is currently director emeritus of the Queens College Hillel Foundation and Adjunct Lecturer in Jewish Studies at Queens College. Rabbi Shur has had a wide and varied career as a lecturer, scholar in residence, and musician at different times in the United States, Canada, South America, Aruba, Bermuda, the Caribbean, Australia, New Zealand, and Israel from 1977 to the present. To date he serves as Cantor during High Holidays at Northbrook Community Synagogue, Northbrook, IL from 1995 to present. His musical productions and CDs include: *The Diaspora Yeshiva Band*, 1974 -1977; *The Moshe Shur Band & A Shur Thing*, 1977- present. Rabbi Shur continues his work in social justice, directing the program, "In the Footsteps of Dr. King," which "seeks to provide students with the knowledge and skills needed to combat bigotry and intolerance in today's society." Students in this program travel to major sites of the civil rights movement and learn from educators who worked with some of the great civil rights leaders.[56]

* * *

Barbara Williams Emerson is the daughter of the well-known activist and director of the SCOPE project, Rev. Hosea L. Williams. Barbara was born in Bainbridge, Georgia on March 4, 1948. She obtained her BA in sociology from New York University and earned a Master of Social Work from Columbia University in Community Organization and Planning and a Doctor of Social Welfare degree from Columbia University in Administration, Planning, and Policy Analysis. For many years, she was the director of the SEEK program at QC and rose to the rank of Dean of Special Programs at the college. In 1994, Barbara was appointed Associate Provost at the New School for Social Research. She got promoted to the position of Vice President for Program Development in the same institution. Barbara later took appointment as the Vice President for Academic Affairs at Audrey Cohen College.

Barbara once explained that as the daughter of Rev. Hosea Williams, she was involuntarily swept into the activist movement, because for her family, "being in the movement was a given."[57] She started as a voter registration organizer at the age of fifteen. Her activist work took her to various states and places including Georgia, Florida, Alabama, Mississippi, Washington D. C., Chicago, and New York. She took part in the March on Washington in 1963 and in the Selma-to-Montgomery March in 1965. She worked mostly in the SCOPE office under the direction of her father and remembers spending "summers and vacations in Atlanta engaged in the demonstration, march, campaign, or project of the day being waged by the force that was Hosea Williams."[58] She was arrested at one of her protests in Grenada, Mississippi in 1966. Barbara has since retired from formal employment but participates in "Hosea Feed the Hungry and Homeless," dinners started by her family. She gives lectures in the United States and internationally on the Civil Rights Movement. She is President of Emerson Consultants, Ltd.

* * *

Peter Geffen was a student at Queens College in 1964 when he heard that his classmate, Andrew Goodman had been murdered by the Ku Klux Klan on the outskirts of Philadelphia, Mississippi, and decided to join the fight as an activist. Accordingly, he traveled down to Orangeburg, South Carolina the following year against his father's wishes to join the SCOPE project to participate in the struggle for civil rights.[59] Geffen's major reason for venturing South and joining SCOPE was rooted in his desire to honor Goodman's memory by continuing the work he had been doing before he was murdered.[60] Geffen went on to provide another reason for his action, "As a Jew, the impact on a young person born after the War of the Holocaust—an experience in which good people stood by as people were deprived of their rights and eventually murdered—there was no way of not looking at the situation and seeing a dramatic parallel."[61]

Geffen went to Orangeburg, South Carolina to participate in SCOPE. In Orangeburg, he was involved in voter registration and taught Black people how to read and write so that they could register to vote. He was among the five hundred volunteers who were beaten, jailed, and threatened with death for their courage in getting Black people to register to vote. Geffen and his colleagues visited churches, Black homes, and wherever Black people lived to encourage them to register to vote because, as he declared many years later, "We shared a dynamic need to change the order of the ways of the world in which we lived." And as he saw it "These were movements of young people."[62] Peter Geffen is a graduate of Queens College and the founder of The Abraham Joshua Heschel School in New York City as well as the founder and president of The *KIVUNIM* Institute. Peter was the recipient of the Covenant Award in 2012.

* * *

Another Queens College student activist who took pride in civil rights advocacy was Joan Nestle. Joan was a versatile activist who had earlier participated in freedom bus rides into Philadelphia and Baltimore. She was an early organizer, activist, and leader who influenced friends to become activists and marched at demonstrations at Queens College. She "sat with CORE (Congress of Racial Equality) comrades at soda fountains while the no-trespassing laws were read to [them], and they were dragged out of restaurants that Black CORE members could not even enter."[63] She documented a vivid description of one of her activist experiences and its aftermath as follows:

> We, the white protestors, acted as a fifth column. Usually under the leadership of a minister, we would enter one of the segregated restaurants, pretending to be quiet couples. Then we would join each other at a table, remembering never to eat or drink anything that was on the table, not even the water. At a given signal, we would all rise, and the respectable

air of the restaurant would be broken by the minister reading a statement announcing who we were and that we would not leave until our Black comrades, who were now picketing and shouting outside the restaurant, were allowed to join us.[64]

Joan began her fight for social justice and social equality in college by supporting the Civil Rights Movement in the 1960s. She marched at demonstrations at Queens College, protested with members of SANE for a sane nuclear policy, and worked with her friends who had founded an anti-HUAC group on campus to fight the House Un-American Activities Committee. Joan and others from QC rode busses from the QC gates to Washington, DC where they were gassed in front of the Pentagon. She and other activists from QC attended meetings of HUAC to defend Paul Robeson and JoAnne Grant's right to travel outside the country. These activists were sometimes called "the scum of the earth."[65] Joan was moved to join the national movement after seeing pictures of a "... Black woman held to the ground by three white sheriffs, a nightstick across her throat, her skirt pushed up above her knees."[66] She described her other horrors to include the murder of Jimmie Lee Jackson, the clubbing and beatings in Selma and Montgomery, the jailing of thousands, and children forced to walk in hate-filled streets. Appalled by seeing mothers, fathers, sons, and daughters gunned down, tear gassed, whipped, water hosed by city police, state police, and the National Guard, she decided to join the national fight for social justice,[67] because all these forces were led against people who just wanted to vote.

Joan and her friend, Judith flew to Atlanta on their way to Selma, Alabama, because she wanted to go, "do battle with another enemy besides [her] own despair, to use [her] body not for lovemaking but for filling the ranks in the struggle to change history."[68] In Selma, they joined other young men and women who were pursuing the same cause. Joan and Judith stayed in the home of a Black family, Mr., and Mrs. Washington, before Judith ultimately moved elsewhere because of her assignment. In their second week, Joan was assigned to a group doing voter registration and community organizing in the poor neighborhoods near Selma. Joan told the story of how during their first week when she and Judith were returning home after 10:00 p.m., they encountered some angry White men in a pickup truck with rifles cradled in their arms. One man shouted at them, "We're going to get you, you nigger lovers."[69] Indeed, as Joan expressed, this was not a joke because, "this was a time and a place where Black children died because they wanted to be free."[70] At the end of the program, Joan joined thousands of marchers from Selma to Montgomery. In her social justice and activist journey, Joan was beaten, spat upon, and stoned.

* * *

Like some of the other activists we have seen thus far who joined the movement because of their backgrounds, Joan's penchant for advocacy has roots in both her upbringing and her identity. Joan was born on May 12, 1940, in New York. She was raised by her mother, Regina Nestle, because Joan's father died before she was born. She attended Martin Van Buren High School in Queens, New York, and studied at Queens College where she obtained her BA degree in English in 1963.[71] She obtained an MA degree in English from New York University in 1968 and enrolled in the doctorate program for two years before accepting an appointment at her alma mater, Queens College. She rose to the rank of professor of English and creative writing and instructor in the SEEK Program. Joan joined the Lesbian Liberation Committee in 1971 and was a foundational member of the Gay Academic Union (GAU) in 1972. In 1973, she and other members of the GAU began the collection and preservation of documents and artifacts having to do with lesbian history. The project, which was later known as the Lesbian Herstory Archives, started in Joan's apartment in 1974. The archives hold more than twenty thousand books, twelve thousand photographs, and more than sixteen hundred periodicals today.[72] The Lesbian Herstory Archives "is home to the world's largest collection of materials by and about lesbians and their communities."[73] It is now housed in a brownstone at 484 14th Street in Park Slope, Brooklyn.

Joan has served as an activist in the lesbian community for many years. She has authored two memoirs,[74] and seven other collections on feminist, lesbian and queer history, and culture.[75] She has won numerous literary awards as well.[76] She retired from Queens College in 1995 and now lives in Australia.

* * *

In our mission to educate the youth of the legacy of the Civil Rights Movement, one of my great concerns is for the unsung heroes, and heroines, those

> *oftentimes forgotten foot soldiers whose backs many stand on. I am concerned that their voices be heard, and their names shouted out. I am concerned that our parents' voices be heard and that their names be shouted out and listed in the pages of history.*
> —Frankye Adams-Johnson

Frankye Adams-Johnson and Isaac Foster are two activists who came to Queens College after they had participated in activism in their own state. Frankye Adams-Johnson (aka Malika) grew up in Pocahontas, Mississippi and attended one of the Black public high schools in Jackson, Mississippi. Frankye's recollection of her childhood is that "life was hardship, Black folks working hard, just trying to figure out how to stay alive from day to day."[77] She once narrated the story of her early life in the following words:

> My mother was a domestic, working for pennies in white folks' white houses on paved streets; we were only allowed to visit her from the back door. It seemed that the feudal plantation owners were more concerned about their cotton being picked than they were of a black child's education. When I started going to the district school, there were many days that the yellow school bus would roll by without me or my siblings on it. Such was the life of a sharecropper's daughter. Such were the events of my life that caused my mind to wander and question God about the unfairness of it all. Such were the events that caused me to yearn for freedom, a word foreign to my young vocabulary, but familiar to my heart.[78]

It is therefore not surprising that at the age of seventeen, Frankye was one of the leading organizers of her high school and two other Black high school walkout and march to Jackson, Mississippi to protest poor conditions in their schools in May 1963. During the protest, she recollected how she was "among the hundreds who were dumped in a garbage truck like garbage and hauled off to the state fairground."[79] But having experienced a semblance of freedom, critical multidimensional consciousness, and voice in the protest, there was no turning back. She noted:

> From that one act of courage, I became fired up by the movement; the movement moved me, and I moved with the movement. I became a regular protester, a regular marcher. Like a soldier in the army, I reported dutifully to the COFO office for my movement assignment for the day, whether it

was marching, passing out leaflets, or door-to-door registration, I was on board the freedom train and loving every bit of it."[80]

This period in the history of Mississippi witnessed the murder of Medgar Evers; police brutality against protesters; trigger-happy, racist police officers water hosing protesters, intense assault from members of the racist White Citizens' Council, assaults by Whites, racist slurs, abuses, and other crimes and misdemeanors perpetrated against protesters. The intense abuse dished out to Blacks culminated in Frankye receiving a back injury at the hands of a racist police officer in July 1963.

In the summer of 1964, Frankye was selected, along with other students, to attend a pre-freshman program at Tougaloo College. While at the college, Frankye was more interested in working for the Student Nonviolent Coordinating Committee (SNCC) in different capacities, from working in Freedom Schools to voter registration. She said, "I was so involved with Freedom Summer activities until the official over the pre-freshman dismissed me from the second session of the program,"[81] but there was no turning back from civil rights activism for Frankye at that point.

In 1967, Frankye Adams-Johnson moved to New York. In 1968 she became an active member of the Black Panther Party. Frankye and her sister started a branch of the party in White Plains, New York. Throughout the 1970s, she was engrossed in the activities of the Black Panthers and in community organizing. Interestingly, in the 1980s, Frankye enrolled at Queens College where she obtained a BA in English and later obtained an MA degree in Creative Writing from City College of the City University of New York. Thereafter, she took up employment as a graduate student at City College and was later appointed an instructor of English. She also taught in other institutions of Higher Learning in the New York City Metropolitan Area.

Frankye returned to Mississippi in 1999. She accepted the appointment with Jackson State University in 2002. As a known playwright, fiction writer, and poet she has published several works in literary journals including: *A Love Supreme, Poetry in Performance 20, City College, Poem for Daddy Sugahboy, Poetry in Performance 19, Maw-Maw*, and others.[82] She received the John Oliver Killens Fiction Award for excerpts from her memoir, *Daughter of the Whirlwinds* in 1986. On March 23, 2012, the Frankye Adams-Johnson Black Panther Party Collection acquired by Jackson State University, was opened at the Margaret Walker Center at

Jackson State University.[83] Frankye Adams-Johnson reads and performs her poetry, produces her plays, and facilitates the *Write On Writers Guild*, which she founded some years ago. She conducts creative writing workshops for various organizations in the Jackson area. She was recommended for an artist fellowship by the Mississippi Arts Commission for her collection of short stories, *No Turning Back*. She served as the chairperson for the Veterans of the Mississippi Civil Rights Movement, whose mission is to educate the youth on the legacy of the Civil Rights Movement, particularly "giving testimony of the unsung heroes, and heroines, those oftentimes forgotten foot soldiers on whose backs many stand."[84]

* * *

Isaac Foster graduated from Queens College in 1972. He came from Mississippi to attend Queens College in 1966. Foster came to Queens College after he had instigated a plantation tractor-drivers' and sharecroppers' strike in 1965–1966 in Tribbett, Mississippi. Born in Sunflower County, Isaac grew up on Mississippi plantations. His father was murdered in 1957 because he wanted to buy his own farm from a Black landowner.

After graduating from high school at the age of twenty-one, he worked at the Greenville Mill but soon lost his job because he tried to organize the workers in the mill to picket the plant. He returned to the plantation in Tribbett and soon instigated the workers there to join the Mississippi Freedom Labor Union (MFLU). Based on Foster's persuasion, twelve tractor drivers at the Andrews Brothers' Plantation joined the MFLU and proceeded to go on strike at the end of May 1965.[85] Foster had helped the men to organize Local 4 of the MFLU with himself as the local's chairman. In retaliation, "A. L. Andrews evicted the tractor drivers and their families, who worked as cotton choppers, from the rent-free houses he provided on the plantation."[86] With time, other planters used the strike as a pretext to replace more cotton pickers, choppers, and poor agricultural workers with mechanical cotton pickers and herbicides, thereafter, evicting the workers and demolishing their homes. The homeless strikers were first accommodated at Greenville Industrial College, which was owned by the Black Mississippi Baptist State Educational Association while the Delta Ministry provided them with food, medical care, and tents for housing.[87] The local health department cited unsanitary and overcrowded conditions as grounds for their eviction from the college, so the strikers were forced to move to a five-acre piece of property on Adams's land.

As the population of the poor increased in Adams's land because of continued evictions and demolition of homes by the landowners, the strikers lived in their camp, which they nicknamed Strike City. The Delta Ministry supplied the strikers with tents, food, and clothing.[88] Isaac Foster lived with the strikers in Strike City along with three Delta Ministry's Freedom Corps members. Foster stayed for a while in Strike City, but due to unforeseen circumstances he withdrew from direct involvement with the organization. In another turn of events, as conditions of the poor worsened due to cuts or delays in federal and state allocations of food to the poor, the Delta Ministry convened a conference at Mount Beulah to "discuss ways to obtain food, employment, and housing."[89] About seven hundred people attended the three-day conference, which styled itself the Poor People's Conference. At the conference, the poor people sent a telegram to President Lyndon B. Johnson in which they described their plight calling for jobs and housing. Having waited for two days without any response from the president, "the poor people voted to send a contingent to occupy Greenville Air Force Base to protest their condition and demand the base for housing."[90] On January 31, 1966, after a resolution at the Poor People's Conference held at Mount Beulah,[91] Isaac Foster led a group of over forty poor Blacks to seize and occupy the barracks of a deactivated Greenville Air Force Base for a live in to protest the poor peoples' living conditions. They demanded food, jobs, job training, income, land, employment of the poor in Operation Help, refunding of the Child Development Group of Mississippi (CDGM), and use of the base for housing.[92] They told the press, "We are here because we are hungry and cold and we have no jobs or land."[93] In a statement released by the poor people, they said, "We don't want charity. We are willing to work for ourselves if given a chance."[94] They went on to say, "We are at the Greenville Air Force Base because it is federal property, and there are hundreds of empty houses and buildings. We need those houses and the land. We could be trained for jobs in the buildings."[95] When they were forcefully evicted from the base by members of an Air Police unit, Isaac Foster told reporters, "The people are going to set up a tent city out at Tribbett and work on getting poor people to come and build a new city. Because we [were] refused by the federal government and evicted, it's important that we start planning our own government."[96]

"TODAY WE FOUND out that we don't have a government," said Unita Blackwell who was one of the three spokespersons of the group. The displaced people wanted to set up a "government of, by, and for poor people..."[97] Unita Blackwell elaborated:

> I feel that the federal government [has] proven that it [doesn't] care about poor people. Everything that we have asked for through these years has been handed down on paper. It's never been a reality. We, the poor people of Mississippi, [are] tired. We're tired of it, so we're going to build for ourselves, because we don't have a government that represents us.[98]

Isaac Foster argued that poor people should begin to build a new country with their own laws and their own enforcement, because the federal government had abandoned them and left them in the dust, hungry and without protection. This is how he made his case, "From nothing we must start building a new country, with our own laws, our own enforcement. No part of the system has any authority or control over us. Our goal is to keep away from depending on the system for anything. And I would like to say that every poor person that will come is welcome"[99] He regretted that the only reason Maj. Gen. R. W. Puryear gave for their eviction was that the buildings they occupied did not have running water or any type of protection, even though the federal government understood that all over Mississippi most of the houses rented by White landlords to poor Blacks were without running water and without protection, and most were in far worse conditions than the deactivated Greenville Air Force Base. In his own direct words, he said, "This can't be your reason for wanting us out because all over Mississippi [Black] homes don't have electricity or water or fire protection."[100]

In his application for a scholarship from the Martin Luther King Jr. Center for Nonviolent Social Change on March 28, 1967, to continue his studies at Queens College, Isaac Foster, ostentatiously displayed his activist credentials.[101] "I am sending you some xeroxed news clippings of my past experiment in the movement,"[102] he wrote.

For a good part of his adult life, Isaac Foster was placed on the Mississippi State Sovereignty Commission watch list. At Queens College, Isaac was in the Search for Education, Elevation, and Knowledge (SEEK) program. While he was a student, he mentored other SEEK students. He also worked in the Queens College Upward Bound Program teaching and mentoring New York City high school students. He died in 1991.

The SEEK Rebellion at Queens College

Activism at Queens College in the 1960s culminated in the SEEK rebellion of 1969. SEEK, an acronym for (Search for Education, Elevation, and Knowledge) was mandated in 1966 by the New York State Legislature to create educational opportunities in the City University of New York for children of working-class parents "to advance the cause of equality and educational opportunity at the City University." The first class started with 175 students at QC. The genesis of the SEEK rebellion at QC was that although the population of students in the SEEK program was almost entirely Black and Puerto Rican, the teaching and administrative staff and the director were all White.[103] The SEEK curriculum lacked Black or Puerto Rican perspectives but had White-orientation. The SEEK students were treated like second-class students because they were not allowed to take science in their first semester and could not vote in Student Government elections. However, other tensions preceded the explosive Spring 1969 semester at QC which I need to mention here. One was the anti-Vietnam War demonstrations staged by White radicals of Students for a Democratic Society (SDS) and their followers that took aim at military and corporate recruiters on campus. As the protesters raised moral indignation about the Vietnam War, so was intimidation and antagonism from the college administration, but the student protests continued. In one incident, about 200 students protested loudly against the military-industrial complex, disrupted a General Electric (G.E.) recruitment, and forced the recruiter off the QC campus. Another demonstration was held against Texaco recruiters as well.[104] As a result of these anti-recruitment demonstrations, three SDS student leaders were suspended by the student court for "contempt of court" because the students insisted on an open trial for their anti-recruitment demonstrations. While the Student Association later dropped the charges against the three students, Dean George Pierson, Dean of Students, insisted on pursuing the charges on his own and refused to reinstate the students. Between March 27 and April 1, there were general student strikes on campus that resulted in student sit-ins in the Social Sciences Building (now Powdermaker Hall) and in Academic 11(now Kiely Hall). These sit-ins were related to the Vietnam War, the need for students to have a voice in college affairs, and the refusal of the college to drop charges against three SDS students who had forced the removal of a General Electric recruiter from campus. During the strike, more than 700 police officers were called in and thirty-eight students and one professor were arrested for trespass and detained in Riker's Island.[105]

A second major campus event was the termination of Sheila Delany's appointment. Sheila was a popular professor of English and Comparative Literature and a Marxist scholar who was denied reappointment and tenure in 1968. Sheila was denied reappointment despite her sterling academic record of scholarly accomplishments. Her case was taken up by the QC chapter of Students for a Democratic Society (SDS). Another major concern on campus was the Max-Kahn secrecy report which the students wanted revoked as official QC policy and urged its revocation as CUNY policy as well. To provide critical adhesive to fight the crackdowns on campus, an ad hoc committee, The Ad Hoc Committee to End Political Suppression was formed to fight for students' rights and academic freedom. The ad-hoc committee took pride in its advocacy for the "Reappointment of Sheila Delany" and demanded the reinstatement of the three SDS members who had been suspended for participating in an anti-recruitment demonstration. They demanded that all administrative and civil charges against the 38 arrested students and one faculty member be dropped. The committee also advocated for the rejection and revocation of the Max-Kahn report adopted by *The Board of Higher Education of the City of New York* on June 5, 1967, which gave CUNY college administrations the right not to disclose the reasons why a faculty was not reappointed. The ad hoc committee criticized this policy and demanded transparency in college personnel matters using Sheila Delany's case as an example.[106] Another event worthy of note was the 1968 crisis at Columbia University. At nearby Columbia University, Students for a Democratic Society and their followers protested Columbia's intention to build a ten-story gymnasium in the recreational space of Morningside Park in Harlem. According to the then Queens College Dean of Students, Dr. George Pierson, a considerable number of Queens College students participated in those tumultuous events in Harlem.[107] It is not surprising then that in January and February 1969, the Black and Puerto Rican Student/Faculty Coalition in the SEEK program at QC felt they had to take it upon themselves to do something to change the status quo because they had proposed autonomy for their program since 1968 with no tangible results. They began to organize and eventually formed the Black and Puerto Rican Student, Teacher, and Counselor Coalition to fight for change in the curriculum and personnel and to take the QC administration head-on to gain power for themselves.[108] They protested and wrote a position paper which called for the removal of the SEEK Director, Dr. Joseph A. Mulholland because, according to them, he was an incompetent director and constituted a poor symbol for the program. Also, they wanted greater autonomy over hiring and the curriculum in the SEEK program.[109] The concerned students argued that since the administrative and clerical staff in the SEEK program were all White, the program did not function in the interest of minorities, and administrators in the program did not really care about minority issues. The main target of their demand was for deep structural changes: to have programs that would enrich the curriculum and present a true picture of minority achievements, rather than a curriculum geared mainly toward Whites. They wanted courses on the Black experience and perspective in the curriculum. The students were resolute in demanding courses, professors, and activities that related to minority interests and backgrounds and were steadfast in their demand for a college curriculum structure that was valid and informative for all students. In short, they wanted the unfair and repressive curriculum in their program scraped. Inspired by the tactics of ingenious revolutionary leaders like Malcolm X, the Black Panthers, and the Young Lords Organization,[110] on January 6, 1969, more than 50 students swarmed into and disrupted business in the Office of the School of General Studies and the Office of Admissions. They also disfigured the catalog room at the Paul Klapper Library. The SEEK demonstrators wanted control of their program, hiring, and admissions. Not satisfied with look warm response from the administration, on January 13, about 15 students with 50 others waiting outside, crashed into the office of the SEEK Director, destroyed telephone lines, removed furniture, and placed them in a nearby lot. On February 4, Dr. Joseph A. Mulholland, the SEEK Director, was replaced by the Dean of Faculty, Dr. Robert Hartle as the new Interim Director of the SEEK program. Things came to a head because the appointment did not augur well with the protesting students. On February 5, 1969, about 100 Black and Puerto Rican students told Dr. Hartle in his office, in a matter-of-fact way, that he was not accepted as the Interim SEEK Director because he was not selected by members of the Coalition. On February 6, the concerned students and members of the coalition met with QC President, Dr. Joseph P. McMurray, and selected Dr. Lloyd T. Delany as the Interim Director of the SEEK program. On February 13, President McMurray made known the appointment of Dr. Lloyd T. Delany as the unanimous choice for the position of Interim Director for the SEEK program. Dr. Delany was an Associate Professor of Educational Psychology, and a well-respected scholar.[111]

The appointment of Dr. Delany as SEEK's Interim Director, did not however bring calm to QC campus, because during the SEEK demonstrations, a group of students who called themselves the *Student Coalition* who were opposed to the sit-ins and occupation of college buildings by some students were mobilizing and organizing counter demonstrations which made for uneasy stand-off on campus.[112] With the Vietnam War and the buildup of the military-industrial complex, activism at QC combined a number of rights; students' rights, civil rights, antiwar, and anti-capitalism emphases. The formation of the Ad Hoc Committee to End Political Suppression reflected the combining and commingling of these sentiments on QC campus.[113] The Ad Hoc Committee to End Political Suppression threatened a college-wide strike on April 21 if their seven demands were not met. The demands included: 1. The reinstatement of the three SDS members who were suspended. 2. Dropping of charges against the three SDS members. 3. Rehiring Sheila Delany. 4. The Max-Kahn report is to be discontinued. 5. All administrative and civil charges against the 38 students arrested during the sit-ins in the Social Sciences Building and in Academic 11 building be dropped. 6. All civil and administrative charges against the one faculty member (Henry Lesnick) arrested during the sit-ins at the college be dropped. 7. The administration must guarantee in writing that no police will ever be called in on campus except if there is direct danger to life.[114]

Dr. Delany served as the Interim Director of the SEEK program until June and then became the SEEK Director. He died in November 1969, but before his death, he had begun long lasting reforms in the SEEK program at QC including diversification of the faculty and staff, and the curriculum. He made structural changes that were more responsive to the needs of Black and Puerto Rican students. An example of the reforms started by Dr. Delany was the appointment of the Ethiopian born Professor of Sociology, Alem Habtu who was brought in to initiate curriculum reforms. Professor Habtu helped to establish the Africana Studies program and created the World Civilization curriculum which integrated African, Asian, and Latin American histories into its curriculum. Although, Dr. Delany died before some of the structural reforms he initiated materialled, nevertheless, the impact of his reforms is still being felt in the SEEK program even today. For example, the SEEK program at QC is housed in a building that bears Delany's name. Besides, faculty and staff in the SEEK program have continued to diversify the curriculum and advocate for changes in the college that are more responsive to the needs of minorities by providing courses, activities, and hiring professors that relate to minority backgrounds and interests.

It is important to note that even as late as May 1969, there were sit-ins in the College Tower from opposing factions of the student political divide.[115] The library and the cafeteria were damaged. Police were called in to clear the buildings but there were no arrests.[116] As June set in, members of the Ad Hoc Committee to End Political Suppression decided that there cannot be a free university in an unfree society and called for "counter-commencement" or a walkout. A counter-commencement was held on June 3 by the QC activists with Dr. Benjamin Spock, the renowned pediatrician and anti-draft activist as the keynote speaker. Others present during the counter-commencement were Dr. Lloyd Delany, Glen Brunman (the Student Association President 1968–1969), Wally Rosenthal, Dr. Louis Kampf, Dr. Ekkehart Krippendorf, Robert Sarlin, and QC's own, Dr. Michael Wreszin. Events in the 1970s are beyond the scope of this book but suffice it to say that the Ad Hoc Committee to End Political Suppression called for anti-war strike at QC on April 21, 1970, due to the exacerbation of the war in Asia. This time the strike was supported by QC faculty and the administration. The QC Academic Senate passed a resolution in favor of the strike by 42–32 with two abstentions.[117] Since its inception, SEEK has served about 20,000 students, some of whom "have gone on to professional and graduate schools to become doctors, lawyers, teachers, administrators, and social workers."[118]

The SEEK rebellion at QC was contagious throughout CUNY. Similar demonstrations took place in other campuses following eruptions at QC.[119] On April 22, 1969, more than 200 Black and Puerto Rican students at City College of New York (CCNY) took over 17 buildings in the South Campus for two weeks demanding that changes be made in the college's admission policy as well as changes in the curriculum.[120] The protest at CCNY arose from the fact that although Blacks and Puerto Ricans made up about 40% of the City of New York high school graduates, there were only 9% of Black and Puerto Rican students in the entire student body at City College in 1969.[121] Student activists at CCNY battled police and CCNY administrators in demanding for open admissions and for the introduction of Black and Latino Studies into their curriculum. In solidarity with their Black and Puerto Rican counterparts, White students occupied the North Campus. Francee Covington, one of the student activists, explained her astonishment in the demographic disparity at CCNY in these words: "This gorgeous campus that was being touted as being one of the world's best public universities had a very low percentage of brown and black people."[122] Similar demonstrations for Open Admission were replicated at Brooklyn College which became known as the "BC19" event. In May 1969, 19 Brooklyn College protesters were arrested by New York City police in their homes on charges of arson and rioting at Brooklyn college after weeks of protests. The arrested students faced felony charges which of course were ultimately dropped, but not before the students had spent 3 days in Riker's Island.[123] There were similar demonstrations at the Borough of Manhattan Community College, Bronx Community College, and other CUNY colleges.[124] The demonstrators for Open Admissions demanded, "increased intake of Black and Puerto Rican students in CUNY colleges; strengthening of remedial programs like SEEK, and the creation of new special programs geared toward preparing the new students of color for a college education."[125] As unrest among the students raged on, the Mayor, John Lindsay and others in the City and the State Governments agreed to the students' demands that eventually opened up CUNY and the City University to many students who would not have had a chance otherwise. It is important to point out that Mayor John Lindsay and Chancellor Albert H. Bowker supported the student protesters. As a result, the Board of Higher Education (BHE) decided to accelerate its original Open Admissions plan to the fall of 1970 which was five years earlier than originally anticipated. According to a recent report, City College is now about 53 percent minority,[126] thereby affirming what Francee Covington predicted, "The way we got involved was to make sure that the people who came after us would have access to this institution."[127] The statistical data published by CUNY Office of Institutional Research and Assessment in 2020 titled, "Total Enrollment by Race/Ethnicity and College: Percentages Fall 2019," reads as follows: American Indian/Alaska Native 0.3%, Asian/Pacific Islander 21.2%, Black 25.2%, Hispanic 30.2%, White 23.1%. Looking back, it is to be said that the SEEK curriculum at CUNY became the model for the entire New York State, in a program called the Higher Education Opportunity Program that was passed into law by the New York State legislature. This program is now established in every college and university in the State University of New York (SUNY) system as well as in many private colleges in New York State.[128]

The changes at QC after the SEEK rebellion were profound and revolutionary. Recalling the events, Professor Frank A. Warren of QC, in his eyewitness account stated:

> I am left with a sense of gratitude to the young student activists. For, when all has been said by the condescending romanticizers and the surly critics about the student activism of the late 1960s and early 1970s, what remains uppermost in my mind is that it was the *Queens College student activists* who were the ones who raised the substantive issues... I cannot forget that it was they who forced the faculty to confront the issue of the role of the College – whether or not it was compatible with its liberal arts purpose to serve as a recruitment center for the military and its corporate allies. It was they who forced the faculty to probe deeply the issue of student and faculty rights. It was they who demanded that we address the issue of racism – in the South, in the North, and at Queens College.[129]

Another QC professor, Dr. Michael Wreszin had this to say about the student protests:

> For me the late '60s and early '70s were the most exciting and intellectually stimulating period in over twenty-three years of teaching at the College. This was due largely to the exploding political and social consciousness of the *activist student body and faculty* determined to register their discontent over the Vietnam War and their desire to transform Queens from an alienated commuter school into a vital, caring, intellectual community.[130]

I must say, in the final analyses, the SEEK rebellion at QC was demonstrably an earth-shattering event that cracked the fault line of the system and brought fundamental changes in QC education policies. A few examples will suffice here: the college curriculum was expanded to include Black and Women studies. Some required courses were abolished except for basic English. Students participated in discussions in various advisory and administrative committees. A different method of evaluating faculty performance through the newly established Queens College Faculty-Student Academic Senate was another welcome innovation.[131] Indeed, Queens College Faculty-Student Academic Senate was the first of its kind in CUNY and perhaps the first in the entire nation.[132]

6 THE REBUILDERS 209

In this chapter, I have focused intensely on highlighting the different activist renditions at QC from 1965 onwards. It begins with the story of students and professors from QC who went to Mississippi in January and during the Spring break in 1965 to rebuild Black churches which had been burned down by White supremacists during Freedom Summer. The chapter discusses another activist undertaking by volunteers affiliated with QC under the auspices of the Summer Community Organization and Political Education (SCOPE) Project. This was a comprehensive voter registration project that was launched in the South by the Southern Christian Leadership Conference (SCLC) headed by Dr. Martin Luther King Jr., in preparation for the Voting Rights Act that was pending before Congress. The chapter also tells the story of a versatile activist, the Lambda Award winning writer and editor, and one of the founders of the Lesbian Herstory Archives, Joan Nestle. The chapter follows up with the stories of two activists (one of them a former member of the Black Panther Party and a winner of the John Oliver Killens Fiction Award) who were involved in activist causes in Mississippi before coming to QC to pursue their college education. It concludes with an important marker, the SEEK Rebellion of 1969 which started at QC before spreading to other CUNY colleges. This rebellion was popularly known as "CUNY's Open Admissions Strike of 1969." The SEEK rebellion resulted in the hiring of more faculty of color, the institutionalization of Black, Hispanic, and Women's Studies programs at QC and in CUNY. As a factual matter, the SEEK curriculum which originated at CUNY became a model for the establishment of a statewide program which became known as the Higher Education Opportunity Program (HEOP) which was passed into law by the New York State legislature in 1969 following the SEEK Rebellion which started at QC.[133]

Civil rights activists Moshe Shur and Peter Geffen (center and right) with Dr. Martin Luther King Jr. in Atlanta, Georgia (Photograph, Courtesy of Peter Geffen)

Protesters in the Hallway of an Occupied Queens College Building in 1969 (Photograph, Courtesy of Harvey L. Silver)

Several Female Protesters in Discussion at Queens College (Photograph, Courtesy of Harvey L. Silver)

Notes

1. "College Mississippi Project Rebuilds Tougaloo Churches." Box 1, folder 2 Robert Masters Collection, Department of Special Collections and Archives, Queens College, City University of New York. Some of the names of the students are spelt differently in this version, for example John Gatti instead of Arthur Gatti and Gus Pereos instead of Gus Peros.
2. Ibid.
3. The following Baptist Churches were repaired: Cedar Grove Baptist Church, St. John's Baptist Church, Church of the Good Hope, and Church of Christian Union.
4. "College Mississippi Project Rebuilds Tougaloo Churches." Box 1, folder 2 Robert Masters Collection, Department of Special

Collections and Archives, Queens College, City University of New York.

See also, "MFP Heads Effort to Build Church." Box 1 folder 2 Robert Masters Collection, Department of Special Collections and Archives, Queens College, City University of New York.

5. Ibid.
6. "College Mississippi Project Rebuilds Tougaloo Churches." Box 1, folder 2 Robert Masters Collection, Department of Special Collections and Archives, Queens College, City University of New York.
7. Telephone interview with Professor Simon, December 7, 2012.
8. Ibid.
9. "Mississippi Baptist Convention Board." Box 1, folder 4, Arthur Gatti Collection, Department of Special Collections and Archives, Queens College, City University of New York.
10. "Letter to Arthur Gatti from Lawrence Scott, April 4, 1965." Box 1, folder 2 Arthur Gatti Collection, Department of Special Collections and Archives, Queens College, City University of New York.
11. Ibid.
12. Meridian is the place where Michael Schwerner and James Cheney were stationed before they were murdered.
13. Ibid.
14. Ibid.
15. "Mississippi Church Rebuilding Volunteers." Box 1, folder 2, Arthur Gatti Collection, Department of Special Collections and Archives, Queens College, City University of New York. Although Steve Zeigfinger is listed as the faculty adviser for this trip, there is no evidence on record that he ever went to Mississippi.
16. Robert Cohen, *Freedom's Orator: Mario Savio and the Radical Legacy of the 1960s*. New York: Oxford University Press, 2009, p. 37.
17. Ibid., pp. 37–38.
18. Ibid., p. 38.
19. See Kevin Donnellan, *GOODMAN*. An Unpublished Essay, 1993.
20. Arthur Gatti—Darklight Publishing LLC. https://www.darklight.nyc/dana-buckley (Accessed 2/27/2020).
21. Ibid.
22. Ibid.

23. Correspondence between Arthur Gatti and the author 8/26/2023.
24. Interview with Dr. Simon, December 7, 2012.
25. Ibid.
26. Ibid.
27. "Mississippi Baptist Convention Board." Box 1, folder 4, Arthur Gatti Collection, Department of Special Collections and Archives, Queens College, City University of New York.
28. Simon Workshops. http://www.simonworkshops.com/index2.html (Accessed 12/12/2012).
29. E-mail correspondence with Dr. Simon 11/14/2012.
30. Simon Workshops. http://www.simonworkshops.com/index2.htmi (Accessed 12/12/2012).
31. Willy Siegel Leventhal, *The SCOPE of Freedom: The Leadership of Hosea Williams with Dr. King's Summer '65 Student Volunteers*. Montgomery, AL: Challenge Press, 2005, p. 45. See also, *The Civil Rights Digital Library/SCOPE project*.
32. Ibid., pp. 43 & 96.
33. *Daily News*, February 13, 2006. See "Series 3: Supplemental Materials." Box 1, folder 13, Dean Savage Collection, Department of Special Collections and Archives, Queens College, City University of New York. See also, "35 Demonstrators Get 30 Days or $50.00 Fines After Trial Here." Box 1, folder 1, Dean Savage Collection, Department of Special Collections and Archives, Queens College, City University of New York.
34. Ibid.
35. This survey is supported by the National Science Foundation but is administered by the National Opinion Research Center. According to Professor Savage, his research has "the potential to provide much better data about where newly minted PhDs take academic or administrative positions."
36. Audrey Williams June, "Do You Know Where Your Ph.D.'s Are?" *The Chronicle of Higher Education*. https://www.chronicle.com/artice/Do-You-Know-Where-Your-PhDs/141777 (Accessed 12/26/19).
37. "Number and Share of Queens College Baccalaureate Graduates Who Pursue Further Education, by Degrees Sought and Program Level, 2013–2019, as of March1." Queens College

Office of Institutional Research. Tables assembled by Dean Savage, Professor Emeritus.
38. Interview with Rabbi Moshe Shur, October 24, 2012.
39. "SCOPE Chapter 33, Mickey Shur, KZSU Project South Interviews," Department of Special Collections and University Archives, Stanford University Libraries, p. 0276-2.
40. Interview with Rabbi Moshe Shur, October 24, 2012. See also SCOPE Chapter 33, Mickey Shur, KZSU Project South Interviews," Department of Special Collections and University Archives, Stanford University Libraries, p. 0276-2.
41. Ibid.
42. Ibid. See also "SCOPE Chapter 33, Mickey Shur, KZSU Project South Interviews," p. 0276-3.
43. *Daily News,* February 13, 2006. See Series 3, Box 1, folder 13 Supplemental Materials, Dean Savage Collection, Department of Special Collections and Archives, Queens College, City University of New York.
44. Ibid.
45. Ibid.
46. "SCOPE Chapter 33, Mickey Shur, KZSU Project South Interviews," Department of Special Collections and University Archives, Stanford University Libraries, p. 0276-7.
47. Interview with Rabbi Shur, October 24, 2012.
48. "SCOPE Chapter 33, Mickey Shur, KZSU Project South Interviews," Department of Special Collections and University Archives, Stanford University Libraries, p. 0276-6.
49. "SCOPE Chapter 33, Mickey Shur, KZSU Project South Interviews," Department of Special Collections and University Archives, Stanford University Libraries, p. 0276-6.
50. "35 Demonstrators Get 30 Days or $50 Fines After Trial Here." Box 1, folder 1, Dean Savage Collection, Department of Special Collections and Archives, Queens College, City University of New York.
51. Ibid., p. 0276-3.
52. Ibid.
53. Interview with Rabbi Moshe Shur, October 24, 2012.
54. "SCOPE Chapter 33, Mickey Shur, KZSU Project South Interviews," Department of Special Collections and University Archives, Stanford University Libraries, p. 0276-1.

55. Ibid.
56. "In the Footsteps of Dr. King." https://www.qc.cuny.edu/community/drking/Pages/Default.aspx. (Accessed 6/8/2021).
57. Barbara Williams Emerson. webspinner@crmvet.org (Accessed 2/20/2020).
58. Ibid.
59. *Daily News,* February 13, 2006. See Series 3, Box 1, folder 13 Supplemental Materials, Dean Savage Collection, Department of Special Collections and Archives, Queens College, City University of New York.
60. *Daily News,* February 13, 2006. See Series 3, Box 1, folder 13 Supplemental Materials, Dean Savage Collection, Department of Special Collections and Archives, Queens College, City University of New York.
61. Ibid.
62. Ibid.
63. Joan Nestle, *A Restricted Country.* San Francisco, CA: Cleis Press Inc. 2003, p. p. 41.
64. Ibid.
65. Correspondence with the author, 8/22/2023.
66. Ibid., p. 42.
67. Ibid., pp. 39–42.
68. Ibid., p. 42.
69. Ibid., p. 50.
70. Ibid.
71. Joan credits her English, Speech and Drama teacher, Mrs. Desser for guiding her to go to Queens College, even though Joan herself doubted her ability to afford college.
72. Joan Nestle: From Wikipedia, the Free Encyclopedia. http://en.wikipedia.org/wik/Joan_Nestle. (Accessed /10/5/2012).
73. "Lesbian Herstory Archives." http://www.lesbianherstoryarchives.org/ (Accessed 10/6/2012).
74. *A Restricted Country.* San Francisco: CA Cleis Press, 2003; *A Fragile Union: New and Selected Writings.* San Francisco, CA: Cleis Press, 1998. See also a talk given by Joan Nestle at her Alma Mater entitled, "The Gifts of Martin Van Buren High School, 1955."
75. *Women on Women: An Anthology of American Lesbian Short Fiction* (with Naomi Holoch). New York: Plume, 1990; *The*

Persistent Desire: A Femme-Butch Reader. Boston: MA: Alyson Publications 1992; *Women on Women 2: An Anthology of American Lesbian Short Fiction* (Editor with Naomi Holoch). New York: Plume, 1993; *Sister and Brother: Lesbian and Gay Men Write About Their Lives Together* (Editor with John Preston). San Francisco, CA: Harper San Francisco, 1994; *Women on Women 3: A New Anthology of American Lesbian Short Fiction* (Editor with Naomi Holoch). New York: Plume, 1996; *The Vintage Book of International Lesbian Fiction*. New York, Vintage, 1999; *GenderQueer: Voices from Beyond the Sexual Binary* (Editor with Clare Howell). Magnus Books, 2020.

76. Lambda Literary Award for Best Lesbian and Gay Anthology-Fiction for *The Vintage Book of International Lesbian Fiction* (2000). Lambda Literary Award for Lesbian Studies for *A fragile Union* (1999). American Library Association Gay/Lesbian Book Award for *A Restricted Country* (1998). Lambda Literary Award for Best Lesbian and Gay Anthology- Fiction for *Women on Women 3* (1997). Lambda Literary Award for Best Lesbian and Gay Anthology—Nonfiction for *Sister and Brother* (1994). Lambda Literary Award for Best Lesbian Anthology for *The Persistent Desire* (1992). Lambda Literary Award for Best Lesbian Anthology for *Women on Women 1* (1990).
77. Veteran of the Civil Rights Movement: Frankye Adams-Johnson (Aka Malika). http://www.crmvet.org/vet/adamsfj.htm (Accessed 9/29/2012), p. 1.
78. Ibid.
79. Ibid.
80. Ibid.
81. Ibid. See also, Frankye Adams-Johnson http://www.jsums.edu/liberalarts/emfl/adamsjohnson.htm (Accessed 9/29/2012).
82. "Margaret Walker Center: Press Release." www.jsums.edu/margaretwalker (Accessed 9/29/2012).
83. Ibid. The Margaret Walker Center doubles as an archive and a museum, and is dedicated to the preservation, interpretation, and dissemination of African American experience. It is also charged with coordinating public programs on campus and throughout the community, along with advocating Black studies at Jackson State University.

84. Frankye Adams-Johnson (Aka Malika) *Jackson Advocate*, September 29, 2012, p. 3.
85. Leon Howell records in *Freedom City*, p. 89 that the strike was in June 1965, but Mark Newman, in *Divine Agitators*, states that the strike was at the end of May 1965, p. 95.
86. Mark Newman, *Divine Agitators: The Delta Ministry and Civil Rights in Mississippi*. Athens, GA: The University of Georgia Press, 2004, p. 96.
87. Ibid, p. 97.
88. Ibid.
89. Ibid, p. 104.
90. Ibid.
91. This conference was called because of dire consequences: the poor would lose their jobs if 35% decrease in crop allotments to planters by the federal government were implemented. Such a move would throw 6,500 tractor drivers and mechanics out of work. The move would put about 30,000 people out of work and out of the plantations to make matters worse, grants for the poor were also withheld by the federal government and the state. See Newman, *Devine Agitators,* p. 104.
92. See Newman, *Divine Agitators,* p. 105.
93. Cited in Leon Howell, *Freedom City: The Remarkable Story of the Dispossessed Negroes Who Struggled to Create a Hopeful New Community in Rural Mississippi*. Richmond, Virginia: John Knox Press, 1969, p. 30.
94. Ibid., p. 31.
95. Cited in Howell, *Freedom City*, p. 31.
96. An edited transcription of a press conference held in the Greenville office of the Delta Ministry on Tuesday, February 1, 1966, p. 501. See also *Birmingham Alabama News*, "The Commercial Appeal," Memphis Tenn., February 2, 1966.
97. "Disillusioned Squatters forming," *Birmingham, ALA, News*, February 2, 1966, p. 1.
98. An edited transcription of a press conference held in the Greenville office of the Delta Ministry on Tuesday, February 1, 1966, p. 501. See also *Birmingham Alabama News*, February 2, 1966.
99. An edited transcription of a press conference held in the Greenville office of the Delta Ministry on Tuesday, February 1,

1966, p. 502. See also *Birmingham Alabama News*, February 2, 1966; The Commercial Appeal, Memphis, Tenn., February 2, 1966. Also see Newman, *Divine Agitators*, 129.
100. Cited in Howell, *Freedom City*, p. 32.
101. See "Letter from Isaac Foster Regarding a Scholarship," The Martin Luther King Jr. Center for Nonviolent Social Change. http://www.thekingcenter.org/archive/document/letter-isaac-foster-regarding-scholarship (Accessed 11/26/ 2012).
102. Ibid.
103. Annie E. Tummino, "Commemorating a Legacy of Dissent: Revisiting Campus Activism 1968–1970." City University of New York: CUNY Academic Works, 2020.
104. In Stephen Stepanchev (ed.), *The People's College on the Hill: Fifty Years at Queens College, 1937–1987*. Shirley Strum Kenny, President, 1988, p. 28.
105. The 38 students and one faculty were released from Riker's Island on June 30, 1969 after they had served fifteen days. Seven women were fined and released.
106. See, "Strike Monday if Seven Demands Aren't Met." Box 1, folder 3, & Box 11, folder 4, Michael Wreszin Collection, Department of Special Collections and Archives, Queens College, City University of New York. See also in the same box a flyer captioned "This afternoon seven hundred student and faculty attended a rally." It is important to also see the Max-Kahn report adopted by, *The Board of Higher Education of the City of New York* on June 5, 1967.
107. Annie Tummino, "Commemorating a Legacy of Dissent: Revisiting Campus Activism 1968–1970." CUNY Academic Works, 2020. https://academicworks.cuny.edu/qc_pubs/464.
108. Ibid. The SEEK demands were rejected. See Stepanchev (ed.), *The People's College on the Hill*, p. 28.
109. Annie E. Tummino, "Commemorating a Legacy of Dissent: Revisiting Campus Activism 1968–1970." City University of New York: CUNY Academic Works, 2020. See also, Eugene Fontinell, "Painful Things Past." In Stephen Stepanchev, ed. *The People's College on the Hill: Fifty Years at Queens College, 1937–1987*. Shirley Strum Kenny, President, 1988, p. 77.
110. According to Annie Tummino, a QC SEEK Student, Felipe Luciano co-founded the New York chapter of the Young Lords

Organization in 1969. The Young Lords is a Puerto Rican nationalist and Civil Rights organization.
111. See Annie Tummino, "Commemorating a Legacy of Dissent: Revisiting Campus Activism 1968–1970." CUNY Academic Works, 2020. https://academicworks.cuny.edu/qc_pubs/464.
112. Eugene Fontinell, "Painful Things Past." In Stephen Stepanchev, ed. *The People's College on the Hill: Fifty Years at Queens College, 1937–1987*. Shirley Strum Kenny, President, 1988, p. 78.
113. Interview with Mark Levy, 4/04/12.
114. "Strike Monday if Seven Demands Aren't Met." Box 10, folder 3, Michael Wreszin Papers. Department of Special Collections and Archives, Queens College, City University of New York.
115. The other faction was a conservative student group that called itself the *Student Coalition*. See Fontinell, "Painful Things Past," In Stephen Stepanchev, ed., p. 78.
116. Stephen Stepanchev (ed.), *The People's College on the Hill: Fifty Years at Queens College, 1937–1987*. Shirley Strum Kenny, President, 1988, p. 28.
117. "Gains at Home but the War Rages On." In Stephen Stepanchev, ed. *The People's College on the Hill: Fifty Years at Queens College, 1937–1987*. Shirley Strum Kenny, President, 1988, p. 71.
118. Ibid.
119. Interview with Mark Levy, 4/04/12. I agree with Mark Levy that the SEEK Rebellion started at QC before it spread to CCNY, because the SEEK Rebellion at QC started in January 1969 while the City College protest was in April 1969, even though City College is often credited with leading the protest for Open Admissions in CUNY.
120. Remembering the Fiery 1969 City College Student Protest." https://www.ny1.com/nyc/all-boroughs/news2019/04/17/1969-city-college-student-protest-50th-annivesary-civil-rights.
121. "Remembering the Fiery 1969 City College Student Protest." https://www.ny1.com/nyc/all-boroughs/news2019/04/17/1969-city-college-student-protest-50th-annivesary-civil-rights (Accessed 7/19/23).
122. Cited in "Remembering the Fiery 1969 City College Student Protest." https://www.ny1.com/nyc/all-boroughs/news/2019/04/17/1969-city-college-student-protest-50th-anniversary-civil-rights p. 2. (Accessed 7/19/23).

123. Puerto Rican Studies at Brooklyn College. https://cdha.cuny.edu/collections/show/402 (Accessed 10/5/2023).
124. Christopher Gunderson, "The Struggle for CUNY: A History of the CUNY Student Movement, 1969–1999." https://eportfolios.macaulay.cuny.edu/hainline2014/files/2014/02/Gunderson_The-Struggle-for-CUNY.pdf
125. Bhargav Rani, "Revolution and CUNY: Remembering the 1969 Fight for Open Admissions." https://gcadvocate.com
126. "Remembering the Fiery 1969, p. 2.
127. Ibid.
128. "Gains at Home but the War Rages On." In *The People's College on the Hill: Fifty Years at Queens College, 1937–1987*. Shirley Strum Kenny, President, 1988, p. 71.
129. Frank A. Warren, "Our Students Taught Us Well." In Stephen Stepanchev, ed. *The People's College on the Hill: Fifty Years at Queens College, 1937–1987*. Shirley Strum Kenny, President, 1988, p. 73. (Italics added).
130. Michael Wreszin, "The Campus Gains a Conscience." In Stephen Stepanchev, ed. *The People's College on the Hill: Fifty Years at Queens College, 1937–1987*. Shirley Strum Kenny, President, 1988, p. 75. (Italics added).
131. "Gains at Home but the War Rages On," p. 71.
132. See Eugene Fontinell, "Painful Things Past." In Stephen Stepanchev, ed. *The People's College on the Hill: Fifty Years at Queens College, 1937–1987*. Shirley Strum Kenny, President, 1988, p. 76.
133. See "Gains at Home but the War Rages On." In *The People's College on the Hill: Fifty Years at Queens College, 1937–1987*. Shirley Strum Kenny, President, 1988, p. 71.

CHAPTER 7

Those Who Volunteered and Why They Volunteered

> *I first went down South as a volunteer with SNCC in the fall of '61. I became a staff member in '62. Jewish participation began to grow, particularly after the (1963) March on Washington. By 1964 maybe 10–15 percent*

One precautionary note is that although I wrote this book to tell the QC story, in this chapter, I will not limit myself to QC data because the QC sample is a very small sample, and the data is not representative of the population that participated among the various volunteer groups. To be sure, in Virginia, teachers were drawn from the United Federation of Teachers (UFT) (thirty of them), and during Freedom Summer, among the purported one thousand students from across the country who participated, there were nearly one hundred fifty lawyers, three hundred ministers, one hundred physicians, nurses, and psychologists who were also involved and did great and important work during that summer. In my attempt to answer this particular question therefore, I will draw from QC data as well as from national data and resources when necessary and wherever I can find them. To be precise, Gertrude (Trudy) Weissman Orris, Isaac Deutscher, Vivian Leburg Rothstein, Debra Schultz and Chude Allen referenced in this chapter were not students at QC and were not affiliated with QC in any way.

> *of the SNCC staff was Jewish, but no one really knows how many volunteers were Jewish because we never asked on the application forms*
> —Dorothy M. Zellner

I have written this book because there is much that is unknown about the contributions of Queens College student activists whose life stories should no longer remain untold. Lee Cogan, in *The People's College on the Hill: Fifty Years at Queens College, 1937–1987*, argued that the dream of Dr. Paul Klapper, the first president of Queens College was to establish "a community of scholars serving others."[1] Cogan went on to state that, "Because [Queens College] students went out into the larger community each day, as residents, family members, and jobholders, they were always part of the real world, and responded to it immediately and fully."[2] He concluded that since Queens College students were "proud of the quality of their education, they were eager to translate it into service, and to live the lives it enabled them to appreciate."[3] True to its motto, *We learn so that we may serve*, Queens College students responded rather quickly to the appeal from Rev. L. Francis Griffin for volunteers to help with preparing Black children for the opening of "Free Schools" in Prince Edward County, Virginia in 1963 where schools had been shut down by orders of the state from 1959–1964). Queens College students and alumni also responded to the call by SNCC and COFO for volunteers in Mississippi in 1964 as well as calls by SCOPE for volunteers to register voters in some Southern states in the summer of 1965. These QC activists took pride in their advocacy for social justice for Blacks in Virginia and Mississippi and in other southern states—despite the risks. I am sure Mark Levy, one of the volunteers for the Mississippi Freedom Summer 1964 Project from Queens College, spoke for most of his fellow volunteers when he said,

> None of us went to Mississippi expecting we might be killed. But we were well informed about the history of incidents in the state and knew and accepted that risk to try to focus the nation's attention on segregation, poverty, and injustice in Mississippi, on the social and political impact on everyone in the North and South because of the unchallenged power of the "Dixiecrats," and on the hope of the Civil Rights Act of 1964. We were committed to changing the status quo.[4]

In a similar vein, in an interview with Bret Eynon on March 5, 1985, Mario Savio, one of the participants in Freedom Summer and a former

Queens College student, spoke of the dangers in Mississippi reminiscent of Mark Levy's statement above. This is what he said: "For me—think about it—there was a very brief span of years, just two, three years all together, from the first picket line that I saw in New York to here I am in Oxford, Ohio, talking with this buddy I've just met about the possibility that in the next couple of weeks we would be killed."[5] And Michael Wenger talked about their venture in Prince Edward County, Virginia in these words:

> I'd been scared initially about going to Prince Edward County. I had worried about being verbally assaulted, threatened, even physically beaten. But any thought of not coming back alive had been buried beneath layers of privilege and self-protective denial.[6]

* * *

In this book, I have argued that the participation of students in activism cannot be reduced to a single common narrative,[7] because numerous theories and postulates have been advanced by scholars for social movement participation. While Eric L. Hirsch argued that consciousness-raising, collective empowerment, polarization, and group decision-making are the necessary ingredients for protest movements to germinate and grow,[8] Doug McAdam posits that "a prior history of activism and integration into supportive networks acts as the structural 'pull' encouraging the individual to make good on his or her strongly held beliefs."[9] It is interesting to note that from the available archival records, it is clear that most of the students who volunteered to go to Virginia and Mississippi and down South from QC were White, and a good number of them were Jewish. A major question I have often been asked by those who are aware of my research, is why many of the QC students and students throughout the country, (particularly those who were White and Jewish),[10] were attracted to the concept of social justice aimed at destroying White power? I did not find a simple or measurable answer to this question but James Farmer (one of the founders of the Congress of Racial Equality) maintained that, "In addition to the stratosphere of top leadership in the NAACP, wherever in the United States there was a driving force for equal rights for Blacks, American Jews were a part of it."[11] And Julian Bond, communications director of SNCC 1961–1965, told Jonathan Mark of The *New York Jewish Week,* "that there had been no specific outreach to Jews, but there was a great [spirit of] volunteerism in Jewish America, people who thought, 'This is important, I need to be involved in this.' Rather than us specifically appealing to Jews, this was something that appealed to Jews. It was an observable phenomenon, out of all proportion to the percentage of Jews in the general population."[12] The motivation and inspiration for participation by each of the student activists are interwoven in their personal stories throughout this book, though I will go into a little detail here, specifically for the White and Jewish students. Although Lucy Komisar credits Allard Lowenstein, Michael Harrington and the political and moral education she received at Queens College for changing her worldview toward activism, it was at the Young People's Socialist League (YPSL) meetings that Lucy took her first steps toward political activism.[13] Elliot Linzer came to student activism through his membership in CORE and the Young People's Socialist League (YPSL). Arthur Gatti was an active member of CORE and Students for a Democratic Society (SDS), two of the most prominent organizations that worked for social, racial, and economic justice. He was also affiliated with the anti-Vietnam War movement, the National Mobilization Committee to End the War in Vietnam, the Youth International Party, and the War Resisters League. Joan Nestle was a strong member of CORE and Andrew Berman was both a CORE member and a member of the SDS. Other CORE members were Michael Wenger and Stan Shaw. Many of the activists from QC had a prior history of activism or were involved in some form of movement participation. For example, many of those who volunteered for Freedom Summer from QC had protested at the New York World's Fair and marched against discrimination at New York City's Woolworth's on Thirty-fourth Street or attended the March on Washington.[14] Andrew Goodman was in the picket lines at the New York World's Fair and marched in demonstrations for equal rights at New York City's Woolworth's on Thirty-fourth Street. This was also true of Mark Levy, who began his activism during his days in student politics and took his first steps toward social justice activism in the student union. According to Mark Levy, his sense of being able to work with others to bring about change determined for him the type of activism he was willing to invest his time and resources in.[15] Similarly, Mario Savio (who was not Jewish) went to Albany with a group of students to protest a proposed fee raise at CUNY colleges. He joined the picket line for civil rights demonstration and antidiscrimination at the New York Woolworth's and served as a picket captain during the student strike of November 16, 1961, at

Queens College. This strike was organized by the Student Association president, Kenneth (Kenny) Warner. One of the QC activists I interviewed told me that he joined the movement because social change was in the air in the 1960s. According to him, the Civil Rights movement was growing and winning victories: the Montgomery bus boycott, sit-ins at lunch counters, freedom rides, desegregation of schools, and the March on Washington. The injunction to Americans by the young and charismatic President John F Kennedy to "ask not what your country can do for you—ask what you can do for your country," was very inspirational and electrifying to many students. Some students believed that possibilities that did not exist before now seemed within reach, making it the most exciting thing youths could engage in.

It has also been said that integration into supportive networks acts as the structural draw that encourages some students to participate in activism. Yes, a few of the student activists I interviewed for this book told me that they joined the movement because some people they knew and respected reached out to them and invited them to join.[16] As Doug McAdam discovered in a series of his studies, student activism was quite often consistent with the core values the students learned at home.[17] Progressive politics animated Michael Wenger because his parents were progressives who hosted a fundraising event for Aaron Henry, head of the Mississippi Freedom Democratic Party (MFDP) in Michael's former high school. Henry even spent the night in Wenger parents' home.[18] Another student in this category was Andrew Berman whose early life was much influenced by his parents' leftist politics. While in college, Berman took interest in peace, social justice, and civil rights causes and joined organizations that emphasized the exchange of ideas concerning social change. Also, according to one writer, Andrew Goodman was born into a leftist Jewish family "steeped in intellectual and socially progressive activism and were devoted to social justice."[19] Indeed, as noted by Jerusha O. Conner, some of the student activists of the 1960s came "from middle and upper class affluent homes run by liberal, well-educated parents who encouraged criticism and intellectual discussion and practiced permissive child rearing."[20] Jon N. Hale argued that many of the 1960s movement volunteers had parents who were active in the civil rights movement themselves or were advocates of social justice.[21]

Indeed, Michael Wenger and Stan Shaw explained that the Queens College volunteers, some of whom were Jewish, had parents who were Holocaust survivors or had, lost relatives in the concentration camps. Many came from families with deep roots in the progressive community, with parents who taught them by word and deed that social justice was an essential component of a healthy society and that they had a responsibility to be engaged in the pursuit of social justice.[22]

Some volunteers like Nancy (Cooper) Samstein heard firsthand accounts of the Holocaust concentration camps from family members and neighbors and were determined never again, and so they identified with victims of oppression as part of their democratic civic voices to combat injustice.[23] Nancy in a newspaper publication maintained that her late husband, Mendy Samstein, who was an organizer for the Student Nonviolent Coordinating Committee, "had been greatly affected by the horrors of the Holocaust, and that he did not want to permit that kind of destruction of a race to happen again."[24] Nancy was also very bothered by the anti-communist witch-hunt her father and her father's friends suffered as officers of the postal workers' union in America.

A considerable number of the volunteers like Betty (Bollinger) Levy (deceased), Dorothy M. Zellner, and Nancy (Cooper) Samstein were "red-diaper babies," "sons and daughters of Jewish intellectuals or labor unionists whose parents or relatives had joined revolutionary and socialist movements and communicated to their children and wards radical political values that made the Civil Rights movement an attractive option."[25] Betty (Bollinger) Levy's mother was a union leader affiliated with the Congress of Industrial Organizations whose union was subpoenaed to testify before Congress.[26] Dorothy M. Zellner falls into this category because, as she once said, she was the daughter of immigrant Jewish leftists who were much influenced by "the young Jewish fighters of the Warsaw Ghetto who fought the Nazis in a last spurt of defiance and despair."[27] Jean L. Konzal attributes her activism to being born into a working-class Jewish family with deep roots in the progressive movements of the early twentieth century. She credits her aunt Jean (after whom she was named), a self-educated woman who became active in radical movements and wrote a damning report of the oppression of African Americans that she witnessed on her trip to Louisiana. Jean Konzal was also very troubled by the memory of the lynching of Emmett Till. She narrated her puzzlement in the following words: "I remember weeping inconsolably at the cruelty evidenced in that image."[28] This was after seeing the gruesome photograph her father brought home from the *New York Post*, as a child.

Debra Schultz has pointed out that, "Progressive Jewish culture communicated a number of social justice messages. One of them was that anti-Black racism was wrong."[29] She went on to say, "My family instilled in me the conviction that being Jewish created an obligation to discern and fight for 'what is right.'"[30] Progressive Jews were urged by their religious obligation to fight for justice and righteousness in what Debra Schultz calls ethical and humanist principles inherent in Judaism.[31] This consideration must have influenced Rabbi Moshe Mitchell Shur, (director emeritus of Queens College Hillel Foundation) who participated in the SCOPE project, because as he said in a *Daily News* interview of February 13, 2006, "This was something of an injustice, and with my Jewish background, if you see an injustice, you have to do something about it."[32] Peter Geffen, a former student of Queens College also told the same newspaper this as his reason for participating in the SCOPE project: "As a Jew, the impact on a young person born after the War of the Holocaust —an experience in which good people stood by as people were deprived of their rights and eventually murdered—there was no way of not looking at the situation and seeing a dramatic parallel."[33] Indeed, a recent writer has commented that "Jews know from Leviticus, 'Do not stand idly by the blood of your neighbor,'" and therefore, "Jews have a history of standing shoulder to shoulder with blacks during the civil rights movement and Jews are at the forefront of social justice causes."[34] Writing about some of the women who went South to work in the Civil Rights movement, Debra L. Schultz stated, "they were secular Jews in a black Christian movement working in the anti-Semitic and virulently racist South."[35] And Dorothy Zellner noted that "she went south because she believed Jews fought injustice in the garment industry, in the Spanish Civil War, in the Warsaw Ghetto, because the Talmud told them to."[36] Mark Levy, writing about Freedom Summer and QC declared:

> Looking at the lists of QC civil rights volunteers involved in activities on campus, in Mississippi, and in Virginia, the fact that a disproportionately large number were Jewish should be recognized. That tradition—religious, cultural, and historical—certainly influenced me and helped shape our liberal and humanistic values, and commitment to social justice. The awareness of discrimination in the world was an important part of growing up. Some of us came from progressive and activist Jewish families... others

came from ones quieted by immigrant and holocaust experiences as well as by the McCarthy-era political atmosphere. It was those core Jewish values, I feel, that strongly shaped many of our individual decisions to step forward to become active. We felt, at least in the 1960s, that we also had support from many rabbis, synagogues, and Jewish community organizations.[37]

Certainly, there were some who took to activism because they were generally supportive of the goals and ideals of the movement and had a personal identification with its ethos, or because they felt an obligation "to do something," which in other words meant fighting for both American and Jewish social justice ideals that would give life focus and meaning.[38] Mark Levy said that he went South "because he thought the best way to fight anti-Semitism was to fight discrimination against all people."[39] He told students at Forest Hills High School in 2010 that his parents passed on important and related values to him namely: To believe that discrimination against anyone was bad; to believe in social justice, and to feel a personal obligation to care for others.[40] Indeed, of no less concern was the rise of anti-Semitism and discrimination in the United States against Jews. This is what Gertrude (Trudy) Weissman Orris told Debra Schultz in an interview: "Well, I always felt that I knew what racism was because of being a Jew and being discriminated against. So, racism to me was very much like being a Jew and being discriminated against."[41] And as Isaac Deutscher, (cited in Debra Schultz), once wrote, "[I]t has been Jews' historic marginality that has led to a broader perspective, more clarity about society's injustices, and identification with the oppressed…"[42] It is also possible that some Jewish people were able to readily empathize with Blacks because of the negative portraits and renditions of Jewishness by Whites. Jonathan Kaufman argues that "Jews had turned to black causes out of sympathy fueled by the radical politics of Eastern European immigrants, by their own experience with discrimination, and by the horror of the Holocaust."[43] Ostensibly, he believes that, "A constellation of factors—economic, political, social—provided fertile soil for religious ideas of social justice and opposition to oppression to take root."[44] Michael Lerner and Cornel West made the point that an extraordinary bond existed between Blacks and Jews in America, which enhanced their desire for cooperation because "Both Jews and Blacks are a pariah people—a people who had to make and remake themselves as outsiders on the margins of American society and culture… Both groups have been hated and despised peoples…"[45] It is worth noting that both groups had experienced genocide and great violence against their communities, both in the form of the Holocaust and slavery. As an outsider looking in, Vivian Leburg Rothstein proclaimed this to Debra Schultz "(T)he Holocaust was the defining fact of my childhood. I was raised totally in a community of refugees. That's what propelled me into oppositional politics. I was used to being outside the mainstream. That made it easier to be critical and to identify with the oppression of Blacks."[46] Both of these group's status as "Other" made it possible for Jewish people to identify with the plight that Black people suffered. Mark Levy in a commencement address to students at Forest Hills High School in 2010 noted, "My parents were the children of immigrants. The Holocaust in Europe and anti-Jewish discrimination, right here, in the U.S. were two important facts in my family's life." Therefore, it was important to him to try to "repair the world, to make it a better place for everyone."[47]

On the other hand, some of the White volunteers who were Christians like Chude Allen wanted to go to Mississippi to fight for the right of both Blacks and Whites to live together based on the Christian principle of redemptive suffering, that is, sacrificing oneself for something greater so as to redeem the nation from its sin of racism.[48] These Christians realized as Martin Luther King, Jr. had noted, "No one is free, until we are all free." The Christian volunteers were willing to forgo everything and suffer all indignities—mobs, beatings, ambush by the Ku Klux Klan, and even death for the cause to free America based on the Christian tenet of brotherhood of all humankind.[49]

It must be said that some of the volunteers simply saw wrong and decided to right it. Joan Nestle was moved to join the movement by seeing pictures of women, men, and children being held to the ground, water hosed, and beaten by white sheriffs. She was also an active CORE member. Joseph Liesner joined the movement because he heard stories of various murders in the South. Rita Schwerner and her husband, Michael, were moved into action after they had seen on television the bombing of the Sixteenth Street Baptist Church in Birmingham, Alabama that killed four young girls. After seeing this brutal event, Michael Schwerner noted that he had chosen service to the poor and the disenfranchised as his life's work and was so thoroughly identified with the civil rights struggle. Mario Savio told Bret Eynon in the "Student Movements of the 1960s Project" interview, that his consciousness (and indeed that of the nation) was raised when he saw on television people being hit over the head, people holding one another against fire hoses; billy clubs and police dogs raining down on men, women, and children. This as he saw it, was so very unreal against what he had been raised to believe about American democracy.[50] And as he later said, "identifying your efforts with people who very obviously were oppressed… just appeals to human beings."[51] He saw Freedom Summer as a unique opportunity to change America. In answer to a question why she got involved while other students were standing by? Lucy Komisar said, "It was a sense of morality, and it's very hard to figure out where that comes from. I think my parents always, being liberal, had some of that sense about social justice; I guess they passed it on to me."[52] Peter Geffen participated in SCOPE because "Andrew Goodman's memory had to be honored by continuing his work and not ignoring what he was doing."[53] There were those who joined the Movement because social change was in the air and they wanted to be part of it.

This chapter examines the motivational factors in movement participation by QC student activists of the 1960s through their own voices and the records they left behind. I conclude that there is considerable individual variation in what accounts for movement participation. And according to McAdam, "As social phenomena, social movements are large and diverse enough to provide a broad umbrella under which a wide variety of participants can huddle."[54]

Notes

1. Lee Cogan, In Stephen Stepanchev ed. *The People's College on the Hill: Fifty Years at Queens College, 1937–1987*. New York, Queens College, 1988, p. 9.
2. Ibid.
3. Ibid.
4. Mark Levy, "About Freedom Summer'64 and QC," p. 4.
5. "Student Movements of the 1960s Project: The Reminiscences of Mario Savio." Box 2, folder 7, Arthur Gatti Collection, Department of Special Collections and Archives, Queens College, City University of New York, p. 29.
6. Michael Wenger, *My Black Family, My White Privilege: A White Man's Journey through the Nation's Racial Minefield* Bloomington, IN: iUniverse, Inc. 2012, p. 42.

7. Jerusha O. Conner, *The New Student Activists: The Rise of Neoactivism on College Campuses.* Baltimore, MD: Johns Hopkins University Press, 2020.
8. Eric L. Hirsch, "Sacrifice for the Cause: Group Processes, Recruitment, and Commitment in a Student Social Movement." *American Sociological Review,* Vol. 55, No. 2, April, 1990, pp. 243–254.
9. Doug McAdam, "Recruitment to High-Risk Activism: The Case of Freedom Summer." *American Journal of Sociology,* Vol. 92, No. 1, 1986, pp. 64.
10. Jonathan Mark writing for New York Jewish Week of July 16, 2014, estimates that about 50% of the 1000 students who participated in Freedom Summer were Jewish. See Jonathan Mark, "Freedom Summer Memories: Black-Jewish Alliance Was Brief, Beautiful." *New York Jewish Week,* July 16, 2014.
11. James Farmer, "Foreword." In Jack Salzman, Adina Back and Gretchen Sullivan Sorin, eds. *Bridges and Boundaries: African Americans and American Jews.* George Braziller in association with The Jewish Museum, New York, NY: 1992, p. 13.
12. Mark, "Freedom Summer Memories," *New York Jewish Week,* July 16, 2014.
13. Lucy Komisar: A Personal History of Civil Rights and Feminism, Talk at Panel on "Women, Queens College, and the Civil Rights Movement," March 16, 2009, Queens College. See Doug McAdam, *Freedom Summer.* New York, NY: Oxford University Press, 1988, p. 49.
14. In Doug McAdam's study of Freedom Summer 1964, about 76% of the participants had taken part in earlier protests. Doug McAdam, *Freedom Summer.* New York, NY: Oxford University Press, 1988. See also, Doug McAdam, "Recruitment to High-Risk Activism: The Case of Freedom Summer." *American Journal of Sociology,* Vol. 92, No. 1, 1986, p. 82.
15. Similarly, Mario Savio (who was not Jewish) went to Albany with a group of students to protest a proposed fee raise at CUNY colleges. He joined the picket line for a civil rights demonstration and antidiscrimination at the New York Woolworth's and served as a picket captain during the student strike of November 16, 1961, at Queens College, organized by the Student Association president, Kenneth Warner. (See Cagin and Dray, *We are not Afraid,* p. 103.

16. Interview with Mark Levy, 4/2/2012; 9/19/12; 11/02/12; 3/14/12; 12/4/18; 3/8/20. Interview with Joseph Liesner 10/20/12.
17. Doug McAdam, *Freedom Summer*, p. 49.
18. Wenger, *My Black Family*, p. 43.
19. Andrew Goodman, http://en.wikipedia.org/wiki//Walden_School_(New_York_City) (Accessed 8/19/2013).
20. Cited in Conner, *The New Student Activists*, p. 5.
21. Jon N. Hale, *The Freedom Schools: Student Activists in the Mississippi Civil Rights Movement*. New York: Columbia University Press, 2018, p. 89.
22. Michael R. Wenger and Stan F. Shaw, "Northerners in a Jim Crow World: Queens College Summer Experience." In Terence Hicks and Abul Pitre eds. *The Educational Lockout of African Americans in Prince Edward County, Virginia (1959–1964): Personal Accounts and Reflections*. Lanham, MD: University Press of America, 2010, p. 56.
23. Cagin and Dray, *We Are Not Afraid*, p. 49.
24. *The Daily Star*. http://old.thedailystar.com/opinion/edits/2007/01/ed0131.html (Accessed 7/14/2012).
25. See Wenger and Shaw, "Northerners in a Jim Crow World," p. 56. See also Debra L. Schultz, *Going South: Jewish Women in the Civil Rights Movement*. New York: New York University Press, 2001, p. 146.
26. See Jon N. Hale, *The Freedom Schools*, p. 89.
27. Dorothy M. Zellner, "My Real Vocation." In Faith S. Holsaert et al. eds. *Hands on the Freedom Plow: Personal Accounts by Women in SNCC*. Urbana, IL: University of Illinois Press, 2010, p. 311.
28. "Questions for Queens College Students Regarding Prince Edward County Project." Box 1, folder 3, Jean L. Konzal Papers, Department of Special Collections and Archives, Queens College, City University of New York.
29. Debra L. Schultz, *Going South*, p. 147.
30. Ibid., p. xiv.
31. Debra L. Schultz, *Going South*, p. 108.
32. *Daily News* February 13, 2006.
33. Ibid.
34. Leah Donnella and Robert Wilkes, "Race in America: A Conversation." *Divided We Fall*, July 16, 2019, p. 2.

35. Debra L. Schultz, "Why I Tracked Them Down: Our Unsung Civil Rights Movement Heroines." *Lilith,* Fall, 1999, p. 12.
36. Dorothy M. Zellner, http://cosmos.ucc.ie/cs1064/jabowen/IPSC/php/authors.php?auid=25409 (Accessed 12/20/2018).
37. Mark Levy, "About Freedom Summer and QC." (n.d).
38. Schultz, *Going South,* pp. 1–28.
39. Mark Levy. http://cosmos.ucc.ie/cs1064/jabowen/IPSC/php/authors.php?auid=25409 (Accessed 12/20/2018).
40. Mark Levy, "Forest Hills High School—June 2010 Commencement Address."
41. Shultz, *Going South,* p. 158.
42. Cited in Schultz, *Going South,* p. 162.
43. Jonathan Kaufman, *Broken Alliance: The Turbulent Times Between Blacks and Jews in America.* New York: Charles Scribner's Sons, 1988, p. 33.
44. Ibid., p. 33. See Schultz, *Going South,* p. 21 for a similar but different version of the same interpretation.
45. Michael Lerner and Cornel West, *Jews & Blacks: A Dialogue on Race, Religion, and Culture in America.* New York: Penguin Books, 1996, pp. 1–2. See also Isabel Wilkerson, *Caste: The Origins of Our Discontents.* New York, Random House, 2020.
46. Debra L. Schultz's interview with Vivian Leburg Rothstein cited in Debra L. Schultz, *Going South,* p. 1.
47. Mark Levy, "Forest Hills High School–June 2010 Commencement Address."
48. See Chude Allen, "My Parents said Yes!" In Jacqueline Johnson ed. *Finding Freedom: Memorializing the Voices of Freedom Summer.* Oxford, Ohio: Miami University Press, 2013, p. 25. Note that Chude Allen, Gertrude (Trudy) Weissman Orris, Isaac Deutscher, Debra Schultz and Vivian Leburg Rothstein were not from Queens College or connected to Queens College in any way. They are only used in this book for illustration purposes.
49. Ibid., pp. 25–27. See also Doug McAdam, *Freedom Summer,* pp. 50–51.
50. Mario Savio, "Student Movements of the 1960s Project: The Reminiscences of Mario Savio", Oral History Research Office, Columbia University, 2000, p. 12.

51. Cited in Robert Cohen, *Freedom's Orator: Mario Savio and the Radical Legacy of the 1960s.* New York, NY: Oxford University Press, 2009, p. 50.
52. Lucy Komisar, "Tully Oral History." McCain Library & Archives, The University of Southern Mississippi, 1998, p. 8.
53. Peter Geffen, *Daily News*, February 13, 2006.
54. Doug McAdam, "Gender as a Mediator of the Activist Experience: The Case of Freedom Summer." *American Journal of Sociology*, Vol. 97, No. 5, 1992, p. 1212.

CHAPTER 8

Conclusion

Throughout this book, I have studied and written on various activists from Queens College in the 1960s. As we moved through the beginning of Queens College as a hotbed of student activism to the SEEK Rebellion, we learned how and why QC students got involved in social justice activism. Here, I would like to take just a few moments to give a very brief synopsis of student activism at QC: from its very beginnings to where it is currently.

College student activism in the United States is not new. It dates to 1638 when students at Harvard College protested the leadership of President Nathaniel Eaton. This was followed by Harvard's Bad Butter Rebellion in 1766. Numerous other student protests followed such as anti-British, anti-Stamp Act protests. There were protests sparked by religious sentiments during colonial days. Campus protests in the intervening years between 1800-1930 mirrored national feelings and included students advocating for anti-slavery or state's rights, the abolitionist movement, problems with university presidents, problems with town's authorities, students' demand to have a say in university decision-making, et cetera. In the 1940s and 50 s, student protests centered around World War II patriotism, anti-McCarthyism, racial conflicts, racial violence, desegregation, and *in loco parentis*. As we've seen in this book, in the 1960s, college students protested segregation, systemic racism, pushed

© The Author(s), under exclusive license to Springer Nature Switzerland AG 2024
M. O. Bassey, *Student Activism in 1960s America*, Palgrave Studies in the History of Social Movements,
https://doi.org/10.1007/978-3-031-54794-2_8

for increase in college and university diversity, civil rights, voting rights, inclusive environment for students of color, changes in college discriminatory policies, as well as the inclusion of student voices in administrative decision-making in universities and colleges. Students also protested the Cold War, the Vietnam War, free speech, and against tuition increases. The 1960s and 1970s are said to have marked the peak of student activism in the United States,[1] as large numbers of college students protested systemic racism, racial and gender inequalities, as well as the Vietnam War. For some Americans, political involvement of young adults was a good thing, but for many others, it was not. Many people in the United States criticized student involvement in matters too complicated for them to comprehend. From the 1990s to the present, student activism has continued to center around systemic racism, student voice in college administrative decisions, social issues, sexual assault, gender inequality, LGBTQ+ rights, ROTC programs, gun control, gun laws and safety, tuition increases, economic inequality, migrant rights, elimination of student debt etc.

* * *

Is there anything the present generation of student activists can learn from the activists of the 1960s? Unfortunately, systemic racism is as entrenched today in America as it was in the 1960s when QC students went to Virginia and Mississippi to make racial equality and social justice government priorities. The QC student activists of the 1960s I interviewed for this book; all told me that most of the gains that followed Freedom Summer have been undone. This is perhaps why Mark Levy, one of the Freedom Summer activists from QC concluded in a speech at the National Convention of the American Federation of Teachers in Los Angeles on July 12, 2014 that, "The Civil Rights Movement is not Over."[2] Yes indeed, according to Monmouth University opinion poll taken in 2020, about 75% of Americans said discrimination was a problem in the country and about 57% said that African Americans were more likely to suffer from police brutality.[3]

What lessons can be learned today from the activism of 1960s? Another way of asking this question is: what does activism of the 1960s mean for our new generation of student activists in 2024? And what does student activism look like today? As we have seen from the above polls some of the major issues like systemic racism remain the same or even worse. Indeed, some of the issues African Americans and some minorities are facing today mirror the same types of issues they faced in the 1960s. As one editor put it, "far too little has changed."[4] However, it appears that because, so little has changed in race relations in America, and there seems to be little visible student actions, many believe that the present generation of students is abandoning activism,[5] and Millennials have been blamed for a lack of engagement with the world. Some people even think that since we are living in these interesting times, student protesters should organize and strategize like their counterparts in the 1960s.[6] Those who are of this persuasion even think that student activism is dead.[7] This is quite to the contrary because in an annual UCLA survey of undergraduates in the United States in 2016, 1 in 10 students said they would participate in protests in college.[8] This is the highest rate of student participation in activism of any kind since 1967 when thousands of students demonstrated on university campuses.[9] After surveying about 3,000 high school and college students in Massachusetts, Connecticut, and Mississippi, Meira Levinson noted, "We're in a groundswell moment of youth activism."[10] Jerusha O. Conner argues that the years 2015–2018 saw a surge in student campus activism which again brought national attention to what was happening in Black and White communities as "student activists staged dramatic acts of resistance to campus policies, protested guest speakers, and forced administrators to engage in long-overdue conversations about institutionalized racism and sexism."[11] We cannot forget so soon activist group like the Occupy Wall Street movement in New York City in 2011 that brought attention to income inequality in America. Indeed, there have been youth activist groups such as Dream Defenders, March on Washington for Gun Control in 2013, People's Climate March in 2014, the Black Youth Project 100 (BYP100), the Assata's Daughters, Million Hoodies Movement for Justice, Women's March of January 21, 2017, the March for Science on April 22, 2017, Concerned Student 1950 from the University of Missouri that pressured the president of the university to resign because he failed to condemn racist acts on campus. Others include March for Our Lives and Black Lives Matter.[12] This is just to mention only a few large-scale protest movements. Indeed, between 2015 and 2021, there were hundreds of demonstrations by student activists in many university campuses across the United States against institutional policies and guest speakers[13] that "forced administrators to engage in long-overdue conversations about institutionalized racism and sexism."[14] According to Genevieve Carlton, "In the past decade, the United States has witnessed a 'renaissance of student activism.'" As she sees it, "college students are more active than ever before, successfully fighting against tuition increases and for more equitable campus policies."[15] Today's youths think they must take upon themselves to do something because those in authority have decided not to act for change. But, unlike the near homogeneous student movements of the 1960s, today's student activists are more diverse in their composition and demands, due in part to the changing student demographics. Although self-care and intersectionality have entered today's student activists' lexicon, there is a subgroup of contemporary student activists who "link their social justice work to the pioneering activist efforts of their predecessors…".[16]

Ideally, students are not participating less in activism, rather they are using different approaches such as, "replacing confrontation with dialogue, lobbying, and direct service provision and 'organizing' locally and globally without ever joining hands."[17] This type of activism may require less time commitment and may seem unreal, remote, and situational, but it poses less risk and is less volatile. It may not, however, carry with it the heroism of the past because today's activists use technology to recruit, train, and mobilize people to effect social change. For instance, on February 16, 2018, after a 19-year-old killed 17 students and staff at Marjory Stoneman Douglas High School in Parkland, Florida, Julian Lopez-Leyva, a student at Bunker Hill Community College, held a one-man demonstration in Boston for 17 hours, each hour representing one of the 17 victims murdered. After hearing five survivors of the Marjory High School massacre announce on CNN that they would be organizing a national "March for Our Lives," Lopez-Leyva created a Facebook event for a "March for Our Lives" in Boston. The protest was to require stricter background checks for gun buyers so that Americans will "Never Again" witness another school shooting of that magnitude. Using social media, Lopez-Leyva was able to connect with other student groups in other college campuses, and during the event on March 24 in Boston Common, there were almost 100,000 demonstrators with more than 2 million people participating in about 800 rallies in all the states in the United States and Washington, DC, and in six continents.[18] Within months "March for Our Lives" had grown into a worldwide movement. Kim Long, a chapter leader of "Moms Demand Action for Gun Sense In America," stated "Our young people in this country are brilliant. They're smart, they're articulate, there's not one of those students who didn't stand up and speak that I wouldn't vote for (for) Congress tomorrow."[19]

The effect of "March for Our Lives" has been long lasting as demonstrated in the documentary, *The Price of Freedom* which shows students as powerful agents of change, among other things.

Similarly, Black Lives Matter hashtag was first used on Twitter by Patrisse Khan-Cullors in 2013 after George Zimmerman was acquitted even though he had murdered an unarmed Black youth, Trayvon Martin. Black Lives Matter became a movement in 2014 when another unarmed Black teenager, Michael Brown was killed by a White police officer in Ferguson, Missouri. The Black Lives Matter platform was launched by Patrisse Khan-Cullors together with Alicia Garza and Opal Tometi, "in order to forward a conversation about what is taking place in Black communities."[20] It went global with branches in many countries. However, people in Minneapolis, Minnesota were galvanized to protest on May 26, 2020, when they saw the gruesome, disturbing, and shocking videos circulating on social media showing how George Floyd was crushed to death under the knee of Derek Chauvin, a White Minneapolis police officer; people gathered in the park in protest under the banner and slogan "Black Lives Matter." Afterward, and within a few weeks and months, people in the United States and the rest of the world gave their support in what became a worldwide movement captioned, "Black Lives Matter." Thousands gathered in Britain, France, and Germany. Many more gathered in Tokyo and Sydney. Parliament Square in central London and the surrounding streets were filled to the brim during demonstrations. In Paris, many people gathered near the Eiffel Tower. The crowds of protesters included a diverse array of people in support for equality and chanting, "Black Lives Matter" and "No justice, no peace." In Australia, thousands protested chanting the mantra, "Black Lives Matter," "How many more?" and "Australia is not innocent," in reference to the Australian government's treatment of the Aboriginal people.[21] According to the *New York Times*, "Black Lives Matter" may be the largest movement in U. S. history. The paper estimated that between 15 and 26 million people in the United States participated in "Black Lives Matter" demonstrations over the death of George Floyd and some others in the year 2020.[22] The *Washington Post* described the "Black Lives Matter" movement as "the broadest in US history"[23] And according to Jesse Hagopian, "The protests dramatically changed the political climate and propelled the Black Lives Matter movement to a level of struggle not seen since perhaps the 1960s and

1970s."[24] This is how one commentator described the "Black Lives Matter" protests in the United States,

> In urban centers, black and white protesters have come forward together in defiance, joined by allies like GOP Senator Mitt Romney and longtime Koch Industries executive Mark Holden. In predominantly white cities across the country, white Americans have shown up by the thousands in solidarity. Even small towns in rural parts of the country have joined in the protests.[25]

Today, because of the use of modern technology, incidents rapidly turn into social movements, and it should be emphasized that the use of modern technology is one of the reasons we are seeing dramatic increases in activism among young people especially among young Black people against police brutality. Eric Braxton noted that, "The killing of unarmed black people at the hands of police is, unfortunately, not a new phenomenon. However, the response from young black people and the way they have used social media to connect, communicate, and organize has helped make the Movement for Black Lives one of the most powerful movements of the last 30 years."[26] As it happened in the 1960s and 1970s, students in the current moment are protesting and advocating for their lives and seeking equality and justice for others. And again, as in the 1960s and 1970s, the nation is divided on whether students should be involved in any type of activism at all. However, since the "March for Our Lives" in 2018 and the "Black Lives Matter" movement in 2020, social activism has again entered people's consciousness. Indeed, in 1969 only 34% of Americans approved of student activism, whereas in 2018, in a Monmouth University opinion poll, 64% of Americans believe that students should advocate for the issues they believe in, and in a Quinnipiac University poll in 2018, 63% of Americans approved of students protesting in favor of stricter gun laws.[27] A recent CBS opinion poll also confirmed that Americans believe students should advocate for themselves, particularly concerning gun violence.[28] Students are receiving more support for their activism now than in the 1960s and 1970s because today, people are seeing things as they happen in real time, due to the use of the Internet and social media.

Under these circumstances, can today's student activists learn from activists of the 1960s? Yes, they can, but maybe not from strategy or organizational standpoint. Indeed, present-day student activists are cognizant of their limitations as one of their leaders once admitted, "We must have been a little crazy to be thinking that we could do something like replicate ... Vietnam-era level of mobilization."[29] In my view, contemporary student activists can learn from the commitment to the cause, sacrifice required, emotional support, and the joy that goes with activism from student activists of the 1960s. They can also enjoy mentorship from the old hands, but their method of operation must be different because as Leah Lievrouw has pointed out, "alternative and activist new media employ or modify existing communication artifacts, practices, and social arrangements of new information and communication technologies to challenge or alter dominant, expected, or accepted ways of doing society, culture, and politics."[30] Jerusha Conner makes the point that as contemporary student activists "work to address the challenges of their day, the new student activists have eschewed competition in favor of building diverse and inclusive coalitions, which make room for a wide range of students' social identities. This intentionality distinguishes their efforts from the more homogeneous student movements of the mid-to-late 1960s..."[31] Also, as an alternative to protest, today's youths are turning more and more to community service as a way of effecting change in their communities. The above characterizations distinguish today's neoactivists (as Jerusha Conner calls them) from the student activists of the 1960s.

Back to the QC nexus, activism as a way of deconstructing and resisting institutional power is at a very low ebb at QC today even as a new set of culture wars are playing out in the polity heightened by rightist political agenda, insurrections, and police brutality.[32] Although there are 136 clubs and organizations registered with the Division of Student Affairs and Enrollment Management at QC, we do not have activist-minded student organizations like SDS, CORE, NAACP, The Student Help Project, or even the Committee to End Political Suppression of the 1960s.[33] Nonetheless, a few student organizations at QC have some element of or have activist bents and intents. These include the *Student Government* and *In the Footsteps of Dr. King*, a non-doctrinaire student organization which provides students with skills needed to combat bigotry and intolerance. This organization allows students to connect with the civil rights struggle of the 1960s. According to Rabbi Moshe Shur, the Director, *In the Footsteps of Dr. King*, offers a unique opportunity for students to travel to major sites of the civil rights and learn under the direction of educators who worked with the great civil rights leaders through the historic landscape of the movement. Another group of QC students with a long tradition of activist engagement are students in the SEEK program. Annie Tummino, in a recent 2020 documentary, "Commemorating a Legacy of Dissent: Revisiting Campus Activism, 1968–1970," maintains that "the SEEK tradition of student activism and engagement is alive and well today,"[34] at QC because, SEEK students occupy significant roles in student government and other organizations on campus. She pointed out that many of the QC SEEK alumni have gone on to pursue gainful political careers. A good example of this is Khaleel M. Anderson who is the youngest Black member of the New York State Assembly.[35] Norka Blackman-Richards, the current SEEK Director, explained to Annie that the long and continuous history of activism among students in the SEEK program at QC was deliberate and intentional because their students are made to be activist-minded as soon as they enter the program and noted:

> The first semester we group the students together and tell them they are the next generation. We ask them, who do you want to be your advocates? Who do you want to be your leaders? Who do you want to speak for you? Students vote on it. We then expect these young people to advocate, to work with the administration, to lead programs for their peers, to tell us what they need. So, we give them a voice and we give them a place[36]

Blackman-Richards believes that social and educational transformation is necessary today to counter oppressive, domineering systems in the same way it was in the 1960s because what is happening today seems to be a repeat of 1969, given the fact that issues of equity and social justice have resurrected in the polity, which to her, looks like lack of progress.[37] Indeed, most of the SEEK students that Blackman-Richards has spoken to and with, tell her that it is important for them to learn about the struggles of the 1960s because it gives them the determination to disrupt fatalistic concepts rooted in hegemony, domination, and oppression. In fulfillment of their civic responsibilities, Blackman-Richards maintains, "our students have been actively organizing, mobilizing and protesting around Black Lives Matter issues but they are also civically engaged, by volunteering at the polls, and leading voting drives."[38] Looking back at the events of 1969, a student activist, Wally Rosenthal, who was described as "the most effective leader of the student action against Queens College,"[39] told Annie Tummino, "We did not take actions against Queens College; we took actions against what we saw as the administration's complicity

8 CONCLUSION 243

with corporations that produced weapons and other products used by the United States military in its horrific assault on the people of Vietnam and other Southeast Asian countries."[40] He also told Annie that they wanted the college to reexamine its role as a recruiting ground for the military-industrial complex.

In reaction to peoples' alienation and marginalization of history, Annie Tummino drove home the point that understanding the past is not just about understanding the ugly past of wars and horrors, "but also to know that ordinary people have always resisted oppression and fought for a more equal, more just, and a more humane world, in many diverse ways."[41] As a way of raising students' consciousness about what happened in the 1960s, the QC Civil Rights archivists make enormous efforts to create exhibits which serve as platforms for outreach to the community, students, faculty, and donors, as a way of accelerating increased community involvement in the archives.[42] Not long ago, the archivists at QC worked with some professors in the history department to incorporate archival instruction into their "America in the 1960s" course. Apart from document analysis and consulting the archives for their research, the students are allowed to write reflection papers on the exhibit for extra credit. The QC archivists are also working with the faculty in English to incorporate primary sources into their "Literature and Human Rights" course. The various exhibits in the QC civil rights archives include Helen Hendricks Oral History, the SEEK History Project, and The Queens College Student Help Project, among others. These exhibits also call for curriculum integration and programming as well.[43] On a more practical level, Sheila Delany, the professor of Medieval Literature whose appointment was terminated at QC in 1968 was invited to campus from Canada to tell her own side of the story and to acquaint the college community with the events that bedeviled the campus in 1968. Unsuspectedly, we learned from Sheila that her termination was not only politically motivated as was earlier assumed, but had sexist undertones as well because Sheila, during the discussion, told the audience that the Chair of the English Department told her, "You could be a fascist or a communist, we don't care if you're charming enough."[44] She also said that she was berated for having an abrasive personality.[45]

It seems apropos to conclude this study by asking some of the 1960s QC student activists what they hope today's student activists should learn from them or what lessons they hope to impart to today's student activists? In an interview with Mark Levy, one of the 1960s student activists from QC, he said,

> One of the things we learned in Mississippi that Summer was that Mississippi was not the only place that had racial and social justice problems—and that the struggle needed to continue in many ways and many places. Whether floating in the air like seeds or growing outward deep in the earth like roots, we who had that experience in '64 would take the message that the movement needs to continue and grow wherever we went.[46]

Mark hopes that telling the story of "ordinary people doing extraordinary things" in previous struggles can add support for young folks assessing and becoming active in the current world. Mark once also said, "One of the tenets of being an organizer and teacher is always to look for opportunities to pass the torch along to potential new activists,"[47] and in one of his writings, he pondered, "How can we best inspire and teach future generations of activists to commit to the fight for social justice?" Looking back on activism in his day, Elliot Linzer told me, "You know the cliché, 'All politics is local,' usually attributed to Tip O'Neill. As I have grown older, more and more I think that it is true."[48] He advised today's student activists to organize around real issues impacting people's daily lives and to build from there to bigger issues, because it is the little things that really matter in people's lives. As he sees it, activism should focus on the possibility of addressing real concerns of the people in the community. He gave an example of how he had to organize his neighbors to request a different bus stop for his and his neighbors' children, because the owner of the property where the previous bus stop was located had become hostile to the school children for always playing in front of his house. Linzer advised today's neoactivists, as Jerusha Conner calls them, to be humble and not to be dogmatic. The issues they pursue should follow from real analysis and real understanding of what is at stake.[49] Michael Wenger, one of the leaders of the Student Help Project and a participant in the *Fast for Freedom* at QC told me that the question concerning what today's student activists could learn from their own experiences, is one he and some of his fellow activists of the 60 s have pondered over the years. He suggested that today's student activists should listen and recognize that nobody has a monopoly on truth and good ideas, because lots of people may have ideas for strategies and tactics that are worth considering. His overarching argument is that today's activists must be open to learning every step of the way. He conceptualizes that it is important for activists in the current moment to have clear and compelling vision, but they should be able to recognize when the goal has been achieved. While he advises today's student activists to be innovative and ambitious, he urges them to set achievable goals that can be attained within a reasonable period. He illuminated the fact that there is a need for creating a critical mass in any movement organization because people who are committed and courageous can make a significant difference, and because, activism depends on building good and effective relationships within and outside its circles to be effective. And indeed, there is so much power when people are a collective. He reminded his audience that it is important to realize that in any organization, honest and effective communication are the panacea because good communication can win the hearts and minds of doubters. Clearly, because activism is so challenging, today's youth organizing groups must constantly assess and reassess their achievements along the way to make changes where necessary. Wenger concluded that it is essential for today's student activists to be ready to commit themselves for the long haul and to recognize that victory may not be as fast and forthcoming as anticipated.[50] Stan Shaw, one of the leaders in the Student Help Project and CORE told me that the student activists of the 1960s were a diverse group. Some followed in their parents' footsteps, while others, like himself, had no support from home for their fight against injustice. What was unique in their circumstance, were the mentors who supported them. Faculty members, Dr. Rachel Weddington, Dr. Sid (Sidney) Simon and Helen Hendricks were trusted counselors and mentors. According to Stan Shaw, Helen Hendricks, who was an Administrative Assistant in the Office of Student Activities, was always available to help student leaders think through their good intentions into productive activities. All these mentors, he said, modeled thoughtful and ethical behaviors. Although their mentors never told them what to do, but they in a Rogerian way, listened to the students' ideas by asking probing questions. In essence, they (the student activists) observed mature behavior and were encouraged to consider outcomes before acting. Stan believes that the twenty-first-century student activists could benefit from having good mentors to guide them, because youths are often very idealistic, impatient, and willing to take unnecessary risks.[51] In a 2015 interview, Frankye Adams-Johnson advised young people to be open to new ideas and to find out what is good for them.[52] In Arthur Gatti's testimony, he thinks that for tangible change to take place, today's student activists must be passionate about what they do. Activism should be undertaken within a broader framework and should be sustained over time. He gave the example of his work as a sous chef and fund raiser in the West Village, New York in the 1980s and 90 s for those suffering from AIDS because of his concern at seeing so many of his friends and neighbors die of the disease. In answer to the question, "what lessons would you impart on today's student activists?" Andrew Berman told me that today's activists are often more tolerant and more successful than his generation was in achieving diversity in areas including race, gender, and LGBTQ. This generation not only tolerates but celebrates diversity. On this, his advice is for them to continue to do so, but to be more internationalist than they were. According to him, in his day, it was relatively rare that Americans met with Vietnamese during the war. The opportunities to do so were relatively rare. Few Americans spoke Vietnamese. Today, American peace activists can travel to Ukraine, West Bank Palestine and meet and develop relationships with folks over there. My advice: "DO SO! Learn some of their culture and language. Explicitly celebrate diversity. Use today's technology, e.g. zoom and other computer skills to connect with people around the world who are direct or indirect victims of war and oppression. Be proud of your activism, but leave some of the ego, some of the stardom behind. That's an area where my generation of activists too often failed." Interestingly, Joan Nestle told me: My activism–not a word I used back then–began in my class positioning, in my beginning understandings of workers and bosses, of what it meant to live day by day hoping to survive in America's 1950s. I came to Queens College with no sense of working class history but my mother had told me of the true heroes, like Paul Robeson and I saw how he stood up to engineered hatred.... At Queens in 1961, I found the CORE chapter on campus, the Congress of Racial Equality, which led me to Freedom Rides in Baltimore and later to Selma, Alabama. SANE had an office on the gate-bound campus, for a sane nuclear policy, and together we refused to go to designated shelters on campus when the sirens rang out–we stood, in silence on the steps of the old library while the FBI took our details under the auspices of the Queens College president. My new friends had founded an anti-HUAC campus group to fight the House Un-American Activities Committee; we staffed table with petitions of protests, and we could see the terror in the eyes of others when asked to say no. We rode busses from those QC gates to Washington, DC and were gassed in front of the Pentagon, we attended meetings of HUAC to defend Paul Robeson and JoAnne

Grant's right to travel outside the country and were called the scum of the earth. Queens College and its students were educating me in so many ways, but I realize Magnus, you must know all of this from your work. These moments, and movements, live in me till this day. They taught me to find and work in communities and to stand alone when needed. You ask me what I would say to activists today–when sadly so much is once again at stake with the even more profound challenge of a planet beginning to collapse under the weight of our greed and our carelessness. I would say thank you beyond words for having the courage, the insight to use the skills of your time to organize for change, I would say never doubt the need for what you do, for the huge gifts you are giving yourselves and your communities, to refuse cynicism, and organized hatreds. All will give your lives deep meaning. You are now in an America that is teetering on the edge of Fascism, find the words, the music, the loves, the ideas, that give you a love of life while you fight for life. Take care of yourselves in the best ways you can and when you need us, find our words—you will be embraced by the deepest human bonds of endeavor, and you will be lonely all at the same time. If I were with you, I would listen to you because you are the main story now. You know, you have no other choice when you see into the coming calamities, than to organize.[53]

As a general note of caution, Manning Marable told us some years ago that, "the [1964] summer mobilization set into motion the subsequent passage of the 1965 Voting Rights Act that extended the electoral franchise to millions of African Americans for the first time in nearly a century."[54] Although some progress has been made, much remains to be done with respect to voting rights and systemic racism in America. Sadly enough, some of the gains made with the passage of the Voting Rights Act of 1965 are being eroded today through voter suppression as many states across the country have passed measures to make it more difficult for some Americans, particularly minorities, to exercise their fundamental right to vote. The tactics used have ranged from dirty tricks that make voting inconvenient, to physical intimidations that prevent people especially Blacks, students, the elderly, and people with disability from casting their ballots.[55] Some of these tactics include limiting forms of acceptable identification for voting, restricting the venues and times for voter registration, and disenfranchising ex-convicts from voting. Indeed, by 2020, there were voter ID laws in place in 36 states and some form of voter restriction in all 50 states in America.[56] Besides, three states in the country have laws requiring proof of citizenship for people to register to vote. Legislation has also been passed in some states to repeal Election Day registration laws and many states have passed legislation to make it more difficult for third parties to register voters.[57] Other concerns include the purging of voter rolls, disenfranchisement of transgender people, disinformation about procedure concerning voting, unequal election resources, closure of DMV offices, and gerrymandering with obvious detrimental effects to democracy.[58] Worse of all, after the 2020 elections, as of February 19, 2021 state law makers have introduced 250 bills in 43 states aimed at making it harder for some people to vote in future elections.[59] Come to think of it, under the *Election Integrity Act* of 2021, it is now a misdemeanor for a non-poll worker to approach voters in line to give them food or water in the state of Georgia.[60]

In my conversations with some of the QC activists of the 1960s, many of them are appalled by today's political discourse. They worry about anti-Social & Emotional Learning (SEL), anti-1619 Project, anti-Critical Race Theory (CRT), and the anti-book campaign rhetoric in the polity. One of them told me, "Between COVID and political attacks, it must be a difficult time for young teachers especially social studies and others who are in fields being attacked." He also said, "The one set of political activities I've engaged in here is around helping fight the right-wing attacks on history teaching and book bans—and supporting local teachers." These activists also worry about the abuse of election laws to suppress votes. And as one of them said to me, "It really boils down to one word ... VOTE." The QC activists of the 1960s also worry about the new set of culture wars, the far-right political insurrections, and police brutality against African Americans. These men and women are activists to the core and have activist mindsets, as they have told me severally: "The struggle is not yet over." Or "It is the responsibility of today's youths to fight to enact change." Or "The answer is for the youths to organize."[61] Some have also told me, "These are very scary times we are living in nationally, statewide and locally." Indeed, many of them have said to me, "We are on the brink of a political precipice." One of them who relocated to a different state even told me, "I've initiated a project to find ... residents and students who went South in the 1960s for civil rights projects like (MS) Freedom Summer 1964 and SCOPE Project 1965." He went on to say, "The one set of political activities I've engaged in here is around helping fight the right-wing attacks on history teaching and book bans—and supporting local teachers." One of the 1960s activists stated: "The lessons of that summer have shaped the

Table 8.1 1960s QC activists in selected occupational groups[65]

Profession	Number	Percentage (%)
College Professors	11	35.48
Lawyers	03	9.67
School Teachers	01	3.22
Clergy	01	3.22
Psychologists	01	3.22
Writers/Artists	04	12.90
Executives	04	12.90
Union Leaders	01	3.22
Technicians	01	3.22
Researchers	01	3.22
Librarians	01	3.22
Computer Scientists	01	3.22
Unknown Occupations	01	3.22
Total	31	99.93[66]

rest of my life and confirmed for me—and for so many of us who were there—our ongoing commitments to social change." Concerning career options, my research provides strong supporting evidence that the career choices of QC student activists of the 1960s are very compatible with the career choices of the Freedom Summer volunteers in McAdam's studies (see Table 8.1).[62] Just as McAdam found in his many studies, most of the subjects in my research are concentrated "in the teaching or other helping professions,"[63] (see Table 8.1). Mark Levy, a QC activist of the 1960s once stated: "That Summer's experience shaped much of the rest of my life and my career—and led to a lifelong commitment to teaching, organizing, and the struggle(s) for social justice."[64]

I want to conclude this work by stating that, as part of a larger social movement of the 1960s, QC students, faculty, and staff, were integral parts of many of the history making civil-minded efforts of the 1960s. From preparing students for the reopening of "free schools" in Prince Edward County, Virginia in 1963 to the larger issue of social justice, the antiwar movement, and the institutionalization of Black Studies, Puerto Rican Studies and Women Studies in CUNY, QC students and faculty were there and played important, pivotal, and significant roles that should be recognized in the same way as the much touted and talked about contributions by students from Ivy League and elite colleges and universities.[67] The contributions of students from Liberal Arts colleges to social justice and significant events in the 1960s should no longer remain unknown to the wider world. This book fills a gaping hole in the historiography of the 1960s student activism in the United States.

Notes

1. acitarel. "A Comparison of Student Activism in American History—Educ 300: Education Reform, Past and Present." May 4, 2018. https://commons.trincoll.edu/edreform/2018/05/a-comparison-of-student-activism-in-american-history/ (Accessed 12/26/2020).
2. Mark Levy, Speech at the National Convention of the American Federation of Teachers, Los Angeles, July 12, 2014.
3. Justin Worland, "The Overdue Awakening" *Time*, June 22–29, 2020, p. 28.
4. Time Editorial, "Where we stand." *Time*, June 22–29, 2020, p. 7.
5. Rob Rosenthal and Lois Brown, "Then and Now: Comparing Today's Student Activism With the 1960s." *HuffPost*, 08/27/2014 Updated Oct 27, 2014 (Accessed 12/26/2020).
6. Ibid.
7. Ibid.
8. Zachary Jason, "Student Activism 2.0: A look Back at the History of Student Activism and Whether Today's Protesters are Making a Difference" p. 2. Fall 2018 (/ED FALL—2018) https://www.gse.harvard.edu/sites/default/files/edmag/pdfs/2018-Fal-20.pdf (Accessed 12/26/2020).
9. Ibid.
10. Cited in Zachary Jason, "Student Activism 2.0," p. 2.
11. Jerusha O. Conner, *The New Student Activists: The Rise of Neoactivism on College Campuses.* Baltimore, MD: Johns Hopkins University Press, 2020, pp. 18–19.
12. See Ibid., pp. 8–17. It is said that the Black Lives Matter hashtag was first used on Twitter by Patrisse Khan-Cullors in 2013 after the acquittal of George Zimmerman in the killing of Trayvon Martin, a Black unarmed young man.
13. See Conner, *The New Student Activist,* pp. 14–18. See also Jesse Hagopian, "Making Black Lives Matter at School," pp. 1–24.
14. Conner, *The New Student Activists,* pp. 18–19.

15. Genevieve Carlton, "Student Activism in College: A History of Campus Protests." https://www.bestcolleges.com/blog/history-student-activism-in-college/ (Accessed 12/26/2020).
16. Conner, *The New Student Activists*, p. 8.
17. Rob Rosenthal and Lois Brown, *HuffPost*, 08/27/2014 Updated Oct 27, 2014, p. 3.
18. Zachary Jason, "Student Activism 2.0."
19. "Teens in Boston Hope to Make a Difference on Gun Legislation"—NBC Boston. https://www.nbcboston.com/news/local/teens-in-boston-hope-to-make-a-difference-on-gun-legislation/127797/ (Accessed 12/28/2020).
20. Cited in Conner, *The New Student Activists*, p. 16.
21. "George Floyd Protests: Live News and Updates." *The New York Times*, June 6, 2020, pp. 3–4.
22. Black Lives Matter May Be the Largest Movement in U. S. History. *New York Times*, July 3, 2020. https://www.nytimes.com/interactive/2020/07/03/us/george-floyd-protests-crowd-size.html (Accessed 12/29/21).
23. Cited in Jesse Hagopian, "Making Black Lives Matter at School." In Denisha Jones and Jesse Hagopian eds. *Black Lives Matter at School: An Uprising for Educational Justice*. Chicago, IL: Haymarket Books, 2020, p. 8.
24. Ibid.
25. Justin Worland, *Time*, June 22–29, 2020, p. 30.
26. Eric Braxton, "Youth Leadership for Social Justice: Past and Present." In Jerusha Conner and Sonia M. Rosen, eds. *Contemporary Youth Activism: Advancing Social Justice in the United States*. Santa Barbara, CA: PRAEGER, 2016, p. 31.
27. acitarel, "A Comparison of Student Activism," p. 3.
28. See Ibid.
29. Cited in Conner, *The New Student Activists*, p. 10.
30. Cited in Charles H. F. Davis111, "Student Activism, Resource Mobilization, And New Tactical Repertoires in the 'Digital Age.'" In Demetri L. Morgan, and Charles H. F. Davis 111 eds. *Student Activism, Politics, and Campus Climate in Higher Education*. New York, NY: Routledge, 2019, p. 117.
31. Conner, *The New Student Activists*, p. 4.
32. Magnus O. Bassey, "Critical Social Foundations of Education: Advancing Human Rights and Transformative Justice Education in

Teacher Preparation." In Ali A. Abdi and Greg William Misiaszek eds. *The Palgrave Handbook on Critical Theories of Education*, pp. 97–111. Switzerland: Palgrave Macmillan, 2022.
33. The clubs and organizations registered with the Division of Student Affairs and Enrollment Management at QC are mostly academic, social, cultural, religious, Greek, and service oriented. One of the very few clubs with activist orientation is the "Liberty in North Korea @QC which has as its objective, "To raise awareness about the corruption and injustice rampant in North Korea."
34. Annie E. Tummino, "Commemorating a Legacy of Dissent: Revisiting Campus Activism 1968–1970." CUNY Academic Works, 2020, Slide # 14. It is also important to point out that the QC SEEK program today has as its motto and guiding principle, "Developing Generations of Scholars and Leaders."
35. Ibid.
36. Ibid.
37. Ibid.
38. Annie E. Tummino, "Commemorating a Legacy of Dissent," Slide # 25.
39. Cited in Tummino, "Commemorating a Legacy of Dissent," Slide #17. This description of Wally Rosenthal was made by the Dean of Students, George Pierson.
40. Annie E. Tummino, "Commemorating a Legacy of Dissent: Revisiting Campus Activism 1968–1970." Slide #17.
41. Ibid., Slide # 25.
42. Annie Tummino and Rachel Kahn, "Campus Unrest at 50: Commemorating the Legacy of Dissent at Queens College." THE ACADEMIC ARCHIVIST, Posted on June 17, 2019, by mlsweet. (Accessed 7/19/23).
43. See Ibid.
44. Ibid.
45. Ibid.
46. Interview with Mark Levy 4/04/2012.
47. Mark Levy, "Mississippi Freedom Summer 1964—A Personal Introduction." (n. d).
48. E-mail correspondence with Elliot Linzer 8/10/2023.
49. Ibid.
50. Correspondence with Michael Wenger 8/19/2023.
51. Correspondence with Stan Shaw 8/21/2023.

52. Frankye Adams-Johnson Oral History Interview conducted by Emilye Crosby, December 6, 2015. YouTube—Library of Congress—February 21, 2020.
53. Correspondence with Joan Nestle 8/22/2023.
54. Manning Marable, in Rita L. Bender, "Searching for Restorative Justice: The Trial of Edgar Ray Killen." *Souls*, Vol. 10, No. 2, 2008, p. 156.
55. Tova Andrea Wang, *The Politics of Voter Suppression: Defending and Expanding Americans' Right to Vote*. Ithaca, NY: Cornell University Press, 2012; Voter Suppression in America. American Civil Liberties Union.
56. NCSL, "Voter Identification Requirements/Voter ID Laws." https://www.ncsl.org/research/elections-and-campaigns/voter-id.aspx (Accessed 1/18/2021).
57. Tova Andrea Wang, *The Politics of Voter Suppression: Defending and Expanding Americans' Right to Vote*. Ithaca, NY: Cornell University Press, 2012; "Voter Suppression in America." American Civil Liberties Union. http://www.aclu.org/voter-suppression-america (Accessed 4/23/2013).
58. Ibid.
59. See Zachary B. Wolf, CNN politics, March 25, 2021.
60. Sante Mastriana, "The Georgia Election Law—Election Security or Voter Suppression?" (/blog_author/sante-mastriana/) CLOSE UP, Washington DC; See also, Zachary B. Wolf and Brian Rokus, CNN politics, March 25 & 26, 2021.
61. These are the kinds of responses I have received from most of the subjects in my study that I have interviewed.
62. Doug McAdam, "The Biographical Consequences of Activism." p. 755; Doug McAdam, *Freedom Summer*, New York, NY: Oxford University Press, 1988.
63. Doug McAdam, "The Biographical Consequences of Activism." p. 755; See also Doug McAdam, *Freedom Summer*, New York, NY: Oxford University Press, 1988.
64. Mark Levy "Mississippi Freedom Summer 1964—A Personal Introduction." (n.d).
65. Many on this list started their careers as teachers or were teaching on the side during the period of their gainful employment.
66. This difference is due to fractions.

67. See Doug McAdam, *Freedom Summer,* New York, NY: Oxford University Press, 1988, p. 5; Bruce Watson, *Freedom Summer, The Savage Season of 1964 That made Mississippi Burn and Made America a Democracy,* New York, NY: Penguin Books, 2010, p. 15, Gwendolyn Zoharah Simmons, "Reflections on the Orientation and My Participation in the 1964 Mississippi Freedom Summer Project." In Jacqueline Johnson, ed. *Finding Freedom: Memorializing the Voices of Freedom Summer,* pp. 49–56. Oxford, OH: Miami University Press, 2013, p. 54.

Bibliography

Primary Sources

Queens College: Department of Special Collections and Archives
Andrew Berman Collection
Arthur Gatti Collection
Barbara (Jones) Omolade Collection
Dean Savage Papers
Debby Yaffe Collection
Elliot Linzer Collection
Jean L. Konzal Papers
Mark Levy Collection
Michael Wenger Collection
Moshe Shur Papers
Phyllis Padow-Sederbaum Collection
Robert Masters Collection
Rosalind (Silverman) Andrews Papers
Stan Shaw Collection
Student Publication Collection

Columbia University Oral History Research Office & Archives
Student Movements of the 1960s Project: Reminiscences of Mario Savio, Interview conducted by Bret Eynon on March 5, 1985, in San Francisco, CA.: Columbia University Oral History office

Mississippi Department of Archives and History
Mississippi Freedom Labor Union Contact List (Electronic Archives online)
Mississippi's Sovereignty Commission File (Electronic Archives online)
Mississippi Freedom Labor Union Contact List

Stanford University Department of Special Collections and Archives
KZSU Project South Interviews: University Archives, Stanford University
SCOPE Chapter 33, Mickey Shur Interview

The King Center Archives
Letter from Isaac Foster Regarding a Scholarship
The University of Southern Mississippi: McCain Library and Archives
Komisar (Lucy) Civil Rights Collection
The Mississippi Free Press, 1962–1963.
Tully-Crenshaw Feminist Oral History Project (Interview with Lucy Komisar, October 1991)

E-Mail Correspondences
Numerous e-mail correspondences

Interviews
Interviews taped and untapped

Secondary Sources

acitarel. "A Comparison of Student Activism in American History—Educ 300: Education Reform, Past and Present." https://commons.trincoll.edu/edreform/2018/05/a-comparison-of-student-activism-in-american-history/ (Accessed 12/26/2020).

Adickes, Sandra E. *The Legacy of a Freedom School.* New York: Palgrave Macmillan, 2005.

Ahmad, Shomial. "Queens College and Civil Rights: Alumni Reflect on Activism 50 Years Ago." PSC CUNY, May 2014 (Clarion/may/2014).

Allen, Chude. "My Parents Said Yes!" In Jacqueline Johnson, ed. *Finding Freedom: Memorializing the Voices of Freedom Summer* (pp. 25–27). Oxford, Ohio: Miami University Press, 2013.

Antler, Joyce. *The Journey Home: How Jewish Women Shaped Modern America.* New York: Schocken Books, 1998.

Archer, Jules. *They Had a Dream: The Civil Rights Struggle from Frederick Douglass to Marcus Garvey to Martin Luther King Jr. and Malcolm X*. New York, NY: Puffin Books, 1996.
Armstrong, Ann Elizabeth. "The Mississippi Summer Project." In Jacqueline Johnson, ed. *Finding Freedom: Memorializing the Voices of Freedom Summer* (pp. 1–9). Oxford, Ohio: Miami University Press, 2013.
Armstrong, Julie Buckner, and Amy Schmidt, eds. *The Civil Rights Reader: American Literature from Jim Crow to Reconstruction*. Athens, GA: University of Georgia Press, 2009.
Asante, Molefi Kete. *Kemet, Afrocentricity and Knowledge*. Trenton, NJ: Africa World Press, 1992.
Auspitz, J. Lee. "Crimson's Ad Protests Ban on Speeches: Queens College Paper Runs Editors' Appeal." Published: Tuesday, November 21, 1961. http://www.thecrimson.com/article/1961/11/21/crimsons-ad-protests-ban-on-speeches/ (Accessed 5/4/2012).
Barton, Keith C., and Linda S. Levstik. *Teaching History for the Common Good*. New York: Routledge, 2004.
Beauchamp, Keith. "Foreword." In Jacqueline Johnson, ed. *Finding Freedom: Memorializing the Voices of Freedom Summer* (pp. i–ii). Oxford, Ohio: Miami University Press, 2013.
Belfrage, Sally. *Freedom Summer*. Charlottesville, VA: University Press of Virginia, 1990.
Bell, Inge Powell. *CORE and the strategy of Nonviolence*. New York: Random House, 1968.
Bell, Lee Anne. "Theoretical Foundations for Social Justice Education." In Maurianne Adams, Lee Anne Bell, and Pat Griffin, eds. *Teaching for Diversity and Social Justice: A Sourcebook* (pp. 1–15). New York, NY: Routledge, 1997.
Bender, Rita L. "Searching for Restorative Justice: The Trial of Edgar Ray Killen." *Souls*, Volume 10, Number 2, 2008, pp. 156-164.
Bestick, G. "Review." *Freedom Summer* by Sally Belfrage.
Biography—Komisar, Lucy (1942-). Contemporary Authors—January 1, 2004.
Biography—Nestle, Joan (1940-). Contemporary Authors—2002. Gale Reference Team.
Bloom, Alexander. *Takin' It to the Streets, a Sixties Reader* (4th edition). New York: Oxford University Press, 2015.
Bond, Julian. "Introduction." In Elizabeth Martinez, ed. *Letters from Mississippi: Reports from Civil Rights Volunteer & Poetry of the 1964 Freedom Summer* (pp. i–xiv). Brookline, MA: Zephyr Press, 2007.
Bradley, Stefan M. *Harlem vs. Columbia University: Black Student Power in the Late 1960s*. Urbana, IL: University of Illinois Press, 2009.
Branch, Taylor. *Parting the Waters: America in the King Years 1954-63*. New York: Simon & Schuster, 1989.

Braungart, Richard G., and Margaret M. Braungart. "Political Generational Themes in the American Student Movements of the 1930s and 1960s." *Journal of Political and Military Sociology* (177–230) Volume 18 (Winter), 1990.

Buechler, Steven M. *Social Movements in Advanced Capitalism: The Political Economy and Cultural Construction of Social Activism.* New York: Oxford University Press, 2000.

Burner, Eric R. *And Gently He Shall Lead Them: Robert Parris Moses and Civil Rights in Mississippi.* New York: New York University Press, 1995.

Cagin, Seth, and Philip Dray. *We Are Not Afraid: The Story of Goodman, Schwerner, and Chaney and the Civil Rights Campaign for Mississippi.* New York: Nation Books, 2006.

Cain, Greg B., and Olga Kiyan. "Lessons Learned from a 28 Year Leave of Absence." *The Harvard Crimson*, March 14, 2019. https://www.thecrimson.com/article/2019/3/14/marshall-ganz/ (Accessed 12/28/2020).

Carawan, Guy, and Candie. *We Shall Overcome! Songs of the Southern Freedom Movement.* New York: Oak Publications, 1963.

Carlton, Genevieve. "Student Activism in College: A History of Campus Protests." *Best Colleges.* https://www.bestcolleges.com/blog/history-student-activism-in-college/ (Accessed 12/26/2020).

Carson, Clayborne. *In Struggle: SNCC and the Black Awakening of the 1960s* (2nd edition). Cambridge, MA: Harvard University Press, 1995.

Chafe, William H. *Civilities and Civil Rights: Greensboro, North Carolina, and the Black Struggle for Freedom.* New York: Oxford University Press, 1981.

Chilcoat, George W, and Jerry A. Ligon. "Developing Democratic Citizens: The Mississippi Freedom Schools as a Model for Social Studies Instruction." *Theory and Research in Social Studies*, Volume 22, Number 2, 1994, pp. 128–175.

Chilcoat, George W, and Jerry A. Ligon. "'Great Potential Curriculumers': Educational Projects that Informed the Curriculum Design of the Mississippi Freedom Schools." Unpublished Paper Presented at the American Educational Research Association Annual Meeting, Division B, Curriculum Studies, Session Number 33.63, New Orleans, Louisiana, April 27, 2000.

Cogan, Lee. *Queens College of the City University of New York, 1937–1962.* Written by Lee Cogan: Harold W. Stoke, President. New York: Queens College, 1963.

Cogan, Lee. *The People's College on the Hill: Fifty Years at Queens College, 1937–1987.* New York: Shirley Strum Kenny, President New York: Queens College, 1988.

Cohen, Robert. "Introduction to Mario Savio Speech." *History, Theory, Culture*, Summer, 2005, pp. 71–74.

Cohen, Robert. *Freedom's Orator: Mario Savio and the Radical Legacy of the 1960s.* New York: Oxford University Press, 2009.

Colca, Carole. "Reflections on a Life-Changing Experience." In Jacqueline Johnson, ed. *Finding Freedom: Memorializing the Voices of Freedom Summer* (pp. 29–36). Oxford, Ohio: Miami University Press, 2013.
Coles, Robert. *Farewell to the South*. Boston, MA: Little Brown & Company, 1972.
Conner, Jerusha O. *The New Student Activists: The Rise of Neoactivism on College Campuses*. Baltimore, MD: Johns Hopkins University Press, 2020.
Conner, Jerusha, and Sonia M. Rosen, eds. *Contemporary Youth Activism: Advancing Social Justice in the United States*. Santa Barbara, CA: Praeger, 2016
Crawford, Vicki L., Jacqueline Anne Rouse, and Barbara Woods, eds. *Women in the Civil Rights Movement: Trailblazers & Torchbearers, 1941–1965*. Bloomington, IN: Indiana University Press, 1993.
Cruden, Alexander, ed. *Perspectives on Modern World History: Student Movements of the 1960s*. Farmington Hills, MI: Greenhaven Press, 2012.
Daily News, February 13, 2006.
Diner, Hasia R., Shira Kohn, and Rachel Kranson, eds. *A Jewish Feminine Mystique? Jewish Women in Postwar America*. New Brunswick: NJ: Rutgers University Press, 2010.
Dittmer, John. *Local People: The Struggle for Civil Rights in Mississippi*. Urbana, IL: University of Illinois Press, 1994.
Dollard, John. *Caste and Class in a Southern Town*. Madison, WI: University of Wisconsin Press, 1989.
Donnella, Leah, and Robert Wilkes. "Race in America: A Conversation." *Divided We Fall*, July 16, 2019.
Donnellan, Kevin. "GOODMAN." Unpublished Essay, 1993.
Egerton, John. *Speak Now Against the Day: The Generation Before the Civil Rights Movement in the South*. New York: Knopf Doubleday Publishing Group, 1994.
Emerson, Barbara Williams. CORE, SCLC, 1963–1972, Georgia, Alabama, New York. webspinner@crmvet.org (Accessed 2/20/2020).
Emery, Kathy, Sylvia Braselmann, and Linda Reid Gold. "Introduction: Freedom Summer and the Freedom Schools." *Introduction to Freedom School Curriculum*. http://www.educationanddemocracy.org/FSCfiles/A_02_Introduction.htm (Accessed 9/30/2012).
EPISODE 5, Mississippi: Is This America? (1962–1964). *Eyes on the Prize*.
Eubanks, W. Ralph. *Ever Is a Long Time: A Journey into Mississippi's Dark Past, A Memoir*. New York, Basic Books, 2003.
Evans, Sara. *Personal Politics: The Roots of Women's Liberation in the Civil Rights Movement & the New Left*. New York: Knopf Doubleday Publishing, 1980.
Families USA. *Wikipedia*. https://en.wikipedia.org/wiki/Families_USA (Accessed 2/21/2020).

Farber, David. *The Age of Great Dreams: America in the 1960s*. New York, NY: Hill and Wang, 1994.

Farmer, James. *Lay Bare the Heart: An Autobiography of the Civil Rights Movement*. New York, NY: Harper Collins, 1985.

Farmer, James. "Foreword." In Jack Salzman, Adina Back, and Gretchen Sullivan Sorin, eds. *Bridges and Boundaries: African Americans and American Jews* (pp. 12–14). New York: George Braziller in association with The Jewish Museum, 1992.

Forman, James. *The Making of Black Revolutionaries*. Seattle, WA: University of Washington Press, 1997.

Frankye Adams-Johnson. Oral History Interview Conducted by Emilye Crosby, December 6, 2015. YouTube—Library of Congress—February 21, 2020.

Freeman, Jo. *The Politics of Women's Liberation: A Case Study of an Emerging Social Movement and its Relation to the Policy Process*. New York: McKay, 1975.

Friedman, Leon, ed. *Southern Justice*. New York: Pantheon Books, 1965.

Garrow, David J. *Bearing the Cross: Martin Luther King, Jr., and the Southern Christian Leadership Conference*. New York: William Morrow, 1986.

Grant, Joanne, ed. *Black Protest: History, Documents, and Analyses; 1619 to the Present*. New York: Fawcett, 1986.

Greenberg, Cheryl L., ed. *A Circle of Trust: Remembering SNCC*. New Brunswick, NJ: Rutgers University Press, 1998.

Gunderson, Christopher. "The Struggle for CUNY: A History of the CUNY Student Movement, 1969–1999." https://eportfolios.macaulay.cuny.edu/hainline2014/files/2014/02/Gunderson_The-Struggle-for-CUNY.pdf (Accessed 10/5/23).

Hale, Jon N. *The Freedom Schools: Student Activists in The Mississippi Civil Rights Movement*. New York, NY: Columbia University Press, 2018.

Harding, Vincent. *Hope and History: Why We Must Share the Story of the Movement*. Maryknoll, NY: Orbis Books, 2009.

Herndon, Michael K. "Reflections of African American Parents, Teachers, and Students in Prince Edward County, Virginia, 1959–1964." In Terence Hicks and Abul Pitre, eds. *The Educational Lockout of African Americans in Prince Edward County, Virginia (1959–1964): Personal Accounts and Reflections* (pp. 83–92). Lanham, MD: University Press of America, 2010.

Hershkowitz, Leo. "Demonstrations and Debates." In Stephen Stepanchev, ed. *The People's College on the Hill: Fifty Years at Queens College, 1937–1987* (p. 66). New York: Queens College of the City University of New York, 1988.

Hershkowitz, Leo. "Andrew Goodman on Freedom's Walk." In Stephen Stepanchev, ed. *The People's College on the Hill: Fifty Years at Queens College,*

1937–1987 (p. 68). New York: Queens College of the City University of New York, 1988.

Hicks, Terence, and Abul Pitre, eds. *The Educational Lockout of African Americans in Prince Edward County, Virginia (1959-1964): Personal Accounts and Reflections.* Lanham, MD: University Press of America, 2010.

Higher Education Today. "Student Activism and Social Change on Campus Before the 1960s." American Council on Education. https://www.higheredtoday.org/2016/03/02/student-activism-and-social-change-on-campus-before-the-1960s (Accessed 12/26/2020).

Hirsch, Eric L. "Sacrifice for the Cause: Group Processes, Recruitment, and Commitment in a Student Social Movement." *American Sociological Review*, Volume 55, Number 2, 1990, pp. 243–254.

Holsaert, Faith S. et al., eds. *Hands on the Freedom Plow: Personal Accounts by Women in SNCC.* Urbana, IL: University of Illinois Press, 2010.

Hooks, Bell. *Teaching to Transgress: Education as the Practice of Freedom.* New York, Routledge, 1994.

Howell, Leon. *Freedom City: The Remarkable Story of the Dispossessed Negroes Who Struggled to Create a Hopeful New Community in Rural Mississippi.* Richmond, VA: John Knox Press, 1969.

Huie, William Bradford. *Three Lives for Mississippi.* Jackson, MS: University Press of Mississippi, 2000.

Hyman, Paula E., and Deborah Dash Moore, eds. *Jewish Women in America: An Historical Encyclopedia*, Volume 1. New York: Routledge, 1998.

In the Footsteps of Dr. King. https://www.qc.cuny.edu/community/drking/Pages/Default.aspx (Accessed 1/21/2021).

James, Michael E. *The Conspiracy of the Good: Civil Rights and the Struggle for Community in Two American Cities, 1875-2000.* New York: Peter Lang, 2008.

Jason, Zachary "Student Activism 2.0: A Look Back at the History of Student Activism and Whether Today's Protesters are Making a Difference." *Search Ed Magazine*, Fall 2018. https://www.gse.harvard.edu/sites/default/files/edmag/pdfs/2018-FAL-20.pdf (Accessed 12/28/2020).

Jeffries, Hasan Kwame, ed. "Understanding and Teaching the Civil Rights Movement." https://www.oah.org/insights/posts/2020/january/understanding-and-teaching-the-civil-rights-movement-new-directions-in-civil-rights/ (Accessed 1/2/2021).

Joan Nestle—Wikipedia, the free encyclopedia. http://en.wikipedia.org/wiki/Joan_Nestle (Accessed 10/5/2012).

Johnson, Jacqueline, ed. *Finding Freedom: Memorializing the Voices of Freedom Summer.* Oxford, Ohio: Miami University Press, 2013.

Jones, Denisha, and Jesse Hagopian, eds. *Black Lives Matter at School: An Uprising for Educational Justice.* Chicago, IL: Haymarket Books, 2020.

June, Audrey Williams. "Do You Know Where Your Ph.D.'s Are?" *The Chronicle of Higher Education.* https://www.chronucle.com/article/Do-You-Know-Where-Your-PhDs/141777.

Kaplan, Lawrence. "McCarthyism at Queens College." *Unpublished paper deposited in Queens College Archives,* n.d.

Kaufman, Jonathan. *Broken Alliance: The Turbulent Times Between Blacks and Jews in America.* New York: Charles Scribner's Sons, 1988.

Kelchen, Robert. "Improving Data on PhD Placements." https://robertkelchen.com/2013/09/23/improving-data-on-phd-placements/ (Accessed 12/26/19).

King, Martin Luther, Jr., Jesse Jackson (Afterword). *Why We Can't Wait.* Signet, 2000.

King, Martin Luther, Jr., Clayborne Carson (Introduction). *Stride Toward Freedom: The Montgomery Story.* Boston, MA: Beacon Press, 2010.

King, Mary. *Freedom Song: A Personal Story of the 1960s Civil Rights Movement.* New York: William Morrow & Co, 1987.

King, Ed, Rev., and Trent Watts. *Ed King's Mississippi: Behind the Scenes of Freedom Summer.* Jackson, MS: University Press of Mississippi, 2014.

Klapper, Melissa R. *Ballots, Babies, and Banners of Peace: American Jewish Women's Activism, 1890–1940.* New York: New York University Press, 2013.

Komisar, Lucy. A Personal History of Civil Rights and Feminism, Talk at Panel on "Women, Queens College, and the Civil Rights Movement." March 16, 2009, Queens College.

Lawson, Steven. F. *Black Ballots: Voting in the South, 1944–1969.* Lanham, MD: Lexington Books, 1999.

Lee, Brian E. "We Will Move: The Kennedy Administration and Restoring Public Education to Prince Edward County, Virginia." In Terence Hicks and Abul Pitre, eds. *The Educational Lockout of African Americans in Prince Edward County, Virginia (1959–1964): Personal Accounts and Reflections* (pp. 19–32). Lanham, MD: University Press of America, 2010.

Lee, Chana Kai. *For Freedom's Sake: The Life of Fannie Lou Hamer.* Urbana, IL: University of Illinois Press, 1999.

Lerner, Michael, and Cornel West. *Jews & Blacks: A Dialogue on Race, Religion, and Culture in America.* New York: Penguin Books, 1996.

Leventhal, Willy Siegel. *The SCOPE of Freedom: The Leadership of Hosea Williams with Dr. King's Summer '65 Student Volunteers.* Montgomery, AL: Challenge Publishing, 2005.

Levy, Mark. "About Freedom Summer '64 and Q.C." Unpublished Paper (n.d.).

Levy, Mark. "Additions to the Q.C. Roll Call Appendix 1" (n.d.).

Levy, Mark. "QC 50s-70s Activist Student Narrative." Unpublished Paper (n.d.).

Levy, Mark. "Proposal for Freedom Summer 1964 and Queens College: A 50th Anniversary Commemoration." Discussion Draft 03/04/2012.

Levy, Mark. "Personal Background Documents about Mississippi Freedom Summer '64: Introduction and Selected Letters and Articles from the Collection of Mark Levy in the Queens College/CUNY Civil Rights Archives." (Edited/Revised as of March 2013).
Levy, Mark. "A Monumental Dissent." In Jacqueline Johnson, ed. *Finding Freedom: Memorializing the Voices of Freedom Summer* (pp. 59–65). Oxford, Ohio: Miami University Press, 2013.
Levy, Mark. "Teaching for Change." https://www.teachingforchange.org/mark-levy-speech-at-aft (Accessed 12/20/2018).
Levy, Mark. "Veterans of the Civil Rights Movement." (Updated 8/16/2011 & August 2017). webspinner@crmvet.org (Accessed 6/2/2019).
Liberato, Ana S. Q., and John D. Foster "Representations and Remembrance: Tracing Civil Rights Meanings in the Narratives of Civil Rights Activists and Hollywood Filmmakers." *Journal of African American Studies*, Volume 15, Number 3, 2010, pp. 367–384.
Linder, Douglas O. "The Mississippi Burning Trial (U.S. vs Price et al.)" http://law2.umkc.edu/faculty/projects/ftrials/price&bowers/account.html (Accessed 9/29/2012).
Loewen, James. *Mississippi: Conflict and Change*. New York: Pantheon, 1980.
Lynd, Staughton, and David Waldstreicher (Foreword). *Intellectual Origins of American Radicalism*. New York, NY: Cambridge University Press, 2009.
Maedke, Janet. "1964: Freedom Summer." http://www.usm.edu/crdp/html/cd/summer.htm (Accessed 9/7/2013).
Mandela, Nelson. *Long Walk to Freedom: The Autobiography of Nelson Mandela*. Boston, MA: Little, Brown and Company, 1995.
Marable, Manning. "Introduction: Searching for Restorative Justice: The Trial of Edgar Ray Killen." *Souls*, Volume 10, Number 2, 2008, pp. 155–156.
Mark, Jonathan. "Freedom Summer Memories: Black-Jewish Alliance was Brief, Beautiful." *The New York Jewish Week*, July 16, 2014.
Martinez, Elizabeth, ed. *Letters from Mississippi: Reports from Civil Rights Volunteers & Poetry of the 1964 Freedom Summer*. Brookline: MA, Zephyr Press, 2007.
Mattson, Rachel. "Framing the Questions: An Interview with Adam Green, The Civil Rights Movement." http://site.ebrary.com/id/10361687?ppg=156.
Maye, Marilyn Allman et al., *Seven Sisters and a Brother: Friendship, Resistance, and Untold Truths Behind Black Student Activism in the 1960s*. Coral Gables, FL: Books & Books, Press, 2021.
McAdam, Doug. "Recruitment to High-Risk Activism: The Case of Freedom Summer." *American Journal of Sociology*, Volume 92, Number 1, 1986, pp. 64–90.
McAdam, Doug. *Freedom Summer*. New York, NY: Oxford University Press, 1988.

McAdam, Doug. "The Biographical Consequences of Activism." *American Sociological Review*, Volume 54, Number 5, 1989, pp. 744–760.
McAdam, Doug. "Gender as a Mediator of the Activist Experience: The Case of Freedom Summer." *American Journal of Sociology*, Volume 97, Number 5, 1992, 1211–1240.
McAdam, Doug, and Ronnelle Paulsen. "Specifying the Relationship Between Social Ties and Activism." *American Journal of Sociology*, Volume 99, Number 3, 1993, pp. 640–667.
McCord, William, and Francoise N. Hamlin (Introduction). *Mississippi: The Long, Hot Summer.* Jackson, MS: University Press of Mississippi, 2016.
McMillen, Neil R. *The Citizens' Council: Organized Resistance to the Second Reconstruction, 1954-64.* Urbana, IL: University of Illinois Press, 1994.
Meier, August, and Elliot Rudwick. *CORE: A Study in the Civil Rights Movement, 1942-1968.* New York: Oxford University Press, 1973.
Mena, Jesus, and Jose Rodriguez. "UC Berkeley to honor Mario Savio, Free Speech Movement with Library Gift, Café." https://www.berkeley.edu/news/media/releases/98legacy/04_29_98a.html (Accessed 10/25/2019).
Meyer, David S., Nancy Whittier, and Belinda Robnett, eds. *Social Movements: Identity, Culture, and the State.* New York: Oxford University Press, 2002.
Mills, Nicolaus. *Like a Holy Crusade: Mississippi 1964: The Turning of the Civil Rights Movement in America.* Chicago, IL: Ivan R. Dee, 1993.
Mississippi, Updated 8/16/2011 & August 2017. http://www.crmvet.org/vet/levym.htm (Accessed 6/2/2019).
Mohl, Raymond A., Matilda Graff, and Shirley M. Zoloth. *South of the South: Jewish Activists and the Civil Rights Movement in Miami, 1945-1960.* Gainesville, FL: University Press of Florida, 2004.
Momeyer, Rick. "A Visit to Oxford." In Jacqueline Johnson, ed. *Finding Freedom: Memorializing the Voices of Freedom Summer* (pp. 39–43). Oxford, Ohio: Miami University Press, 2013.
Moody, Anne. *Coming of Age in Mississippi: The Classic Autobiography of Growing Up Poor and Black in the Rural South.* New York: Dell, 1992.
Moore, Jane Bond. "A SNCC Blue Book." In Faith S. Holsaert et al., eds. *Hands on the Freedom Plow: Personal Accounts by Women in SNCC* (pp. 326–331). Urbana, IL: University of Illinois Press, 2010.
Morgan, Demetri L., and Charles H. F. Davis III. *Student Activism, Politics, and Campus Climate in Higher Education.* New York, NY: Routledge, 2019.
Morris, Aldon D. *The Origins of the Civil Rights Movement: Black Communities Organizing for Change.* New York: Free Press, 1986.
Moses, Robert P., and Charles. E. Cobb, Jr. *Radical Equations: Civil Rights from Mississippi to the Algebra Project.* Boston, MA: Beacon Press, 2002.

Mutua, Athena D. "Restoring Justice to Civil Rights Movement Activists?: New Historiography and the 'Long Civil Rights Era.'" January 2008. http://works.bepress.com/athena_mutua/1 (Accessed 9/7/2019).

Muyskens, James's Web Page. (President of Queens College 2002–2013) Originally published with the title, "Religious Diversity in Queens." In Ellen Freudenheim, ed. *Queens: What to Do, Where to Go (and How Not to Get Lost) in New York's Undiscovered Borough*. New York: St. Martin's Press, 2006.

Myrdal, Gunnar. *An American Dilemma: The Negro Problem and Modern Democracy*. New York: Routledge, 1995.

Navasky, Victor S. *Kennedy Justice*. New York: Scribner, 1971.

NBC Boston. *Teens in Boston Hope to Make a Difference on Gun Legislation*. https://www.nbcboston.com/news/local/teens-in-boston-hope-to-make-a-difference-on-gun-legislation/127797/ (Accessed 12/28/2020).

NCSL "Voter Identification Requirements/Voter ID Laws." https://www.ncsl.org/research/elections-and-campaigns/voter-id.aspx (Accessed 8/25/2020).

Nestle, Joan. "The Gifts of Martin Van Buren High School, 1955." A Short Essay Written for Her High School Commemorative Book Used to Raise Money for the New Students of MVB.

Nestle, Joan. *A Restricted Country*. San Francisco, CA: Cleis Press Inc., 2003.

Newfield, Jack. *A Prophetic Minority*. New York: Dutton Adult, 1966.

Newman, Mark. *Divine Agitators: The Delta Ministry and Civil Rights in Mississippi*. Athens, GA: The University of Georgia Press, 2004.

Oates, Stephen B. *Let the Trumpet Sound: A Life of Martin Luther King, Jr.* New York: Harper Perennial, 2013.

Oberschall, Anthony. *Social Conflict and Social Movements*. Englewood Cliffs, New Jersey: Prentice-Hall, Inc., 1973.

Olson, Lynne. *Freedom's Daughters: The Unsung Heroines of the Civil Rights Movement from 1830 to 1970*. New York: Scribner; Reprint edition, 2002.

Omolade, Barbara. *The Rising Song of African American Women*. New York: Routledge, 1994.

Omolade, Barbara Jones. "Building a New World." In Faith S. Holsaert, et al. eds. *Hands on the Freedom Plow: Personal Accounts by Women in SNCC* (pp. 388–394). Urbana, IL: University of Illinois Press, 2010.

Payne, Charles. "Men Led, But Women Organized: Movement Participation of Women in the Mississippi Delta." In Vicki L. Crawford, Jacqueline Anne Rouse, and Barbara Woods, eds. *Women in the Civil Rights Movement: Trailblazers & Torchbearers 1941–1965* (pp. 1–11). Bloomington, IN: Indiana University Press, 1993.

Payne, Charles M. *I've Got the Light of Freedom: The Organizing Tradition and the Mississippi Freedom Struggle*. Berkeley, CA: University of California Press, 2007.

Perlstein, Daniel. "Teaching Freedom: SNCC and the Creation of the Mississippi Freedom Schools." *History of Education Quarterly*, Volume 30, Number 3, 1990, pp. 297–324.

Queens College (New York, NY). *Queens College of the City University of New York, 1937–1962* [written by Lee Cogan]; Harold W. Stoke, President, New York: Queens College, 1963.

Queens College (New York, NY). *The People's College on the Hill: Fifty Years at Queens College, 1937–1987/* edited by Stephen Stepanchev, Queens College of the City University of New York; Shirley Strum Kenny, President, New York: Queens College, 1988.

Queens College, City University of New York—Wikipedia (Accessed 6/25/2019).

Raines, Howell. *My Soul Is Rested: Movement Days in the Deep South Remembered.* New York: Penguin Books, 1983.

Ransby, Barbara. *Ella Baker & the Black Freedom Movement: A Radical Democratic Vision.* Chapel Hill, NC: The University of North Carolina Press, 2003.

Rappaport, Doreen, and Shane W. Evans (Illustrator). *Nobody Gonna Turn Me 'Round: Stories and Songs of the Civil Rights Movement.* Cambridge, MA: Candlewick Reprint, 2008.

Rehak, Michael. "Remembering The Dream: Queens College Reaches Out for Black History Month." http://www.queenstribune.com/feature/RememberingTheDreamQueensC.html (Accessed 10/6/2012).

Robnett, Belinda. "African-American Women in the Civil Rights Movement, 1954-1965: Gender, Leadership, and Micromobilization." *American Journal of Sociology*, Volume 101, Number 6, 1996, pp. 1661–1693.

Robnett, Belinda. *How Long? How Long? African-American Women in the Struggle for Civil Rights.* New York: Oxford University Press, 1999.

Rosenthal, Rob, and Lois Brown. "Then and Now: Comparing Today's Student Activism With the 1960s." *HuffPost*, August 27, 2014. Updated October 27, 2014.

Rothschild, Mary A. *A Case of Black and White: Northern Volunteers and the Southern Freedom Summer, 1964-1965.* Westport, CT: Greenwood Press, 1982.

Salem, Dorothy C., ed. *African American Women: A Biographical Dictionary.* New York: Garland Publishing, 1993.

Salter, John R., Jr. *Jackson, Mississippi: An American Chronicle of Struggle and Schism.* Lincoln, NE: Bison Books, 2011.

Salzman, Jack, Adina Back, and Gretchen Sullivan Sorin, eds. *Bridges and Boundaries: African Americans and American Jews.* New York, NY: George Braziller in Association with The Jewish Museum, 1992.

Sandel, Michael J. *Democracy's Discontent: America in Search of a Public Philosophy*. Cambridge, MA: The Belknap Press of Harvard University Press, 1996.
Schultz, Debra L. "Why I Tracked Them Down: Our Unsung Civil Rights Movement Heroines." *Lilith* (Fall), 1999.
Schultz, Debra L. *Going South: Jewish Women in the Civil Rights Movement*. New York: New York University Press, 2001.
Seeger, Pete, and Bob Reiser. *Everybody Says Freedom*. New York: W. W. Norton, 2009.
Sellers, Cleveland L., and Robert L. Terrell. *The River of No Return: The Autobiography of a Black Militant and the Life and Death of SNCC*. New York: William Morrow Paperback, 2018
Sessions, Judith A. "Letter from Dean Judith Sessions." In Jacqueline Johnson, ed. *Finding Freedom: Memorializing the Voices of Freedom Summer* (p. iii) Oxford, Ohio: Miami University Press, 2013.
Silberman, Charles E. *Crisis in Black and White*. New York: Random House, 1964.
Silver, James W. *Mississippi: The Closed Society*. New York: Harcourt, Brace & World, 1964.
Silver, James W. *Running Scared: Silver in Mississippi*. Jackson, MS: University Press of Mississippi, 1984.
Simmons, Gwendolyn Zoharah. "Reflections on the Orientation and My Participation in the 1964 Mississippi Freedom Summer Project." In Jacqueline Johnson, ed. *Finding Freedom: Memorializing the Voices of Freedom Summer* (pp. 49–56). Oxford, OH: Miami University Press, 2013.
Smith, Frank E. *Congressman from Mississippi*. New York: Pantheon, 1964.
Smith, Lillian. *Killers of the Dream*. New York: W. W. Norton, 1994.
Smith, Bob. *They Closed Their Schools: Prince Edward County, Virginia, 1951–1964*. Farmville, VA: Martha E. Forrester, Council of Women, 1996.
Stepanchev, Stephen, ed. *The People's College on the Hill: Fifty Years at Queens College, 1937-1987*. New York: Queens College, 1988
Strippel, Jane. "Friends of the Mississippi Summer Project." In Jacqueline Johnson, ed. *Finding Freedom: Memorializing the Voices of Freedom Summer* (pp. 13–22). Oxford, Ohio: Miami University Press, 2013.
Sugarman, Tracy, and Charles McLaurin (Introduction). *Stranger at the Gates: A Summer in Mississippi*. Prospecta Press, 2014.
Terborg-Penn, Rosalyn. "A Black History Journey: Encountering Aptheker Along the Way." *Nature, Society, and Thought*, Volume 10, Number 1 & 2, 1997, pp. 189–200.
The New York Times. George Floyd Protests: Live News and Updates. https://www.nytimes.com/2020/06/06/us/george-floyd-protests.html (Accessed 6/6/2020).

Tillerson-Brown, Amy. "'Grassroots Schools' and Training Centers in the Prospect District of Prince Edward County, Virginia 1959–1964." In Terence Hicks and Abul Pitre, eds. *The Educational Lockout of African Americans in Prince Edward County, Virginia (1959–1964): Personal Accounts and Reflections* (pp. 1–17). Lanham, MD: University Press of America, 2010.

Time Editorial, "Where We Stand." *Time*, June 22–29, 2020.

Titus, Jill Ogline. "Farmville, 1963: The Long Hot Summer." In Terence Hicks and Abul Pitre, eds. *The Educational Lockout of African Americans in Prince Edward County, Virginia (1959–1964): Personal Accounts and Reflections* (pp. 33–45). Lanham, MD: University Press of America, 2010.

Veterans of the Civil Rights Movement—Frankye Adams-Johnson (Aka Malika). http://www.crmvet.org/vet/adamsfj.htm (Accessed 9/29/2012).

Veterans of the Civil Rights Movement—Mark Levy, COFO (SNCC/CORE), 1964, 1965.

Voter Suppression in America. American Civil Liberties Union. http://www.aclu.org/voter-suppression-america (Accessed 4/23/2013).

"Voter Suppression in the United States." https://en.wikipedia.org/wiki/Voter_suppression_in_the_United_States.

Wang, Tova Andrea. *The Politics of Voter Suppression: Defending and Expanding Americans' Right to Vote*. Ithaca, NY: Cornell University Press, 2012.

Ward, Lacy, Jr. "Robert Russa Moton Museum Farmville, Virginia." In Terence Hicks and Abul Pitre, eds. *The Educational Lockout of African Americans in Prince Edward County, Virginia (1959–1964): Personal Accounts and Reflections* (pp. xiii-xv). Lanham, MD: University Press of America, 2010.

Watson, Bruce. *Freedom Summer: The Savage Season of 1964 That Made Mississippi Burn and Made America a Democracy*. New York: Penguin Books, 2010.

We Have No Government. An Edited Transcription of a Press Conference held in the Greenville office of the Delta Ministry, Tuesday, February 1, 1966.

Wenger, Michael R. *My Black Family, My White Privilege: A White Man's Journey Through the Nation's Racial Minefield*. Bloomington, IN: iUniverse, 2012.

Wenger, Michael R., and Stan F. Shaw. "Northerners in a Jim Crow World: Queens College Summer Experience." In Terence Hicks and Abul Pitre, eds. *The Educational Lockout of African Americans in Prince Edward County, Virginia (1959–1964): Personal Accounts and Reflections* (pp. 55–66). Lanham, MD: University Press of America, 2010.

Wesley, Charles H., and Thelma D. Perry. *History Is A Weapon: The Mis-Education of the Negro*. http://www.historyisaweapon.com/defcon1/misedne.html, 1969 (Accessed 8/25/2009).

Wilkerson, Isabel, *Caste: The Origins of Our Discontents*. New York, Random House, 2020.

Williams, Juan. *Eyes on the Prize: America's Civil Rights Years 1954-1965.* New York: Penguin Books, 1988.

Wolf, Zachary B., and Brian Rokus, CNN politics, March 25 & 26, 2021.

Woodruff, Nan Elizabeth. "The Contested Terrain of Historical Memory in Contemporary Mississippi." http://erea.revues.org/1811, 2011 (Accessed 11/4/2013).

Woodson, Carter G. *The Mis-Education of the Negro.* Trenton, NJ: Africa World Press, Inc., 1990. Originally published in 1933.

Worland, Justin. "The Overdue Awakening." *Time*, June 22–29, 2020.

Young, Jasmin A. "Stefan Bradley: Harlem vs. Columbia University: Black Student Power in the Late 1960s" (Book Review). *Journal of African American Studies*, Volume 16, Number 1, 2012, pp. 168–170.

Zellner, Dorothy M. "My Real Vocation." In Faith S. Holsaert, et al. eds. *Hands on the Freedom Plow: Personal Accounts by Women in SNCC* (pp. 311–326). Urbana, IL: University of Illinois Press, 2010.

Zellner, Dorothy M. "King's Words Live in Palestinian City." *Dominican Life, USA.* http://www.domlife.org/2011Stories/mlk_zellner.htm (Accessed 6/16/2012).

Zellner, Dorothy M. (Biographical Details). http://cosmos.ucc.ie/cs1064/jabowen/IPSC/php/authors.php?auid=25409 (Accessed 12/20/2018).

Zinn, Howard. *SNCC: The New Abolitionists.* Chicago, IL: Haymarket Books, 2013.

Index

A
Ackerman, Gary, 5
  in *Fast for Freedom*, 40
The Activist (QC SDS newsletter), 168–170
Adams-Johnson, Frankye (Malika), 197–199, 245
Ad Hoc Committee to End Political Suppression (QC organization), 203–205, 206–208
Adickes, Sandra, 94
African Americans. *See* Blacks
Africana Studies program, 205
Ahmad, Shomial, 85
Alexander, Jonathan, 183
Allen, Chude, 229
Allen, Rev. and Mrs., 101
Altman, Julie, 13
American Civil Liberties Union (ACLU), 34
American Youth for Democracy, 32
Anderson, Khaleel M., 242

Andrews, Rosalind Silverman, 60, 68–69
Anti-Semitism, 228
Antiwar movement against Vietnam War, 2–4, 205
Aptheker, Herbert, 67
Asher, Rikki, 18
Asip, Monsignor, 155
Association of Black Women Historians (ABWH), 68
Australia, 239

B
Baldwin, James, 156
Barbera, Michael, 60
Barbour, Haley, 127
Barnett, Ross, 173
Beauchamp, Keith, 79
Bender, Rita Schwerner. *See* Schwerner, Rita
Berkeley, University of California at, 105–106, 110–113

Berman, Andrew (Andy), 167–171, 223–225
Black and Puerto Rican Student, Teacher, and Counselor Coalition (QC organization), 203
Black Lives Matter movement, 239–240
Blackman-Richards, Norka, 242
Black Muslims, 83–84
Black Panther Party, 198
Blacks
  in CUNY, 207
  education of, 159
  Freedom Summer and, 80
  Jews and, 228
  lunch counter sit-ins by, 161
  in Mississippi, 85–87, 90, 93–94, 98–100, 105–106, 187
  murdered in Mississippi, 121–122
  police killings of, 240
  in Prince Edward County, 56–57, 59–60
  in SEEK, 203–208
  in Southern Civil Rights movement, 37
  see also Civil Rights movement
Blackwell, Unita, 201
Blair, Ezell, Jr. (Jibreel Khazan), 161
Blumberg, Mark, 60
Board of Higher Education (BHE), 207
Bollinger, Carl, 87
Bollinger, Ruth, 87, 90
Bond, Julian, 159, 163, 165, 223–225
Bowers, Sam, 121
Bowker, Albert H., 207
Bradley, Stefan M., 9
Brass, Donna, 60
Braungart, Margaret M., 1, 3
Braungart, Richard G., 1, 3
Braxton, Eric, 240

Bridge Leaders, 14, 15, 128–129, 149–151
Britt, Travis, 156
Brody, Mickey, 55
Brooklyn College, 206–208
Brooks, Steve, 40
Brown, Michael, 239
Brown v. Board of Education (US; 1954), 55
Brunman, Glen, 206
Buckley, William F. Jr., 33
Butts, Charlie, 51, 52

C
Cagin, Seth, 34, 156, 157
Carlton, Genevieve, 237
Carmichael, Stokely (Kwame Ture), 51, 153, 156
Center for Constitutional Rights, 166
Chaney, Ben, 95
Chaney, James, 85, 86, 118
  honored by Obama, 85
  memorial for, 95
  missing in Mississippi, 42, 80–83
  murder of, 100, 121, 125, 128
Chauvin, Derek, 239
Chevigny, Bell Gale, 167
Chicago, University of, 2
Christians, in Civil Rights movement, 229–230
City College of New York (CCNY), 206, 207
City University of New York
  Administrative Council of, 33
  Friends of Women's Studies at, 160
  Open Admissions Strike of 1969 IN, 209
  QC in, 30
  SEEK program in, 203, 205–206
  tuition charged at, 35–36
Civil Rights Archives (QC), 99

INDEX 273

Civil Rights Coordinating Council (CRCC), 151
  Omolade as chair of, 151, 156
Civil Rights movement, 9, 236
  bridge leaders in, 149–151
  Christians in, 229
  Freedom Summer, 79–84
  Hendricks and Weddington's support for, 6–8
  impact on Omolade of, 151
  Jews in, 227–228
  Komisar's activities in, 51–53
  lessons learned in South by, 9
  as motivation for QC students, 225
  QC Roll Call of Queens College Students and Faculty in, 11
  in South, 37
  see also Freedom Summer (1964)
Clinton, Bill, 63
Cogan, Lee, 27, 222
Cohen, Robert, 111–113
Colden, Charles S., 27–28
Columbia University, 3, 9, 203
Committee for a Free City College, 27–29
Committee for a Sane Nuclear Policy (SANE), 67, 246
Committee of Concern (Mississippi organization), 103, 184, 185
Committee to Defend Martin Luther King, 50
Communist Party, 32
Communists, 34
Congress of Racial Equality (national organization)
  Dorothy Zellner in, 161
  Route 40 Freedom Rides organized by, 51
  QC activists in, 222
  Schwerners in, 115–117
Congress of Racial Equality (NYC chapter), 151

Congress of Racial Equality (QC chapter), 11
  Berman in, 166
  creation of, 37
  demonstrations at World's Fair by, 173
  faculty advisers to, 8
  Fast for Freedom supported by, 40
  Freedom Summer and, 79, 151
  Freedom Week sponsored by, 154
  Gatti in, 185
  Linzer in, 171–173
  Nestle in, 246
  QC NAACP becomes, 59–60, 62
  Simon as adviser to, 187
Conner, Jerusha O., 237
  on activists in 2015-2018, 236–238
  on backgrounds of student activists, 225
  on current student activists, 241
  on influence of professors, 42–43
Cooper, Nancy (Samstein), 114–115, 156, 226–227
Council of Federated Organizations (COFO), 94, 109
Council on Foreign Relations (organization), 55
Covington, Francee, 207
Crossley, Nick, 150
Crown (student publication), 5
  Dorothy Zellner as editor of, 161
  suspended by QC administration, 31, 38
Cruden, Alexander, 2–4
Curran, Mary Doyle, 84

D
Davis, Benjamin J., 33
Davis, William P., 184, 187–188
DC Students for Civil Rights (organization), 68

Dearman, Stanley, 127
Dee, Henry Hezekiah, 124
Delany, Lloyd T., 203–206
Delany, Sheila, 203–204, 243
Delta Ministry (organization), 199–200
Democratic Party
　Freedom Democratic Party and, 100
　in Mississippi, 95
　national convention of 1968 of, 3
Deutscher, Isaac, 228
Dewey, John, 19
Diamond, Dion, 173
Dissent Forum (QC group), 50, 53
Doar, John, 53
Dow Chemical Company, 2
Dray, Philip, 34, 156, 157
Dress code at Queens College, 31, 39
DuBois, W.E.B., 161
Dulles, Allen, 122
Dunbar, Les, 162

E
Eaton, Nathaniel, 235
Election Integrity Act (Georgia; 2021), 248
Emerson, Barbara Williams, 189, 193
Epstein, Howard (Howie), 167
Eubanks, W. Ralph, 127
Evers, Medgar, 51–53, 198
Eynon, Bret
　on Savio in Berkeley, 110
　on Savio in Mississippi, 106, 109, 222
　on Savio's arrest, 106
　on Savio's interactions with Jews, 105
　on Savio's motivations, 229

F
Families USA (organization), 63
Farber, David, 1
Farmer, James L. (Jim), 157, 223
Fast for Freedom (1964), 5, 39–41, 60
　Pollack in, 63
　Wenger in, 61
Fast, Howard, 32
Federal Bureau of Investigation (FBI), 31
　arrests in murders of Chaney, Goodman, and Schwerner by, 124
　bodies of Goodman, Schwerner, and Chaney found by, 83
　Evers's killer arrested by, 51–52
　in Mississippi, 98
Fein, Lewis, 185
Floyd, George, 239
Food Research and Action Center (FRAC), 63
Forman, James (Jim), 94, 163
Foster, Isaac, 197, 199–203
Freedom Democratic Party (FDP), 99–101. *See also* Mississippi Freedom Democratic Party (MFDP)
Freedom Rides (Route 40 Freedom Rides), 51
Freedom Schools (Mississippi), 86, 88–94, 109, 159
Freedom Summer (1964), 5, 79–85, 125–128
　bridge leaders for, 149–151
　careers of volunteers in, 248–249
　churches burned during, and rebuilt following, 183
　Cooper in, 114–115
　Dorothy Zellner's recruiting for, 160, 164–165
　Freedom Schools in, 88–93
　Freedom Week and, 154–155

fundraising for, 171
Levy on lessons of, 17, 84–86, 96, 244
Levys in, 87–93
Liesner in, 115–117
Masters in, 97–101
QC volunteers in, 222
Queens College response to, 39–43
recruitment at QC for, 151
Savio in, 104–108, 229
Student Help Project and, 54–60
Weddington and, 64
Freedom to Write Committee (of PEN), 54
Freedom Vote (Mississippi), 109
Freedom Week (QC), 15, 154–156
The Free Press (independent QC newsletter), 38–39, 168, 169
Free Speech Movement (FSM), 2, 110–113
Freire, Paulo, 19
Friends of Women's Studies (at CUNY), 160
Frye, Hardy T., 117

G
Garza, Alicia, 239
Gatti, Arthur, 183–186, 224, 244–247
Gay Academic Union (GAU), 196
Geffen, Peter, 189, 193–195, 227, 229–230
Gliber, Gerald, 59
Goldberg, Mrs., 101
Gold, Ina, 60
Goodman, Andrew
  Cagin and Dray on, 156
  Cooper and, 114
  Geffen and, 193–195, 230
  honored by Obama, 85
  in Mississippi and death of, 79–83, 85
  Mark Levy and, 156
  missing in Mississippi, 40
  murder of, 42–43, 60, 106, 121, 125
  political background of, 224, 225
  recruited by Omolade, 156
  Savio and, 104
Goodman, Carolyn, 81, 84
Goodman, Robert, 81, 82, 84
Grant, JoAnne, 195, 247
Green, Robert Lee, 56–57
Greensboro (North Carolina), 160–161
Greenville Air Force Base (Mississippi), 200–201
Greenwood (Mississippi), 99–101, 165
Gregory, Dick, 117
Griffin, L. Francis, 56, 60, 222
Guggenheimer, Elinor, 54
Gun control actions, 236–239

H
Habtu, Alem, 205
Hagopian, Jesse, 239
Hale, Jon N., 10, 225
Harrington, Michael, 8, 50, 111
Hartle, Robert, 204
Hartman, Sheila, 60
Harvard College, 235
Hausman, Leonard, 60
Hayden, Tom, 186
Heidelberg, Polly, 96
Helman, Marc, 185
Hendricks, Helen, 6–8, 42, 245
Henry, Aaron, 61, 114, 225
Hershkowitz, Leo, 83
Higgs, William L., 51
Higher Education Opportunity Program (HEOP), 207, 209
Hirsch, Eric L., 58, 223

Hodes, Bill, 101
Holden, Mark, 240
Holmes County (Mississippi), 106–108
Holocaust, 114
  children of survivors of, 10, 225
  Geffen on, 193, 227
  Kaufman on, 228
  Schultz on, 161
Hooks, bell, 153
House Un-American Activities Committee (HUAC), 36, 50, 94, 195, 246
Howard (dean), 32
Hubbard, Carolyn, 40, 59
  in Prince Edward County, 60, 61

I
Independent Students for a New Left (ISNL; QC), 167
In loco parentis doctrine, 31
In the Footsteps of Dr. King (QC organization), 241
Irvine, John, 59

J
Jackson, Jimmie Lee, 195
Jarsky, Walter, 183
Jews
  among student activists, 222, 223–229
  Savio and, 105
Johnson, Lyndon B.
  Great Society under, 1
  Leona Levy's letter to, 89–90
  Mississippi Freedom Democratic Party and, 98
  Rita Schwerner meets with, 125
  Voting Rights Act signed by, 85, 191
Johnson, Paul, 122

Jones, Barbara. *See* Omolade, Barbara Jones

K
Kaplan, Lawrence, 32
Katzenbach, Nicholas, 122–124
Kaufman, Jonathan, 228–229
Keating, Kenneth B., 39–41
Kennedy administration, 1, 65
Kennedy, John F., 225
Kennedy, Robert F., 41
Kent State University (Ohio), 3
Kerr, Clark, 111
Khan-Cullors, Patrisse, 239
Khazan, Jibreel (Ezell Blair, Jr), 161
Kiely, Margaret V., 29
Killen, Edgar Ray, 125–126
King, John, 106
King, Martin Luther, Jr., 189, 229
  Committee to Defend Martin Luther King, 50
  March on Washington speech of, 1, 4, 37, 53
  SCLC under, 209
  Shur meets, 191
Klapper, Paul, 28–30, 222
Knap, Ted, 91
Komisar, Lucy, 6, 50, 53–54, 224
  as editor of *Mississippi Free Press*, 5, 12, 51–53
  education at QC, 27, 49
  on Harrington, 8
  motivations for, 230
Konzal, Jean L. Stein, 60, 65–66, 226
Ku Klux Klan, 121, 184–185

L
LaGuardia, Fiorello, 28–30
Lappe, Frances Moore, 129
League for Industrial Democracy (LID), 168

Lenz, Harold, 32
Lerner, Michael, 228
Lesbian Herstory Archives, 196
Levine, David, 93
Levinson, Meira, 237
Levy, Betty Bollinger, 18, 99, 226
   in Mississippi, 86–93, 96–98
   recruited for Freedom Summer by Dorothy Zellner, 164
   Rita Schwerner and, 125
Levy, Leona, 89–90
Levy, Mark, 18, 97–98
   on Civil Rights movement, 236
   on commitment of COFO volunteers, 222
   as coordinator of QC Civil Rights archives, 12
   on Freedom Summer and Mississippi, 84–86, 86–92, 93–96
   on Hendricks, 6, 42
   on Jews in Civil Rights movement, 227–229
   on lessons of Freedom Summer, 17, 236, 248, 249
   on Mississippi Freedom Democratic Party, 97
   on Omolade, 156
   on QC student community, 10, 34
   on QC student rebellion (1969), 206
   political background of, 223–224
   QC Roll Call of Queens College Students and Faculty created by, 12
   QC Special Collections Library and, 86–87
   recruited for Freedom Summer by Dorothy Zellner, 164–166
   Rita Schwerner and, 125
   as Student Association President, 36
   during student strike of 1961, 33–36
   suspension of, 31
Lewis, John, 111, 171
Liesner, Joseph, 115–118, 229
Lievrouw, Leah, 241
Lindsay, John, 207
Linzer, Elliot, 171–173, 224, 244–247
Lively, Walter, 51
Long, Kim, 238
Lopez-Leyva, Julian, 238
Lowenstein, Allard, 51, 54, 82, 114, 156
   Komisar and, 224
   speaks at QC, 82, 114, 156

M

Madden, Robert, 183
Maidanick, Rhoda, 61
Malcolm X, 19, 33, 67
Mandala, Nelson, 158
Marable, Manning, 19, 247
March for Our Lives, 236–239
March on Washington for Jobs and Freedom (1963), 37
   Andrews (Silverman) at, 68
   Emerson at, 193
   Komisar at, 53
   Konzal (Stein) at, 65
   Linzer on staff of, 171
   QC students at, 225
   Schwerners at, 118
March on Washington for Jobs and Freedom (1963), 4–6
March on Washington to End the War in Vietnam (1965), 168
Marjory Stoneman Douglas High School (Parkland, Florida), 238
Mark, Jonathan, 223
Mars, Florence, 126

Martinez, Elizabeth, 108
Martin Luther King Jr. Center for Nonviolent Social Change, 201
Martin, Trayvon, 239
Marxist Discussion Group (QC group), 33
Masters, Robert (Bob), 99–103, 183
McAdam, Doug, 17
  on bridge leaders, 15
  on careers of Freedom Summer volunteers, 248–249
  on motivations of student activists, 230
  on personalities of activists, 149
  on values of student activists, 10, 223, 225
McCain, Franklin, 161
McComb (Mississippi), 106–108, 109
McDew, Charles, 173
McMurray, Joseph P., 204
McNamara, James, 54
McNamara, Robert, 2
McNeil, Joseph, 161
McSorley's Men's Bar (New York), 54–55
Mercado, Lou, 57
Meridian (Mississippi)
  COFO convention in, 94
  Levys in, 87
  rebuilding churches in, 184, 187
  Schwerners in, 115–117, 120
Mexico, 4, 105, 111–113
Mississippi
  church rebuilding in Tougaloo, 183–186
  on Jewish volunteers in, 226–227
  Komisar in, 5, 51–53
  Levys in, 87–96
  Liesner in, 115–117
  Masters in, 99–104
  Murders of Blacks in, 124–125
  QC volunteers in, 222
  response at QC to, 4–5
  Savio in, 104–108
  Schwerners in, 115–117
  Sovereignty Commission of, 126–128
  trials of Killen in, 125–128
  see also Freedom Summer (1964)
Mississippi Freedom Democratic Party (MFDP), 88
  Atlantic city convention of (1964), 97–98
  Cooper in, 114
  Liesner in, 116
  Masters in, 99–101
  Omolade on, 158, 159
  Savio in, 104–106
Mississippi Freedom Labor Union (MFLU), 199
Mississippi Freedom Summer. *See* Freedom Summer (1964)
Mississippi Free Press, 5, 12
  Komisar as editor of, 50, 51–53
Monsonis, Jim, 82–83
Moore, Charles Eddie, 124
Moore, Jane Bond, 165
Moore, Ronnie, 173
Morrissey, Bob, 185
Moses, Robert (Bob), 94, 116, 117, 124
Moss, James A., 162
Moss Point (Mississippi), 115–117
Mulholland, Joseph A., 203, 204
Muyskens, James L., 30

N
NAACP (National Association for the Advancement of Colored People; QC chapter), 33
  becomes CORE, 59–60, 62
National Organization for Women (NOW), 53

INDEX 279

National Student Association (NSA)
  Betty Levy in, 50
  Komisar in, 50, 51
Neshoba County (Mississippi), 121–124
Nestle, Joan, 194–196, 209, 244–247
  background of, 9, 224
  motivations of, 229
Newman House (Queens College), 4, 105, 186
Nonviolence, 89–90
Notre Dame University, 185

O

Obama, Barack, 63
  Goodman, Chaney, and Schwerner honored by, 85
Oberschall, Anthony, 151
O'Brien, Tony, 115–116
Occupy Wall Street movement, 237
Omolade, Barbara Jones, 114
  in Freedom Summer, 59
  Goodman and, 83, 115
Omolade, Barbara Jones, 149–154, 156–161
O'Neill, Tip, 244
Open Admissions policy, 207
Orangeburg (South Carolina), 189–191, 193, 194
Organization of Poets, Playwrights, Essayists, Editors, and Novelists (PEN), 54
Orris, Gertrude (Trudy) Weissman, 228
Orsby, Herbert, 124

P

Padow-Sederbaum, Phyllis, 60, 69
Parental School, 28, 29
Parkland (Florida), 238
Payne, Charles, 149–150

PEN (Organization of Poets, Playwrights, Essayists, Editors, and Novelists), 54
Peros, Gus, 183
Philadelphia (Mississippi), 83, 97, 122
Phoenix (student publication)
  attempts to censor, 50
  creation of, 38
Pierson, George, 202, 203
Pioneers, 14
Pollack, Ronald (Ron) F., 5, 62–63
  in *Fast for Freedom*, 40
  in Mississippi, 185
Poor People's Conference (1966; Mississippi), 200
Price, Cecil, 83, 125
Prince Edward County (Virginia), 5
  Andrews (Silverman) in, 68
  Konzal (Stein) in, 65
  Padow-Sederbaum, 69
  QC volunteers in, 222
  Shaw in, 61–62
  Student Help Project members in, 8–9, 55–61, 64
  Weddington in, 7
  Wenger in, 60–61
  Yaffe in, 66
Puerto Rican students, 203, 204, 205–208
Puryear, R.W., 201

Q

QC Roll Call of Queens College Students and Faculty, 11
Queens (boro), 27
Queens College (QC)
  The Activist and other independent newspapers at, 168–170
  conservative credentials of, 30–32
  current clubs and organizations in, 241

Freedom Week (1964) at, 151–154
history of, 28–35
impact of student activists on, 206–208
SEEK rebellion in, 202–206
student community in, 10, 11, 222–223
student press at, 38–39
student strike of 1961 at, 3, 33–35, 105
Queens College Faculty-Student Academic Senate, 208
Queens College Mexico Volunteers, 4, 112, 114–115, 185
Queens College Mississippi Freedom Project, 183
Queens College Special Collections Library, 86–87
Civil Rights Archives in, 99, 243
Queens College Student Association
antiwar protests and, 202
civil rights actions by, 224
current, 240
Fast for Freedom supported by, 40
Levy as president of, 84, 86
on tuition, 35

R
Racism, 235–236
Rainey, Lawrence, 83, 122, 123
Rampart (student publication), 38–39
suspended by administration, 31
Randolph, A. Philip, 94, 171
Rebuilders, 14
Red-diaper babies
Betty Levy as, 86
Dorothy Zellner as, 161
Mark Levy on, 9
Resnick, Sol, 167
Richmond, David, 161

Robert Russa Moton Museum (Farmville, Virginia), 66
Robeson, Paul, 161, 195, 246
Robnett, Belinda, 15, 150
Romney, Mitt, 240
Rosenthal, Eric, 40
Rosenthal, Wally, 242–244
Rothstein, Vivian Leburg, 229
Rustin, Bayard, 50, 171, 192
Rutledge, Samuel A., 28

S
Safransky, Sy, 89, 90
Salinger, Pierre, 123
Samstein, Mendy, 115, 226
Samstein, Nancy Cooper, 114, 156, 226–227
Sandel, Michael J., 4
SANE (Committee for a Sane Nuclear Policy), 67, 246
Savage, Dean, 189
Savio, Mario, 13, 109–110
at Berkeley, 2, 105–106, 110–113
in Mexico, 110–111, 185
in Mississippi, 103–106, 222
motivations for, 229
political background of, 224
at QC, 103–105
Schenkler, Michael, 59
Schultz, Debra L.
on Dorothy Zellner, 161, 164
on progressive Jews, 226–227
on Rita Schwerner, 118
Schwartz, Howard, 40
Schwerner, Michael
honored by Obama, 85
Levys and, 87
missing in Mississippi, 41, 65, 80–118
motivations for, 229
murder of, 83–85, 100, 116, 118, 121, 125

Rita Schwerner and, 118–120
Schwerner, Rita (Bender), 86, 87,
    118–119, 125–129
  after death of Michael Schwerner,
    117–124
  Mark Levy and, 156
  in Mississippi, 115–117
  motivations for, 229
SCOPE. *See* Summer Community
    Organization and Political
    Education (SCOPE) Project
Scott, Lawrence, 184, 185
Search for Education, Elevation, and
    Knowledge (SEEK) program,
    201–206, 206–209
  current students in, 241–242
Selma (Alabama), 195
Selma-to-Montgomery March (1965),
    193, 195
Shaftel, Oscar, 32
Shaw, Stan F., 8
  on backgrounds of QC volunteers,
    225
  on Civil Rights movement in South,
    37
  on Hendricks, 6
  on mentors for activists, 245
  in Prince Edward County, 9, 58,
    60–61
  in QC CORE, 59, 224
  on Weddington, 7, 64
Shenton, James P., 189, 190
Shlakman, Vera, 32
Shur, Moshe Mitchell (Mickey), 189,
    190–192, 227, 241
Silverman, Rosalind (Andrews), 60,
    68–69
Simmons, Charles, 40
Simon, Sidney B. (Sid), 11
  as advisor to Student Help Project,
    55
  Konzal (Stein) and, 65

  in Mississippi, 183, 184, 187–188
  Shaw on, 245
  Wenger on, 6–8, 14, 43
Smith, Mr. and Mrs., 116
Society of Friends (Quakers), 183
Southern Christian Leadership
    Conference (SCLC), 188, 209
Southern Conference Educational
    Fund (SCEF), 166
Southern Regional Council (SRC),
    162
Sovereignty Commission (Mississippi),
    126–128, 201
Spock, Benjamin, 206
Stanford University, 13
State University of New York
    (SUNY), 208
Stein, Jean L. (Konzal), 60, 65–66,
    226
Stepanchev, Stephen, 37
Stoke, Harold W., 33, 34, 105
Straus, Dudley P., 32
Student Coalition (QC), 204–205
Student Help Project (SHP), 49,
    55–56
  Andrews (Silverman) in, 68
  Betty Levy in, 49
  Fast for Freedom supported by, 40
  Freedom Summer and, 58–59, 80,
    129, 151
  in Prince Edward County, 8–9,
    55–61
  in recruiting volunteers for Virginia
    and Mississippi, 5
  Simon as adviser to, 187
  Terborg in, 67
  Weddington as adviser to, 64–65
  Yaffe in, 66
Student Nonviolent Coordinating
    Committee (SNCC)
  Adams-Johnson in, 197
  becoming all-Black, 166

Cooper in, 106
Dorothy Zellner in, 5, 161–164, 222
formation of, 50
in Freedom Summer, 80
Masters in, 100
Omolade in, 151–153, 156–159
in Prince Edward County, 57
Rita Schwerner working for, 125
Savio in, 105, 106
Student press, 38–39
Students for a Democratic Society (SDS)
  antiwar protests by, 3, 203
  Columbia University chapter of, 203
  on Delany's termination, 203
  Gatti in, 183
  placed on probation at QC, 169–170
  QC activists in, 224
  QC chapter of, 166–167
  QC Independent Students for a New Left becomes chapter of, 167
  SEEK rebellion (1969) and, 202
  Yaffe in, 66
Student Voice (SNCC newsletter), 163–164
Sulkes, Marjorie, 60
Summer Community Organization and Political Education (SCOPE) Project, 188, 209, 222
  Emerson in, 193
  Geffen in, 193–194, 229–230
  motivations of participants in, 227
  Savage in, 189
  Shur in, 188–190

T
Tauber, June, 61

Tax evasion, 55
Teachers Union, 31–32
Terborg-Penn, Rosalyn M., 30–32, 39, 67
Theobald, John J., 31–32
Thomas, Norman, 50
Till, Emmett, 116, 124, 173, 226
Tometi, Opal, 239
Tougaloo (Mississippi), 183–187
Trailblazers, 14
Tuition, 35–36
Tummino, Annie, 242
Ture, Kwame (Stokely Carmichael), 51, 153, 156
Turner-Collins, Dessie, 97

V
Venceremos Brigade, 170
Veterans of the Mississippi Civil Rights Movement (organization), 199
Vietnam War, 1, 2, 68, 170, 173, 185, 186, 202, 205, 208, 224, 236
  protests against, 2–4, 203, 207
  QC Fast for Peace in, 168
Virginia. *See* Prince Edward County
Voter registration, 155
  during Freedom Summer, 99–102
  Geffen's work on, 193
  Liesner's work on, 115
  Nesle's work on, 195
  Savio's work on, 103–106
  SCOPE Project for, 188–191, 209
Voting, 2, 52, 102, 158, 236, 242, 247, 248
  current attempts to limit, 247–248
  Komisar on, 51–52
Voting Rights Act (1965), 85, 191, 209, 247

W

Wallace, George, 122
Ward, Lacy, Jr., 69
Warner, Kenneth (Kenny), 34, 105, 112, 225
Warren, Frank A., 208
Weddington, Rachel, 64–66
  as advisor to Student Help Project, 55
  Konzal (Stein) and, 65
  in Prince Edward County, 5, 7, 59–61
  Shaw on, 245
Weiner, Harvey, 38, 170
Weinstock, Rosalind, 59
Wenger, Michael R., 5
  in QC CORE, 224
  on backgrounds of QC volunteers, 225
  on Civil Rights movement in South, 37
  in *Fast for Freedom*, 40, 42
  on Goodman, 85
  on Hendricks, 6
  on murders of Blacks, 124
  political background of, 224
  in Prince Edward County, 8, 57–60, 222
  on QC student community, 11
  on Simon, 6–7
  on today's activists, 244–247
  on Weddington, 64
West, Cornel, 228
White privilege, 59, 95, 109
Whites
  in Black Lives Matter protests, 239
  in Mississippi, 95, 101
  in Prince Edward County, 59
  Rita Schwerner on attitudes of, 118
  as SEEK program faculty, 202, 203
Williams, Hosea L., 189, 192

Wisconsin, University of, 3
Women
  as bridge leaders, 149–151
  in City University of New York, 160
  in Civil Rights movement, 226
  employment discrimination against, 53
Women Strike for Peace (QC chapter), 36–37
Woodson, Carter G., 158–159
World Civilization curriculum, 205
World's Fair (Flushing, 1964-65), demonstrations at
  Berman at, 167
  Goodman at, 82
  Linzer at, 171
  QC students at, 157, 223
  Simon at, 187
Wreszin, Michael, 206, 208
Wu, Frank H., 1

Y

Yaffe, Deborah (Debby), 60, 66–68
Young, Andrew, 192
Young People's Socialist League (YPSL), 224
  Komisar in, 50, 51
  Terborg in, 67

Z

Zeigfinger, Steve, 185
Zellner, Bob, 122–123, 173
Zellner, Dorothy (Dottie) Miller, 5, 160–165
  Levys recruitead by, 87
  political background of, 226, 227
  in SNCC, 223
Zimmerman, George, 239
Zinn, Howard, 14, 206
Zitron, Celia, 31

Printed in the United States
by Baker & Taylor Publisher Services